T0250711

Lecture Notes in Computer Science 569

Edited by G. Goos and J. Hartmanis

Advisory Board: W. Brauer   D. Gries   J. Stoer

A. Beaumont   G. Gupta (Eds.)

Parallel Execution of Logic Programs

ICLP '91 Pre-Conference Workshop
Paris, June 24, 1991
Proceedings

Springer-Verlag
Berlin Heidelberg NewYork
London Paris Tokyo
Hong Kong Barcelona
Budapest

Series Editors

Gerhard Goos
Universität Karlsruhe
Postfach 69 80
Vincenz-Priessnitz-Straße 1
W-7500 Karlsruhe, FRG

Juris Hartmanis
Department of Computer Science
Cornell University
5148 Upson Hall
Ithaca, NY 14853, USA

Volume Editors

Anthony Beaumont
Gopal Gupta
Department of Computer Science, University of Bristol
Queen's Building, University Walk, Bristol BS8 1TR, UK

CR Subject Classification (1991): D.1.6, D.1.3, F.4.1, D.3.2, D.2.5

ISBN 3-540-55038-0 Springer-Verlag Berlin Heidelberg New York
ISBN 0-387-55038-0 Springer-Verlag New York Berlin Heidelberg

Typesetting: Camera ready by author
Printing and binding: Druckhaus Beltz, Hemsbach/Bergstr.
45/3140-543210 - Printed on acid-free paper

Preface

Logic programming refers to execution of programs written in Horn logic. Among the advantages of this style of programming are its simple declarative and procedural semantics, high expressive power and inherent nondeterminism.

In recent years, there has been a large increase in the number of programmers choosing to write applications in Logic programming languages such as Prolog. This is in part due to the high performance gained by the current sequential language implementations. However, the inherent parallelism present in logic programming languages makes them ideal candidates for parallel implementations which will significantly increase their speed of execution. There are three essential issues in parallel execution of logic programs:

1. Which form(s) of parallelism—among the many sources of parallelism available (or-parallelism, and-parallelism, stream parallelism, data-parallelism, etc.)—will be exploited?

2. Will parallelism be explicitly programmed by programmers, or will it be exploited implicitly without any help from them?

3. Which target parallel architecture will the logic program(s) run on?

Consideration of the various alternatives available, for each of the issues above, leads to a wide spectrum of choices for designing a parallel logic programming system. This is indeed demonstrated by the radically different approaches taken in the various papers collected in this volume.

These papers were presented at the workshop on Parallel Logic Programming held in Paris on June 24th as part of the 8th International Conference on Logic Programming. The workshop was quite a success with over 50 participants. There were 15 speakers, including 2 invited speakers.

We would like to thank all the authors for participating: without their submissions there wouldn't have been any workshop. We would also like to thank David H.D. Warren for his help and support, Philippe Codognet, ICLP Workshop Chair, for giving us the opportunity to organise this workshop and for answering our numerous questions.

University of Bristol   Anthony Beaumont
October 1991   Gopal Gupta

Table of Contents

DEBUGGING PARALLEL STRAND PROGRAMS

Martin Gittins
The Strand Group, Ver House, Markyate, AL3 8JP, England.

Introduction

This paper describes a new debugger for such programs using the language Strand[1].

Strand [2] is a commercially available language at the weakest level of parallel logic languages. Implementations exist for a wide variety of machines, both parallel and sequential. For some time the lack of a debugger has been a barrier to widespread usage, and the availability of such tools is critical to the success of parallel logic systems. AM is a truly concurrent debugger for Strand Programs, soon to be released to beta test sites. It is anticipated that it will continue to develop in the light of widespread experience.

AM use a model of a running Strand Program that it described as a hog pen. Each processor maintains its own hog pen, populated by active processes. Processes are let out of the hog pen for processing under the control of the debugger.

An important issue in the design of debuggers is the focus of attention, and significant emphasis in AM is concerned with this issue. For true parallel machines the focus issue has the extra dimension of physical location as the normal issues concerning code focus. AM allows programmers to view the active processes and progress the computation, either across all processes or to only follow one process.

Strand

This section describes the basic features of Strand as relevant to the discussion of the debugger. As mentioned above Strand is the weakest of the logic programming languages in the sense that it has fewest of the 'logic' features that characterise such languages. There is not sufficient space to provide a complete overview of Strand here but for more details see [1,2]. A more direct comparison to logic programming languages is given in [3]. The design considerations for Strand were that it should be simple and efficient on true parallel machines. Largely this has been achieved. It was NOT a design consideration that it should be a logic language, rather it appears that the logic formalism provides the best option for designing an architecture independent language.

The syntax is based on the familiar 'Edinburgh' syntax, such that a clause has the form:

Head:- $G_1, G_2, .., G_n$ | $B_1, B_2, ... , B_m$.

where the G_1 to G_n are the guards and the B_1 to B_m the body calls. When reducing a process, clauses are examined until one clause is found where all the guards succeed and the parameters match. This system then commits to this clause and the body calls spawned as new processes. Note that exactly one clause is selected and, if more than one clause is capable of selection, the user can not *a priori* determine which clause will be selected. In other words Strand is a committed choice non-deterministic (ccnd) language.

The guards can only be chosen from a set of system supplied guard kernels. This very reduced set of guards ensures that the language is flat, no guards bind variables.

It is often the case that a guard, for example a numeric comparison, can not fail or succeed because a data value is not available. If no clauses can commit, but one or more can not make a determination because of lack of data the reduction attempt suspends. When the data is available, the selection process is restarted from the beginning. This feature imparts a strong dataflow character to the language. A major difference from most other ccnd languages is that Strand does not support unification, but rather supports the concept of matching and binding. Clause selection will result in a set of bindings that are local to the body of the clause only. If it is required to bind to variables passed as parameters then the binding must be performed by kernels. The most common such kernel being the assignment operator ':=', but others exist. For example consider a simple database of facts:

```
father(john,david).
father(david,graem).
```

In most logic languages a call of the form: father(john,X) results in X being bound to david. In Strand this binding will not happen unless the programmer explicitly adds an assignment. The simple database then looks like:

```
father(john, X):- X := david.
father(david,X):- X := graem.
```

This means that the facts can not be used in 'reverse' and that calling father(X, graem) will not work. To simplify the writing of such fact style clauses it is possible in Strand to add a mode declaration that will cause the compiler to generate the explicit bindings:

```
-mode father(?,^)
father(john, david).
father(david,graem).
```

Note however that the bindings are still one way, so this is not unification. It is possible of course to assign one variable to another, giving the effect of the variables being 'unified', in the sense of representing the same object.

The data structures supported in Strand are similar to those in Prolog, that is to say lists and tuples. List are represented as literal lists:

```
[a,b,c,d]
```

or as list pair structures of head and tail:

```
[Head | Tail]
```

Tuples are represented within curly braces: {a,b,c}, or can be manipulated by special kernels. Notice that separate kernels are provided for getting and putting a tuple argument to reflect the distinction in Strand between assignment and reading a value.

On all machines, both shared and distributed memory, Strand uses a common variable space to manage and control computations. All variables exist in the same space and may be assigned or read from any processor. This is a very attractive property because it means that Strand code can be written largely independently of the location of code and data at run time. The single assignment semantics mean that it is always safe to copy data to processors where it is required. The only issues in code design that have to take account of the distributed nature of a true parallel implementation arise because of the lack of instantaneous communications and infinite memories.

No attempt is made to automatically allocate processes to processors. It is considered that this is the responsibility of the programmer. However the language is designed to make this task easier. All processes, by default, execute on the processor upon which they are created. If it is required to execute on a different processor the call is annotated with a '@' symbol followed by an indication of the processor required. This may be an absolute reference to the processor by number or a relative reference using a form of relative addressing. For example:

    open_database(Cmds)@3,

will cause the open_database call to be executed on processor 3. The processor number may be computed at run time:

    vector_sum(Array,Sum)@Index,

where Index is computed at run time to be an integer. [Processor numbers are always interpreted modulo the number of processors].

Alternatively a call of the form:

    spawn_worker(Input,Params)@fwd,

where a string is used as the processor reference, performs the call on the processor that has the next highest number to the current processor. Relative directions such as 'fwd', are interpreted in the context of a virtual topology. A virtual machine can be created at run time, this is a set of processors (perhaps a sub-set of the total set of processors) and a virtual topology. Process creation using the topologically defined directions then exist only within the virtual machine.

A complete Strand system consists of a number of modules, each module is a collection of procedures defined in a single source file. Each module contains a list of procedures exported by that module, and only these procedures may be called from outside the module, others being private. Inter-module calls have the form: Module:Call, e.g.

    blackboard:start(In),

calls start/1 in module blackboard, typically defined by the file blackboard.std. Modules are normally loaded automatically by the system when required, but may be manipulated as first class data objects and, for example, passed between processors by variable assignment. A number of kernels provide basic loading and handling for modules.

Strand comes with a run-time environment that handles a number of the features of the language, mainly module manipulation and I/O. The environment is itself a more or less standard Strand program, and includes amongst other features a shell that prompts the user for input and keeps track of running computations. (A computation is a Strand call from the top-level.)

A Strand example is shown below, taken from the debugger code. This is part of the code used to determine if a list of processors (the first parameter) contains the local processor ID, the second parameter. A call to is_this_me(proc_spec,Id,X) assigns a value to X indicating if Id is included in the specification. A three valued logic is used, 1 for included, -1 for not included and 0 for don't know. Exclusion dominates inclusion, for example is_this_me([2:8,-[3,6]],3,X) assigns -1 to X.

Note the use of a mode declaration for combine/3.

```
is_this_me([],_,R):- R:=0.              % the empty list means nobody
is_this_me([X|More],Me,R):-             % a list, check the head and
tail
     is_this_me(X,Me,RX),
     is_this_me(More,Me,RM),
     combine(RX,RM,R).
is_this_me({':',L,H},Me,R):-            % a X:Y tuple, I'm in the range
     Me >= L, Me =< H | R := 1.
is_this_me({':',_,_},_,R):-             % ... or not
     otherwise | R := 0.                % note the use of otherwise


     %combine encodes the combination rules,
     % 1 means yes
     % 0 means don't know
     % -1 means no, and takes priority over yes
-mode combine(?,?,^).
combine(-1,_,-1).
combine(_,-1,-1).
combine(0,0,0).
combine(1,0,1).
combine(0,1,1).
combine(1,1,1).
```

Not discussed here, but an important aspect of Strand is the ability to call C and Fortran routines. These may be viewed as conventional/existing routines incorporated into a Strand application, or as a mechanism to extend the capabilities of Strand, for example adding support for a database or windows. It is possible to write both guard and body kernels in foreign code.

Other Debugging Facilities

Strand offers other debugging facilities, mainly organised around the concept of resolvent collection. Modules can be compiled in resolvent mode, and then a running computation aborted with resolvent collection. For large, particularly multi-processor computations the number of entries in such a resolvent list may be vary large, to help in such circumstances a resolvent analysis tool (RAT) is provided that will 'read' a resolvent list and present a precis of the content and allows closer examination of the individual entries.

In addition a lint facility checks for singleton variables and other errors that are detectable at compile time, for example unreachable code.

Debugging Model

The model used by AM is based on the concept of a hog-pen. The active processes are kept in a local hog-pen, each processor using its own hog-pen. Effectively a hog-pen defines a virtual processor, and it is possible to request more hog-pens that the number of physical processors that exist. In this case the hog-pens are allocated to processors on a round-robin basis.

Each hog pen has a gate that allows processes to be reduced under the control of the debugging system. The hog-pen gate can be open, counting or closed. If counting it will allow a specific number of processes to pass through the gate. If open it will allow an unspecified numbers of processes to pass. The gate is closed initially, and can be opened by a number of commands. Once open or counting it can be closed by command, or more typically by a shutter process, this is a process that is marked to prevent it passing though the gate until confirmed by the user.

Once out of the gate a process is reduced, or it may be sent to another virtual processor for execution. If a process suspends, the process is not returned to the hog-pen but is suspended in the normal manner until its input parameters are available.

Normally user commands are sent to all hog-pens, and by default all hog-pens act upon the command. It is possible to direct commands at subsets of the hog-pens, thus enabling attention to be focused on specific physical location(s). Normally all hog-pens act in parallel and the programmer does not have to take particular notice of the location of the processes.

AM Operations

Operations consist of four types:

1.handling of modules

these are concerned with transforming debuggable modules (debug) , or loading previously transformed modules (load). Modules may be specified to be run outside of the control of the debugger, in which case all calls to such modules are passed to the normal Strand environment. Of course such calls share the same variable space as those run under control of the debugger.

2. displaying information

Primarily about the state of the program or debugger such as the hog pen contents (active), the state of the databases (show), or the state of the hog-pens (status)

3. tracing information

These are concerned with turning trace information on (trace, shut and monitor), or turning it off (untrace, unshut, unmonitor). Three bits of information are maintained and any procedure can have any combination, including none. The effects are independent and are as follows:

shut
This causes an attempt to reduce the procedure to shut the hog-pen gate at the point BEFORE the shut procedure is reduced. Only the hog pen on the local processor is shut.

trace
This causes the name and parameters to be printed when an attempt is made to reduce the procedure, regardless of whether the process suspended.

monitor
This prints the results of reduction of a procedure as a series of reductions, each one of the form:

    parent_process -> child_process

The reduction is printed when the process is actually reduced, i.e. following any suspension if it occurs. If the process does not suspend then trace and monitor print at the same time.

4. controlling execution

These control the execution of the program through the operation of the hog pens. (open, shut, count). Plus, of course, the ability to start new computations. Some special operations allow a specific call to be processed out of turn (count), or to run outside of the debuggers control (detach). It is even possible to put aside the current hog pen and start a new one with a specified process as the initial content (sub-tree).

A listing of commands for AM is given in the Appendix. In order to reduce the amount of typing all commands have a number of aliases, usually including the initial letter of the command.

Using the debugger

The debugger is started from the Strand shell in the same manner as any strand computation, by calling am:begin. This produces a 'Debug>' prompt which expects one of the commands shown above. Pressing <return> returns to the normal shell prompt, the shell remains active and accessible throughout a debugging session. Responses from AM are preceded by the processor number generating the response.

A new process can be created by calling it, as from the shell, for example to create a call to hanoi:go, one would type:
Debug>hanoi:go(5)

Note that the module name and colon are compulsory. When a reference to a new module is made, AM will ask if it should be in debug or normal mode. The new process is immediately reduced. To see the results of the reduction one can examine the active list:
Debug>active
hanoi:gen(X121732)
   etc

To allow the computation to proceed a number of options can be used. The most uncontrolled is open, which runs the computation until the next shut point, or the active list is empty.
Debug>open
 <program output here>

Information of the execution of the program is normally collected, perhaps restarting the program a number of times. Finally to quit the debugger, type quit:
Debug>quit
AM quitting

A transcript of a debugging session follows (user input in shown in full version and bold):

1>**am:begin**
     After Midnight. Version 0.1
     Copyright (c) Strand Group
     1 Node invoked
[started,1]
Debug>**hanoi:go(6)**
     Do you want to run hanoi in debug or normal mode?
     In debug mode? y
Debug>**active**

```
     [1]hanoi:go(6)
     [1]End
Debug>count(3)
Debug>shut(gen/2)
     [1][hanoi:gen/2,shut]
Debug>trace(move/6)
     [1][hanoi:move/6,trace]
Debug>open
     [1]Stop point: hanoi:gen(6,Var)
Debug>active
     [1]hanoi:gen(6,Var)
     [1]hanoi:move([],Var,1,3,2,Var)
     [1]hanoi:say_goodbye(Var)
     [1]End
Debug>open
     [1]Trace: hanoi:move([],[6|Var],1,3,2,Var)
     [1]Stop point: hanoi:gen(5,Var)
Debug>untrace(move/6)
     [1][hanoi:move/6]
Debug>monitor(move/6)
     [1][hanoi:move/6,monitor]
Debug>open
     [1]Stop point: hanoi:gen(4,Var)
Debug>active
     [1]hanoi:gen(4,Var)
     [1]End
Debug>open
     [1]Stop point: hanoi:gen(3,Var)
Debug>open
hanoi:move([],[5,4,3|Var],1,2,3,Var)=>move([],[4,3|Var],1,3,2,Var)
hanoi:move([],[5,4,3|Var],1,2,3,Var)=>move(Var,[5,],1,2,3,Var)
hanoi:move([],[5,4,3|Var],1,2,3,Var)=>move(Var,[4,3|Var],3,2,1,Var)
Stop point: hanoi:gen(2,Var)
hanoi:move([],[5,4,3|Var],1,2,3,Var) => []
...
```

Design Considerations

The conceptual model is one of the most critical aspects of the design. The model used
by AM developed naturally as the project proceeded. The original concept was to
implement a model closer to the 'spy and leap' model used in Prolog debuggers.
However these are inappropriate concepts for concurrent execution. Spy and leap are
also closely tied to the Byrd Box model of Prolog execution. In Strand with the absence

of backtracking the Byrd Box model is not appropriate, Strand clauses effectively only have a single 'port'.

Debuggers exist for one reason: to find software bugs. In theory all bugs can be removed by examination of the source code. In practice this is impossibly difficult for a large program. The reason for this is that any non-trivial program is too hard to grasp in complete entirety at sufficient detail. The whole concept of abstraction, and its manifestation in procedures, objects etc. is an attempt to resolve this issue. With a parallel system the situation is made more complex by its parallel nature, with nodes operating more or less asynchronously. Therefore it essential that a debugger allows the programmer to focus attention on a very small part of the program execution, and shift that focus when, and where, necessary. A significant part of the AM design is thus concerned with allowing the uninteresting (i.e. bug-free) sections of code to run quietly, but the interesting sections to be examined closely.

It is also clear that performance of the system is critical if large programs are to be debugged. Several principles became clear during the development of the system. The emphasis on performance needs to be in the correct place. The run loop is critical as every process reduction requires one pass through this loop. One important measure of performance is the number of actual reductions compared to the number of reductions executed without the debugger. On the other hand the front end and database update are not critical.

Care needs to be taken regarding the number and size of messages send between physical processors. Two optimisations try to reduce this overhead. Firstly the database is replicated on every node. The original design placed a single database on the front end, but this required an exchange of messages between each node and the front end for every reduction. Clearly a large amount of communication traffic for any parallel system. The second optimisation is that all references to processes for printing are converted to strings locally. This is primarily to avoid the potential of passing large data structures to the front end for printing.

Implementation

Implementation is via a source-to-source transformation that is performed on the fly when a file is compiled in debug mode. This technique is used because it avoids the requirement of maintaining a separate transformed source file and the possibility of confusion that might result.

The basic mechanism is to transform all clauses in the file into 'reduce' clauses, where the original argument list becomes one of the arguments to the new clause. The body returns a list of calls rather than executing the call themselves. The technique is an extension of the method described by Foster and Taylor, chapter 9 in [1].

The on the fly transformation is done by calling a modified compiler, which parses the input file as normal, and then calls the transformation program to generate the transformed source, and finally compiles the results of the transformation, writing the compiled output to a file with the suffix '.dam' rather than the normal '.sam'.

Each clause transformed as follows, if the original clause is:

    <Head> :- <Guards> | <Body Calls>.

it is transformed to:

    reduce(Head,X,Q):- <Guards>|X:= [<Body Calls>].

It other words the guards are used to control execution, as in normal running, but when the clause reduces it returns a list of Body Calls rather than spawn those as new processes. The guards themselves, and the body calls are not changed from the normal form. This is true for both calls to user defined procedures as well as kernels and system calls to the environment.

A number of slightly different variants on this basic theme were tried in the process of development of the debugger. The transformation is relatively easy to change and further changes may still occur.

The final parameter to the reduced clause is a quit flag. One of the features normally expected of a debugger is the ability to clean up after a debugging session, either because the user quits or the program under test fails. This requires a reasonable amount of attention, and one of the requirements is that any suspended processes are removed, hence on termination all processes are forced to exit by setting the quit flag. A 'catch-all' clause is also added to catch any process failures.

AM exists in distributed form, with a single front end process to parse user input, and allow aliases to be defined for commands. Associated with each physical processor is a debug node that control execution of the debugged code on the local processor. Virtual nodes are allowed. By default all nodes respond to debug commands, but commands can be addressed with annotation derived from Strand's turtle graphic annotation. For example the following command:

    Debug>open@[2:9,-[4,8]]

will cause processors in the range 2 to 9, except numbers 4 and 8, i.e. numbers 2,3,5, 6,7 and 9 to open, all others will ignore the command.

The overall design of the AM run-time system is as shown in the diagram below. Each box is a separate perpetual process, and the links between them are streams. The system is divided into two parts, a front end and a set of node execution units. The single front end is primarily concerned with processing input from the user, and its major task is recognising commands, checking the syntax, removing aliases and posting the command to the execution units. All normal commands are send to all execution units, the only exception is that run requests are only send to node 0 unless the user explicitly stipulates a list of processors to be used. Commands that are directed at specific nodes are in fact send to all nodes, and it is up to the nodes to decide if they should respond or not using the 'is_this_me' code shown earlier. At first sight this seems wasteful, but in practice the critical nodes would have to process the message anyway, and the non-effected nodes might as well as the processor is probably idle anyway. It has the major advantage of allowing the front end to only maintain a single broadcast stream and avoid the overhead of maintenance of a set of individual streams. The front-end also maintains a variable server in a similar manner to the Strand environment. This enables variable bindings at the level of the AM prompt to be created and maintained. This is purely for convenience of the programmer to create and use temporary data structures etc.

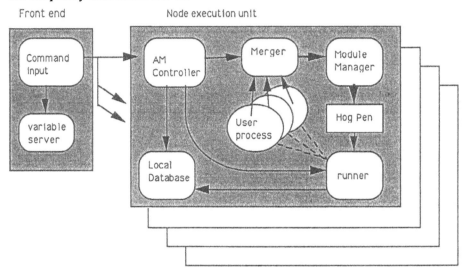

Each node has three major perpetual processes and the user's transformed code. The AM controller is mainly responsible for routing messages to the correct component in the execution unit. The database maintains a record of the current shut, trace and monitor points. This is optimised to minimise the number of reductions required to look up a particular procedure, particularly in the case where a small number of entries exist in the database. It is organised as a hierarchy of tuples, with a top level index based on arity, then module, and finally procedure name. This data structure is relatively expensive to update, but fast to test. Note that each node maintains its own database. This is primarily to reduce communication traffic. It is also useful occasionally, to allow different control on different nodes.

The remaining processes in the execution unit are concerned with the main run loop. This loop takes processes from the hog pen and reduces them, eventually placing the resulting offspring processes in the hog pen for later reduction. Recall from the description above that the hog pen gate can be open or shut. When open the runner process takes processes, one at a time, from the hog pen and attempts to reduce them. This goes

through a number of steps:
1. the database is interrogated to see if any of the trace,shut or monitor bits are set.
2. if the trace bit is set, the trace message is printed
3. if the shut bit is set a message is printed and the gate closed
4. the runner checks to see in the process is a kernel call, if it is the kernel is called, the kernel calling process may suspend.
5. if not a kernel the runner checks to see if it is a user-defined kernel
6. if not a process is forked to execute the reduce/3 call, passing in the process as the first parameter.
7. if the monitor bit is set a monitor process is forked that waits for the reduce/3 call to complete.

All the outputs from the reduce/3 calls are merged together to provide the input to the module manager. The outputs need to be merged to allow for any suspensions of the reduce/3 calls. Any run requests from the user are also merged into this stream.

The module manager performs two tasks, it checks for remote calls (those with an '@' sign), and performs module look up. Any remote calls are send to the front end to be forwarded to the 'correct' node. The stream used for this (referred to as the hotline), is not shown in the figure above for reasons of clarity. The second task is to determine if the module referenced in the call should be loaded in debug or normal mode. The module manager maintains two lists, one of debug modules and one of non-debug modules. In the event that the module is not in either list, the module manager asks the front end to request from the user how this module is to used. This request is also routed through the hotline, hence the reason that these two seemingly dissimilar tasks are handled by the same process.

If the module is a loaded debug module, the module manager replaces the module field with a pointer to the actual module, otherwise it leaves the string. The runner process can then test this field, and if it finds a string, it uses a normal strand environment call to run the module as normal. Of course, any off-spring processes from such a call are not handled by AM.

Further Design Issues

Some design issues remain to be settled. One is the trade-off concerning whether or not to allow kernels to be trapped. The current implementation supports this, but it would be faster to test for kernel calls before performing the database look up and thereby avoiding the database look when calling kernels. The saving is not large per reduction cycle, but kernels make up a significant number of calls so the overall effect is likely to be noticeable. On the other hand it is not clear how much benefit is gained from being able to shut or trace kernels.

A second design issue concerns suspended processes. How critical is it to be able to 'see' suspended processes? The current implementation does not provide a mechanism to examine suspended processes. However a trial version of AM has been written that includes such a feature, but at the cost of some loss of performance.

The issue of 'focus of attention' discussed earlier is covered by AM with a number of strategies. Not only can modules be executed in normal or debug mode as required, it is also possible to detach an individual process from the control of the debugger. This request is handled by the runner and the detached call spawned directly. The other dimension is the ability to specify separately if required, what is happening of different nodes. Here the target is not to pre-empt the user's imagination.

Performance

Some measurement of the performance, in terms of the number of reductions required has been made. Measurements were made on several programs to determine the overhead of running AM. Each was measured using the normal Strand system and then measured running through AM. No tracing or monitoring was activated and all measurements were made on a Sun 3/260 workstation with 16 MBytes of memory. The table below shows the times and reduction counts for two programs run without AM and with AM. The overhead factor is also given, this is the AM performance divided by the non-AM performance. Note that these measurements indicate that the reduction ratio covers a wide range, from 1:1.3 to 1:50.

Program	Time (secs)	AM Time (secs)	Over'd Factor	Red'ns	AM Red'ns	Over'd Factor
Hanoi	0.84	4.06	4.8	17,744	22,570	1.3
Hanoi*	0.06	0.90	15	853	3,560	4.1
NQueens(6)	0.84	77	92	6,407	273,993	43
NQueens(8)	18	1,850	103	118,812	5,829,963	49

The wide variation in overhead was greater than expected. On closer examination two factors account for most of the variation, The first is the effect of system calls to the Strand environment, primarily those associated with output. Such calls take the same number of reductions if called from the debugger, as when called normally. To determine the effect of this a variant on the Towers of Hanoi that does not produce any output, Hanoi*, was created. As expected this showed a greater overhead, but still less than the NQueens. The second factor is the large number of arithmetic calls in the NQueens code (from the attach checking; the algorithm used is a naive one). These have a large impact on the overhead because the arithmetic expressions are interpreted by the debugger. Further work is planned to reduce this overhead.

Retrospective and Future Developments

The AM system certainly seems to provide a useful debugging environment, and addresses a number of issues. The major issue being the focus of attention, this AM does quite well by allowing a number of different mechanisms to narrow the focus. The other major issue, of performance, seems at the moment to provide a more varied result. It would be possible to increase performance significantly for particular machines, but the intent is to provide a portable debugger that runs on all Strand implementations. In particular the transformation technique seems to operate well and give a good combination of performance and flexibility. The design of the run-time system has been critical and significant effort has gone into its implementation. The 'dataflow' flavour of the current design fits the style of Strand well and is typical of large Strand programs.

Some issues continue to be addressed; the major ones are the handling of the output as the number of processors becomes large; and the performances issues surrounding those programs that perform particularly badly under the current implementation. An area that has not yet been explored is the potential for incorporating some of the ideas of RAT into AM. This would provide more facilities for investigating the variables that link processes together, and the ability to look at a shut computation from a static perspective.

The next major stage in the development of AM is the addition of a graphics front end based on X-windows. Recently a version of Strand has been developed that has a much improved interface to Sun's Open Look™. This will allow the addition of some extra debugging facilities, in particular the ability to follow variable assignments more easily. With a textual front end it is very hard to devise a usable mechanism to manipulate variables. The extra dimension of a graphical display will allow this to be more easily achieved. This should develop a more user-friendly environment and make AM a more powerful debugging tool.

References

[1] Foster,I. and Taylor, S, "*Strand: New Concepts in Parallel Processing*", Prentice-Hall, 1990.
[2] *Strand User Manual; Buckingham release*, Strand Software Technologies, 1990.
[3] Foster,I. and Taylor, S, "*Strand: A Practical Parallel Programming Tool*", North American Conf on Logic Programming, MIT Press, 1989.

Appendix: AM Command Summary

A Summary of Commands is as follows, several commands make reference to proc-id, this is a procedure id, and has the form:

module:procedure/arity,

the module may be omitted in which case the most recently referenced module name is used instead, this is referred to as the current module.

debug(module)
transforms, compiles and loads the nominated module.

load(module)
loads a previously compiled module.

count
reduces the next process in active list.

count(N)
reduces the next N processes in the hog pen.

count(Name) or count(Name/Arity)
reduces the next process in the hog pen with the specified name and arity.

open
opens the hog-pen gate and allows processes to be reduced until next shut point is reached, or the hog pen is empty.

active
lists the hog pen contents in the order in which they will be allowed out. This may be affected by specific count or detach requests.

shut proc-id
makes proc-id a shut point. Proc-id is a triple consisting of module name, procedure name and arity, and may be written (Module,Procedure,Arity), or (Module:Procedure/Arity). The module name may be omitted, in which case it defaults to the most recently loaded module (the current module).

unshut proc_id
removes proc-id from the list of shut points

unshut all
removes all shut points.

trace proc-id
traces all reductions of proc-id

untrace proc-id
removes proc-id from the trace list

untrace all
removes all trace points.

shut
shuts the hog-pen gate

branch proc_id
reduces to completion/suspension the first occurrence of proc-id in the hog pen list. All reduction steps are printed.

shutters
Displays a list of shut points

traces
Displays a list of trace points

monitors
Displays a list of all monitor points.

show
Displays the status of all shut, trace and monitor points.

detach proc_id
runs the first occurrence of proc_id in the hog pen, detached from the debugger, and hence to completion or a state of suspension. Detached processes run outside of the debugger's control and it is not possible to re-attach them, or any of their child processes. Detached process share data with debugger controlled processes.

sub_tree proc_id/Nth
reduces the specified process, and uses the new processes it spawns as a new hog pen. The existing hog pen is set aside until joined sometime later. This allows the close examination of a small piece of code to be performed in isolation. Sub-tree can be performed as many times as required, each sub-tree being undone by a join.

join
The current hog pen is merged with the most recently set aside hog pen by a sub-tree. If no set aside hog pen exists the command has no effect.

Constraint Handling, Garbage Collection and Execution Model Issues in ElipSys

Michel Dorochevsky, Kees Schuerman, André Véron, Jiyang Xu
Parallel and Distributed Systems Group
European Computer-Industry Research Centre
Arabellastr. 17, D-8000 München 81, Germany
e-mail: elipsys@ecrc.de

Abstract

This paper presents the constraint handling and garbage collection parts of Elip-Sys and gives an overview of its execution model. ElipSys[1] is a logic programming system being developed at ECRC. It combines parallelism, constraint satisfaction on finite domains, and tight database coupling. Constraints in ElipSys are handled in a way that significantly improves the expressiveness and declarativeness of logic programming and offer an increase in efficiency through parallelism. The garbage collector tackles the additional complexity of the parallel execution environment and takes into consideration also the data generated by the constraint solver. The ElipSys execution model is designed to be appropriate to a range of parallel architectures, from shared to distributed memory machines.

1 Introduction

ElipSys [7] is a logic programming system being developed at ECRC combining parallelism, constraint satisfaction on finite domains, and tight database coupling. The Elip-Sys project addresses issues at all levels: from language design to implementation. Of particular note is the work to improve the expressiveness and declarativeness of logic programming, and the design of an execution model that is appropriate to a range of parallel architectures, from shared to distributed memory machines. These ingredients should enable ElipSys to effectively tackle large real-world applications.

As it is defined, the ElipSys project has greatly benefited from the research efforts of three former projects at ECRC: MegaLog [5], a platform for developing knowledge base management systems, CHIP [9], a constraint handling system in Prolog and PEPSys [4], a parallel logic programming language. ElipSys is part of the ESPRIT project EP2025, the European Declarative System (EDS), which aims at providing the hardware, a distributed

---

[1] ECRC Logic Inference Parallel System

memory multi-processor system, and the software required to build the next generation of corporate information servers [12, 10].

The ElipSys system is designed to exploit *coarse-grain* parallelism in order to achieve efficiency in both shared and distributed memory environments. OR- and independent AND-parallelism are the two forms of parallelism available in ElipSys. Independent AND-parallelism is simply transformed to OR-parallelism.

OR-parallelism is felt to be well suited to search algorithms and to complement constraint handling on finite domains by providing parallel enumeration facilities. Of particular interest is the opportunity to get super-linear speed-up when exploring search trees with, for instance, branch-and-bound algorithms [14, 13]. Moreover, in a distributed computing environment, communication is to be avoided as much as possible. OR-parallelism leads to parallel computations which interact either seldom or in a well controllable way with each other. ElipSys is aimed at supporting efficiently traditional Prolog-like computations.

In the current design of ElipSys, the control of parallelism is made through user annotations and dynamic control. In the future, annotations should be minimised or better eliminated by using techniques of static program analysis and improving dynamic control based on more intelligent scheduling policies.

This paper is divided into 5 sections. Following this introduction, section 2 presents an overview of constraint handling in ElipSys. Section 3 highlights the most interesting aspects of the ElipSys execution model. Section 4 discusses garbage collection in ElipSys with particular emphasis on the interactions with constraint handling. The conclusions are given in section 5.

2 Constraint Handling

Finite domains are encountered frequently in real-world applications, especially in search problems. Although they can naturally be expressed and programmed with standard logic programming languages, the efficiency of such programs is often far from satisfactory. As demonstrated in many recent research and development results, both declarativeness and efficiency of a logic programming system can greatly benefit from the use of a dedicated constraint solver. The constraint solver of ElipSys is largely based on that of CHIP, a sequential constraint logic language developed at ECRC which provides finite domains in addition to other domains of computation [9].

2.1 Programming with Constraints

ElipSys integrates the finite domain constraint solving techniques of CHIP with OR-parallelism into a production quality system, following an experimental implementation based on PEPSys [14].

In addition to the parallel implementation of finite domain constraints, a major contribution of ElipSys is its emphasis on declarative semantics, which has resulted in a language that clearly separates the control from the logic of programs. ElipSys is backed by a type system, whose theory and semantics are based on standard first-order logic, with the restricted second-order extensions to define parametric types. Finite domains are therefore no more than particular kinds of types, from the semantics point of view.

We take the N-queens puzzle as an example to demonstrate how ElipSys allows a declarative programming style while providing competitive performance. The following program specifies the problem with rather standard Prolog syntax:

```
queens(Board, Domain) :- place(Board, Domain), safe(Board).

place([], Domain).
place([X|Y], Domain) :- X :: Domain, place(Y, Domain).

safe([]).
safe([F|T]) :- safe1(T,F,1), safe(T).

safe1([],X,Nb).
safe1([F|T],X,Nb) :- X =\= F, X =\= F+Nb, X =\= F-Nb,
       Nb1 is Nb+1, safe1(T,X,Nb1).

?- queens([Q1,Q2,Q3,Q4], 1..4).
```

where $X::M..N$ is defined such that X is an integer in the range $[M, N]$. Although this program mirrors the formal specification of the problem, it is extremely inefficient because it implements a generate-and-test algorithm. In order to obtain a more efficient program for solving the problem, users are normally forced to rewrite the program, taking the control into consideration.

With ElipSys, however, the same program performs much more efficiently (in fact more efficiently than any of the programs written in standard Prolog for solving the same puzzle that we have seen). This is because the type checking predicate '::'/2 and the arithmetic comparison '=\='/2 are implemented in such a way that they detect finite domain types and apply constraint handling methods whenever possible. The algorithm actually used by the above program is the so-called *generalised forward checking* [13].

The declarative meaning of the goal X::Type is not changed. Operationally, when X is free and *Type* represents a finite domain, instead of instantiating it to a value in *Type* immediately, the goal is handled in two separate phases: in the first phase X is instantiated to an internal structure, called a *domain structure*, that represents *Type* and is used by the constraint solver; in the second phase X is further instantiated to a value remaining in that domain structure. When the goal is initially invoked, only the first phase is performed, i.e. X is first instantiated to a domain structure. In the mean time the goal is also delayed, and will only be reactivated when there is no other work available in the system or at the time hinted by the user, which will be discussed below. When the goal is reactivated, it performs only the second phase, namely, enumerating remaining elements in the type.

A domain structure can be understood as a logical variable constrained to take values only from a finite set of values (initially the entire domain of the given type). When further constraints are imposed on the variable, elements of the set may be removed. When there is only one possible value left in the set, the variable is then instantiated to it. For simplicity, we call a variable constrained by domain structures a *domain variable.*

When an enumeration phase is entered, there may be several uninstantiated domain variables. One of them is chosen by the constraint solver and is instantiated to a value in the domain. A system ordering (temporal order) is normally used in selecting uninstantiated domain variables.

It is, however, sometimes very important for efficiency which ordering is used, as explained in [13]. In order to gain the flexibility of using different enumeration algorithms, users can influence the constraint solver by supplying alternative methods through *heuristics* in the form of declarations. For instance, the above program can be augmented by the following declaration:

```
:- heuristic queens(Board, Domain) with first_fail(Board).
```

where first_fail/1, among several others, is a standard heuristic built-in to ElipSys and selects first the variable whose domain structure has the least number of remaining elements. The constraint solver then uses this alternative enumeration method for the variables listed in Board.

There are certainly applications that need specific heuristics in order to improve the efficiency. Indeed for the queens puzzle a so-called *middle first* (place a queen as close to the middle of the board as possible) is known to perform better than the first-fail method. User defined heuristics can also be supplied to the constraint solver using the same syntax:

```
:- heuristic queens(Board, Domain) with middle_first(Board).
```

Heuristics are meta-logical predicates defined using normal Prolog clauses. Several domain related meta-logical predicates are built-in for defining heuristics.

2.2 Implementation of Constraints

The constraint solver of ElipSys is based on that of CHIP, with significant modifications in the binding structures in order to run in a parallel environment.

Of particular importance is the implementation of *backtrackable assignment* (BA) variables, which are available internally to implement various data structures of the coroutining and finite domain machineries. In contrast to normal logical variables, a BA variable can be destructively assigned to different values many times. The previous values are restored upon backtracking.

Backtrackable assignment variables and a good implementation are a prerequisite for the efficiency of constraint handling. During the constraint propagation phase it is necessary to efficiently modify in place the constraint data structures.

Despite the overhead introduced by the shared environment machinery, the finite domain constraint solver of ElipSys is comparable in efficiency to the one of CHIP. This is mainly due to an improved handling of the BA variables which avoids the use of time stamps [1].

2.3 Constraints Measurements

To show the efficiency of the constraint handling, we compare three versions of the queens solver in ElipSys with three versions of the program for the same problem in standard Prolog. The three ElipSys programs use no heuristics, the first-fail heuristic, and the middle-first heuristic, respectively. The three standard Prolog programs use generate-and-test, standard backtracking, and forward-checking algorithms, respectively. The last version is generally considered a very good implementation in standard Prolog. BIM Prolog, which is one of the fastest known Prolog systems on SUN 3/60, is used for the standard Prolog programs in the comparison. Table 1 shows the execution times for the N-queens programs.

N queens problem — first solution —SUN 3/60					
	BIM Prolog			ElipSys		
N	Generate & test	Standard backtracking	Forward checking	GFC standard	GFC first-fail	GFC middle-first
8	304.3	0.18	0.12	0.20	0.24	0.08
12		0.74	0.34	0.60	0.50	0.18
16		49.50	14.20	20.60	0.32	0.26
20		1450.56	321.70	500.88	0.76	0.44
30					3.34	1.12
40					1.88	1.52
50					254.66	2.26
60					9.64	3.30
70					248.34	6.38
80					1888.18	9.80
90					>1 hour	7.24
200						34.33

Table 1: Comparison with standard Prolog BIM V2.5. Times are in seconds.

Table 2 shows the execution times and speed-ups of the N-queens program for all solutions on a Sequent Symmetry. The relative performance improves with the size of the problem and when the problem is big enough the speed-up obtained is almost linear to the number of processors. We do not include data for big Ns here because the number of solutions increases drastically. We could provide data for single solutions with big N, but this sometimes gives superlinear speed-up and sometimes no speed-up, varying from run to run due to the randomness of the parallel exploration of the search tree. Heuristics are not used, since they do not improve the efficiency much when N is small.

N queens problem (all solutions, no heuristics)					
	Number of processors (Sequent Symmetry)				
N	1	2	4	8	10
	time	speedup	speedup	speedup	speedup
8	3.51	1.9	3.3	5.1	5.8
9	14.92	2.0	3.7	6.9	8.3
10	58.77	2.0	3.9	7.6	9.4
11	281.23	2.0	4.0	7.9	9.9

Table 2: Speed-up through parallelism. Times are in seconds.

3   Execution Model

The ElipSys execution model clearly distinguishes between binding environment and code, and scheduling and control issues. This allows the design of a well-understood and explicit interaction mechanism. The binding environment and code rely on shared memory whereas scheduling and control are message based.

The ElipSys execution model comprises a scheduler and several inference engines [8]. The engines process threads of ElipSys computation, i.e. *el-threads*, the units of sequential computation. The execution of an el-thread involves the creation of more el-threads. Several el-threads are available for processing in parallel by the engines. The distribution of the el-threads among the engines is done by the scheduler.

An el-thread binds its *private variables* in place (i.e. in a location of the local or the global stack) and binds *shared variables* in a binding array [17]. Each engine has its private binding array for storing shared variable bindings. Shared variables have an associated stack location which contains an index in the binding arrays. The shared binding environment in ElipSys is *read only*.

The code area, i.e. the memory area where the ElipSys abstract machine code is stored, is shared by all engines. Although ElipSys allows an application to change its code dynamically, this feature is seldom used, so writes to this area are very infrequent.

3.1   ElipSys System Architecture

ElipSys has a multi-threaded system architecture (see figure 1). It comprises several workers sharing memory and communicating via messages. Each worker consists of a set of engines, a memory manager and part of the scheduler, which is distributed among all the workers. A worker is the unit of processor allocation and is mapped to an operating system task. The engines can be mapped to operating system threads.

Latencies in the underlying hardware and software cause blocking of engines, e.g. a memory fault blocks an engine until the associated page of memory has been brought in from a remote processing node or secondary storage. The scheduler of a worker keeps available a sufficient number of runnable engines (i.e. engines with a ready el-thread) to be able to mask latencies by means of switching between engines.

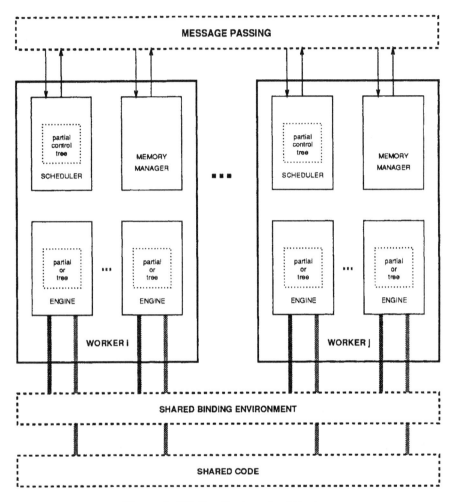

Figure 1: ElipSys System Architecture

The scheduler manages the distribution of el-threads over the workers in order to achieve a good speedup and high utilisation of allocated resources, i.e. *high locality, good balance of load*, and *coarse grain parallelism*. The scheduler dispatches work and exchanges load information between different workers by means of message passing. Coarse grain parallelism is strived for by selecting work for remote workers from the top of the search tree. The principle of locality leads to allocating work from the bottom of the search tree to the local engines.

The memory manager manages a private heap and a shared heap. It provides functions to allocate and free memory blocks. Memory allocation is a local operation, i.e. a worker cannot allocate memory blocks from remote heaps. Private memory blocks cannot be freed remotely. A worker can however free memory blocks from remote shared heaps. This involves message passing between the local and the remote memory managers. The workers share a common address space which implies that the memory managers have to synchronise, by means of message passing, when they want to expand their heaps.

The main characteristic of ElipSys is that it has the same execution model and system architecture on both shared and distributed memory machines. On distributed memory machines, ElipSys uses *Distributed Shared Memory (DSM)* for the binding environment and the code. A *strong coherent DSM* ensures that at any time all the copies of shared data are coherent. In a *weak coherent DSM* the coherency establishing operations (e.g. invalidating or copying data) are done lazily and are possibly triggered by the application.

The *read only* property of the ElipSys shared binding environment implies that every engine has only a few pages with a single writer and multiple readers (i.e. there is one such page per stack). The other pages have multiple readers and no writers or they have a single reader/writer. A strong coherent DSM for the binding environment requires therefore less network traffic than one would in general expect. The very structured nature of an ElipSys computation (traversal of a tree) allows however the use of weak coherent DSM. The synchronisation and coherency mechanisms of the weak coherent DSM can be connected to the scheduling and control machinery of the system. Using a weak coherent DSM should lead to less messages than using a strong coherent DSM [15, 6]. Experimenting with weak coherent DSM is part of the future work on the ElipSys system.

3.2   ElipSys Implementation

A first prototype of ElipSys is already running on a 12 processor Sequent Symmetry, a shared memory machine. This implementation is however not yet multi-threaded, i.e. a worker comprises only a single engine. This does not cause a serious performance loss on shared memory architectures where latency is not a real issue. In distributed computing environments one has however to cater for considerable network latencies.

A network of Sun workstations running the Mach operating system kernel is used as a testbed for distributed ElipSys, in particular to experiment with distributed shared memory. A few workers are allocated per workstation. In the current implementation latency is masked by switching between workers (i.e. task switching), as opposed to switching between engines (i.e. thread switching) in a multi-threaded implementation. We expect to have preliminary results of distributed ElipSys by the end of the year.

4   Garbage Collection

As in sequential logic programming systems, garbage collection in ElipSys plays an essential role for supporting real-world applications. The implementation of ElipSys is based on WAM [16] technology. For sequential WAM based systems, *mark-and-compact* garbage collection represents the state-of-the-art. The principles of this garbage collection technique are well explained in [3]. The garbage collection algorithm used in ElipSys is an extension of this method without significant increase in complexity compared to the standard model.

In this section we will first describe the aspects of garbage collection related to the constraint data structures and then briefly present how garbage collection is performed in parallel.

4.1   Garbage Collection of Constraints Data Structures

The implementation of coroutining and constraints in ElipSys introduces new data structures on the stacks which are subject to garbage collection. In particular a new kind of variables, the above mentioned *backtrackable assignment* (BA) variables, has been added to ElipSys at the implementation level.

The introduction of BA variables slightly increases the complexity of the garbage collection algorithm (see [11] for more details). Delay and domain variables represent quite complex data structures which are allocated dynamically on the global and trail stacks, and inside the binding arrays. The structures of delay and domain variables differ from each other depending on the type of domain. It is therefore essential to make the garbage collector independent from the coroutining and constraint data structures. This is achieved in ElipSys by representing delay or domain variables as standard *inference engine term* data structures which have to be tagged properly. Fig. 2 shows the simplified representation of a domain variable compared to a standard structure.

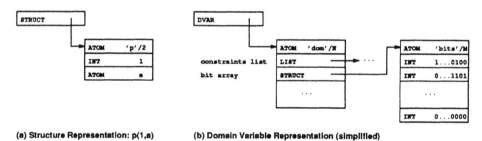

(a) Structure Representation: p(1,a)   (b) Domain Variable Representation (simplified)

Figure 2: Structure and Domain Variable Representation

The design decision to use the generic inference engine term data representation has proved extremely valuable in the past: the integration of coroutining in ElipSys, done after the garbage collector had been completed for constraints, did not require any change in the garbage collection component of ElipSys. The only drawback of this data representation is a slight increase in memory consumption compared to other implementations which rely on more compact and less general representations [9, 1].

Table 3 shows the amount of garbage collected during the execution of four programs using constraints: *bridge* (scheduling problem with disjunctive constraints), *color* (graph colouring problem), *layer* (channel routing problem in digital circuit layout) and *rna-folding* (biological application to predict secondary structure of a ribosomal RNA sequence). The figures are taken from a sequential execution but apply equally well to the parallel case. For each stack the number of collected KBytes, the number of scanned KBytes and the garbage ratio are given. This ratio, the amount of garbage reclaimed,

Benchmark	Global Stack			Binding Array			Trail Stack			Total
	coll	scan	[%]	coll	scan	[%]	coll	scan	[%]	[%]
bridge	3.8	105.8	4	46.9	63.6	74	13.3	133.4	10	21
color	4.6	153.3	3	7.3	44.4	16	1.0	122.0	1	4
layer	176.1	455.7	39	229.0	279.0	82	75.7	219.6	34	60
rna-folding	347.5	360.6	96	210.8	213.8	99	78.9	82.1	96	97

Table 3: Amount of Collected Garbage [in KBytes]

differs very much from program to program. Pure constraint programs like the graph colouring problem *color* seem not to generate any garbage at all[2]. The figures on the other benchmarks indicate that more realistic application programs like *bridge* or *rna_folding* cannot do without garbage collection.

4.2 Garbage Collection in Parallel

ElipSys follows an independent garbage collection approach, an idea first presented by [2], where neither synchronisation nor communication is necessary between parallel threads of computation. Garbage collection is done in an incremental way, i.e. garbage collection restricts itself to those parts of the stacks which have not yet been garbage-collected previously and is triggered *before* creating a parallel branch. A single, incremental garbage collection step is therefore restricted locally to one thread of sequential computation and can be performed completely independently from any other parallel work.

This approach fits very well with the overall requirement of ElipSys to be suited for execution on distributed memory machines as well as shared memory architectures. In distributed memory environments, communication between processing elements must be avoided as much as possible. Initial results have proved the validity of the ElipSys garbage collector design (more details can be found in [11]).

5 Conclusions

We have presented the most interesting aspects of the logic programming system ElipSys. Constraint handling has been improved at language level, compared to the previous CHIP system, by a stricter separation of logic from control and increased declarativeness. The parallel implementation of constraints has shown to be efficient and offers new possibilities for parallel exploration of search problems. The garbage collector significantly increases the functionality and usability of ElipSys for real-world applications. To our knowledge, it is the first working garbage collector within the type of constraint logic systems based on CHIP [9]. Finally, the execution model of ElipSys has been carefully designed to be suited for various parallel architectures, i.e shared and distributed memory machines. Prototypes of a number of commercial applications are currently being implemented on ElipSys.

---

[2]Fortunately the garbage collection overhead is negligible in that case.

Acknowledgements

We would like to thank Mike Reeve for commenting earlier versions of this paper. This work was partially funded by the ESPRIT II project EP2025, the European Declarative System (EDS).

References

[1] A. Aggoun and N. Beldiceanu. Time Stamps Techniques for the Trailed Data in Constraint Logic Programming Systems. In *Seminaire de Trégastel sur la Programmation en Logique*, France, 1990.

[2] Khayri A.M. Ali. Incremental Garbage Collection for Or-Parallel Prolog based on WAM. In *Proceedings of the Gigalips Workshop*, April 1989.

[3] Karen Appleby, Mats Carlsson, Seif Haridi, and Sahlin Dan. Garbage Collection for Prolog Based on WAM. *Communications of the ACM*, 31(6):719–741, June 1988.

[4] U. C. Baron, J. Chassin de Kergommeaux, M. Hailperin, M. J. Ratcliffe, P. Robert, J.-C. Syre, and H. Westphal. The Parallel ECRC Prolog System PEPsys: An Overview and Evaluation Results. In *Proceedings of the 5th Generation Computer Systems Conference*, November 1988.

[5] Jorge B. Bocca. MegaLog — A platform for developing Knowledge Base Management Systems. In *Proceedings of the International Symposium on Database Systems for Advanced Applications*, pages 374–380, April 1991.

[6] Lothar Borrmann. A virtually shared memory model with customized coherency. In Peter Mueller-Stoy, editor, *11th ITG/GI Conference on Architecture of Computing Systems*. VDE Verlag - ISBN : 3-8007-1688-7, March 1990.

[7] Sergio A. Delgado-Rannauro, Michel Dorochevsky, Kees Schuerman, André Véron, and Jiyang Xu. ElipSys: An Integrated Platform for Building Large Decision Support Systems. Technical Report DPS-104, ECRC, January 1991.

[8] Sergio A. Delgado-Rannauro, Michel Dorochevsky, Kees Schuerman, André Véron, and Jiyang Xu. ElipSys Execution Model. Technical Report DPS-86, ECRC, January 1991.

[9] M. Dincbas, P. Van Hentenryck, H. Simonis, A. Aggoun, T. Graf, and F. Berthier. The Constraint Logic Programming Language CHIP. In *Proceedings of the International Conference on 5th Generation Computer Systems*, pages 693–702, December 1988.

[10] M. Dorochevsky, M. Paci, M. J. Reeve, K. Schuerman, A. Véron, K.-F. Wong, and J. Xu. EDS: A Host for ESQL and ElipSys. In *Proceedings of the 3rd Workshop on Parallel and Distributed Processing*, Sofia, Bulgaria, April 1991. Elsevier Science Publisher B.V.

[11] Michel Dorochevsky. Garbage Collection in the OR-Parallel Logic Programming System ElipSys. Technical Report DPS-85, ECRC, March 1991.

[12] G. Haworth, S. Leunig, C. Hammer, and Reeve M. The European Declarative System, Database and Languages. *IEEE Micro*, 10(6):20–23, December 1990.

[13] Pascal Van Hentenryck. *Constraint Satisfaction in Logic Programming*. MIT Press, 1989.

[14] Pascal Van Hentenryck. Parallel constraint satisfaction in logic programming: Preliminary results of CHIP within PEPSys. In Giorgio Levi and Maurizio Martelli, editors, *ICLP'89*, pages 165–180, Lisbon, June 1989. MIT Press.

[15] Kai Li and Paul Hudak. Memory coherence in shared virtual memory systems. *ACM Transactions on Computer Systems*, 7(4):321–359, November 1989.

[16] David H.D. Warren. An Abstract Prolog Instruction Set. Technical Note TN-309, SRI, October 1983.

[17] David S. Warren. Efficient Prolog memory management for flexible control strategies. In *The International Symposium on Logic Programming*, pages 198–202, 1984.

CONTROLLING SEARCH WITH META-BRAVE

P.Kefalas and T.J. Reynolds
Department of Computer Science
University of Essex
Colchester CO4 3SQ, UK
e-mail reynt,kefap@essex.ac.uk

Abstract

We outline the Brave system: a Horn-clause language **Brave**, a dialect of Prolog designed for OR-parallel execution, plus **meta-Brave**, containing extra-logical features. Brave has been stripped of Prolog's cut, **assert** and **retract**, enforcing a declarative programming style which enables easier parallelisation. However, we need replacements for those predicates, in particular to code parallel versions of search algorithms, where guidance of the search in one subtree requires information from another subtree. Meta-Brave features directives which allow algorithmic knowledge about the domain to be stated independently from the Brave application program. This guidance is provided in three main ways: partial results are selectively remembered (**lemmas**), conditions of early failure of subproofs are stated (**pruning**), the style of search is altered (**strategies**). We show how this combination of features makes the Brave system specially suited to writing clear programs, for example search algorithms taken from Artificial Intelligence. In this paper we investigate how OR-parallelism can be exploited in hill-climbing, genetic algorithms and best-first search. By simulation we analyse the parallelism obtained.

1 Introduction

We outline the logic programming system Brave plus Meta-Brave (more fully described in [1]). Brave is a minimal Prolog designed for OR-parallel execution. Brave lacks the **cut**, **assert** and **retract** of Prolog because we believe they compromise parallel execution. However, in common with other workers [2][3][4][5], we believe we need replacements, in particular to code parallel versions of search algorithms, where guidance of the search in one subtree requires information from another subtree. Rather than include this meta-control in Brave itself, we provide a meta language in which we may express guidance of search as a separate declarative programming activity. We believe this separation leads to clearer programs, without inhibiting the free exploitation of parallelism. Meta-Brave can guide search using three main mechanisms: partial results are selectively remembered (lemmas), conditions for early failure of subtrees are stated (pruning), the style of search is altered (strategies). We show how this combination of features makes the Brave system specially suited to writing clear programs for example search algorithms taken from Artificial Intelligence. In [1] results were presented for the application of Brave to the branch and bound algorithm and alpha-beta pruning of game trees. In this paper we present results for hill-climbing, genetic algorithms and best-first search.

2 Brave

Brave has no cut (!), but allows the if-then-else construction:

$$p :- q \rightarrow r ; s$$

replacing a number of uses of cut. Unlike Prolog's equivalent construction, the condition q in Brave's if-then-else must have only one solution. There are two terminators for OR-cases :

>**dot** (.) terminates OR-cases to be tried sequentially,

>**colon** (:) terminates OR-cases to be tried in parallel.

These terminators are semantically transparent, only possibly altering the order of solutions. There are a number of instances where sequential execution to find one solution for a goal is required and finding extra (identical) solutions is over-computation. This is indicated in Brave by the call:

>**single(g1,g2,..)**

As with Prolog

>**bagof(term, goal, L)**

is used to collect solutions of **goal** into a list , but we also add :

>**expand(t, L)**

to expand a list in parallel. This enables the exploitation of data parallelism. The use of **expand** fattens trees, reducing the maximum memory required for any particular processor.

3 Meta Brave and search problems

The command

>**:- lemmapattern(predicate,lifetime,type) if condition.**

directs that any result for **predicate** be retained as a lemma, provided **condition** is satisfied. The operation is asynchronous. The **condition** is written as a conjunction of goals to be executed sequentially, for one solution. Lemmas are held in a special database and may be accessed explicitly by the condition of a meta-directive through use of the meta-predicate **lemma/1**. The command

> **:- lookup(predicate).**

forces consultation of the lemma-base whenever **predicate** is called (with subsumption check). The command

> **:- prune(goal) if condition.**

causes **goal** to be failed if **condition** can be satisfied at least once. The meta-directive:

> **:- strategy(predicate, breadth-first).**

has the effect of suspending calls to predicate until all processes are suspended, then allowing all calls to predicate to proceed, thus inducing a breadth-first search. The meta-directive:

> **:- strategy(predicate(..,X,....), best-first(X,N)).**

has a similar effect, but also asks that calls to predicate be ordered according to the (integer) X, before the best N of them are allowed to proceed.

4 Example Programs

We present three programs with an evaluation of their parallel performance obtained from a simulator. The simulator runs Brave Abstract Machine code produced by compilation. In one cycle of the simulator an abstract machine instruction is executed at every processor which has work. We take into account overheads due to lemma creation and lemma retrieval. We also count 50 abstract instructions per processor task switch. However we do not take into account the costs of remote references, which would occur in a distributed memory architecture. Neither do we take into account the cost of distributing the lemmabase. Studies of these overheads await the results of practical trials on an actual parallel architecture, which we are currently pursuing.

4.1 Parallel Best-First Search

There is a problem in parallelising best-first search: a global best-first requires a synchronisation point to sort all unexpanded nodes, and then re-distribute them. Alternatively each processor can apply its own local best-first without synchronisation. Between synchronisations two main sources of parallelism can be exploited:

(a) the evaluation function can be executed concurrently,

(b) more than one best node can be expanded at a time.

The Brave program to perform global best-first search is not much different from a multiple depth-first search program (only the heuristic evaluation has been added):

```
bf(Node, HValue, [Node | RestPath] ):-
        (leaf(Node) ->
                    RestPath = []
        ;
                    arc(Node, Children),
                    expand(NewNode, Children),
                    heuristic(NewNode, HeuristicValue),
                    bf(NewNode, HeuristicValue, RestPath)
        ).
```

However it is the strategy meta-directive which determines that the execution should proceed in a best-first fashion:

```
:- strategy(bf(_,V,_)), best-first(V,1)).
```

This instructs the underlying implementation to switch strategy: all calls to **bf/3** suspend until there are no more active branches in the execution tree. At that point, only the best processes, according to the value of **V**, proceed while the others remain suspended. Each processor takes one process. This is tunable to the application but the number of re-distributed processes is equal to the number of processors available in the machine. In the Brave program, there is no need to explicitly keep a structure for the nodes that belong to the frontier set. Instead, the suspended processes form the frontier set. Termination is a problem for such a search, which may be solved by the meta-directives:

```
:-lemmapattern(leaf(Node), permanent, success).
:-prune(bf(_,HeuristicValue,_)) if
            lemma(leaf(Node)).
```

In a parallel best-first algorithm, the only way of implementing a loop check is to publish the nodes that have already been expanded:

```
:-lemmapattern(arc(Node,_), permanent, success).
:-prune(arc(Node,_)) if
            lemma(arc(Node,_)).
```

We have applied best-first to the N-puzzle. Three types of heuristics are used :

(a) the number of tiles which are in a different place from that in the final board,

(b) the sum of the manhattan distances for each tile from its final position,

(c) heuristic (b) plus a breadth-first component, ie. the distance from the initial state.

Figures 1 and 2 show the speedups obtained for the same random configuration of the initial board. Figure 1 indicates a super linear speedup using heuristic (a). Figure 2 corresponds to the same problem tested with the more refined heuristic (b). This shows that a small problem may seem larger, with more scope for parallelism, if a naive heuristic is employed. Figure 3 shows data taken for an 8-puzzle with a much more difficult initial position. It indicates that the potential for parallelism grows with the difficulty of the problem. Figure 4 shows the speedup obtained for 15-puzzle tested with heuristic (c).

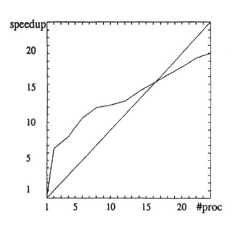

Figure 1 : Best-first on 8-puzzle with the naive heuristic (a).

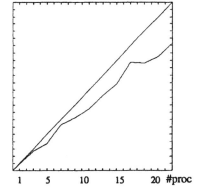

Figure 2 : Best-first on 8-puzzle with the refined heuristic (b). The same problem as is Figure 1.

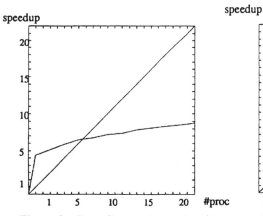

Figure 3 : Best-first on 8-puzzle with the refined heuristic (b). A more difficult problem than in Figure 2.

Figure 4 : Best-first on 15-puzzle with A*-like heuristic (c).

4.2 Hill-Climbing

We look at two methods for exploiting OR-parallelism in hill-climbing :

(a) the evaluation is performed simultaneously for all children nodes,
(b) separate local searches start from different initial states.

Program 1 in the appendix shows Brave coding for a hill-climbing algorithm. The method of 2-opting is used to solve the Travelling Salesman Problem. Firstly, we investigate how much parallelism is available in 2-opting itself. Hill-climbing is performed for only one candidate tour of length 15 (Figure 5(a)) and 25 (Figure 5(b)). The source of parallelism in

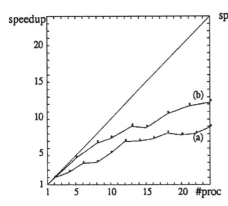

Figure 5 : Parallelism in the 2-opting procedure. One initial state: (a) Tour of 15 nodes, (b) Tour of 25 nodes.

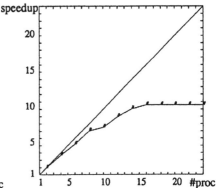

Figure 6: Multi-Hill-Climbing. 15 initial candidate tours.

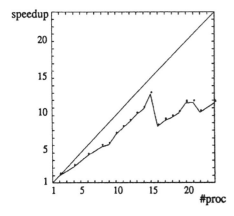

Figure 7 : Fully parallel Hill-Climbing. Still 15 initial candidate tours.

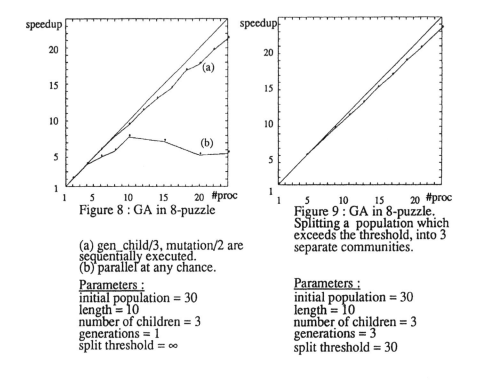

Figure 8 : GA in 8-puzzle

(a) gen_child/3, mutation/2 are
sequentially executed.
(b) parallel at any chance.

Parameters :
initial population = 30
length = 10
number of children = 3
generations = 1
split threshold = ∞

Figure 9 : GA in 8-puzzle.
Splitting a population which
exceeds the threshold, into 3
separate communities.

Parameters :
initial population = 30
length = 10
number of children = 3
generations = 3
split threshold = 30

2-opting is the ability to check all disjoint arcs for qualification in parallel. Figure 6 shows the speedup obtained by initiating hill-climbing with 15 different candidate tours. Notice that in this case, we restrict the parallel examination for qualification, ie. the **mutate/2** procedure is executed sequentially. The speedup for more than 15 processors remains constant since only 15 processors can be successfully utilised while the rest remain idle. It is also worth pointing out that the task switching is reduced to a minimum because each processor is exclusively working on one candidate tour. For Figure 7 the two sources of parallelism are combined. The number of task switching operations is increased but the speedup obtained is slightly better than both previous cases.

4.3 Genetic Algorithms (GAs)

There are three sources of OR-parallelism in GAs:

(a) more than one pair of parents may be selected to breed in parallel,
(b) within the breeding process itself potential offspring may be prepared in parallel,
(c) multiple populations may be developed simultaneously.

We have applied the GA listed in the appendix to the 8-puzzle problem. A member of the population is a list of legal moves from the initial board :

[u,d,d,r,l,...,l]

The performance of any board is the sum of the manhattan distances of that board from the goal board. Figure 8 shows the result of applying the GA to an initial population of 30 structures of length 10, ie. 10 legal moves performed on the initial configuration of the 8-puzzle. Every pair of parents produces 3 children, that is 90 new members per generation. The second clause ga/3 is omitted so that splitting the population into communities does not occur. Thus Figure 8 shows only the OR-parallelism obtained by the parallel generation of children. We have been experimenting with two alternatives: one is to restrict parallel execution of calls which perform the breeding (Figure 8.(a)) while the other allows parallelism at any point (Figure 8.(b)). The speedup obtained in the former case is higher due to lack of task switching and consequently idle time. The total number of idle cycles per processor falls down by a factor of 400 while the total cycles are reduced to 1/3 of the cycles of the latter case. It is clearly shown that when the grain of computation increases the speedup obtained is higher. Figure 9 shows the speedup obtained by a GA in which a split of the population in three parts takes place after its size exceeds 30 individuals. The speedup is higher than in previous case. This implies that parallelism due to the separate communities dominates over the parallel breeding.

References

[1] T.J. Reynolds, P.Kefalas "OR-Parallel Prolog and Search Problems in AI Applications". *Proceedings of the 7th International Conference on Logic Programming*, ed. D.H.D. Warren and P.Szeredi, MIT Press, pages 340-354,1990

[2] S. Haridi, P. Brand. "ANDORRA Prolog - An Integration of Prolog and Committed Choice Languages". *Proceedings of the FGCS '88 Conference*, ICOT, pages 745-754, 1988

[3] B. Hausman, A. Ciepielewski, A. Calderwood. "Cut and Side Effects in Or-Parallel Prolog". *Proceedings of the FGCS '88 Conference*, ICOT, pages 831-840, 1988

[4] E. Lusk et al., D.H.D. Warren et. al, S. Haridi et al. "The Aurora OR-Parallel Prolog System". *Proceedings of the FGCS '88 Conference*, ICOT, pages 819-830, 1988

[5] P. Szeredi. "Using Dynamic Predicates in Aurora - a Case Study". *Internal Report, Dept. of Computer Science, University of Bristol*, 1990

Appendix

Program 1.

```
hill_climb_two_opts( InitialRoutes, ImprovedRoute, Distance):-
    expand( Route, InitialRoutes ),
    opts( Route, ImprovedRoute ),
    evaluate( ImprovedRoute, Distance ).

opts( Route, ImprovedRoute ) :-
    arc( Route, Mutation ),
    (Route = Mutation ->
        ImprovedRoute = Mutation ;
        evaluate( Mutation, Cost ),
        opts(Mutation,ImprovedRoute)
    ).

arc( Route, MutatedRoute ):-
    bagof( MR, mutate(Route,MR), NewRoutes),
    ( NewRoutes = [] ->
        MutatedRoute = Route ;   expand( MutatedRoute , NewRoutes)).

mutate( Route, Result) :-
    disjoint( Route,arc(A,B), arc(C,D)),
    qualified( Route, arc(A,B), arc(C,D) ),
    opting( Route, A,B,C,D, Result).


disjoint( [C1|Rest], arc(A,B), arc(C,D) ) :-
    append( [C1|Rest], [C1], RoundTour ),
    disjoint_arcs_aux( RoundTour, arc(A,B), arc(C,D) ),
    D \= A.

disjoint_arcs_aux( [A,B|Rest], arc(A,B), arc(C,D) ) :-
    any_arc( Rest, arc(C,D) ).
disjoint_arcs_aux( [_|Rest], arc(A,B), arc(C,D) ) :-
    disjoint_arcs_aux( Rest, arc(A,B), arc(C,D) ).

any_arc( [C1,C2|_], arc(C1,C2) ):
any_arc( [_|Rest], Arc ) :-
    any_arc( Rest, Arc ):

qualified( Route, arc(A,B), arc(C,D) ) :-      % 2-opting
    cost( A, B, C1 ),
    cost( C, D, C2 ),
    cost( A, C, C3 ),
    cost( B, D, C4 ),
    C12 is C1 + C2,
    C34 is C3 + C4,
    C12 > C34.

/*    meta-directives.                         */

:- lemmapattern(qualified(Route,_,_)).
:- prune(qualified(Route,_,_)) if
                        lemma(qualified(Route,_,_)).
```

Program 2.

```
ga(0, Society, Society).
ga(N, Population, FinalSociety):-
        N \= 0,
        split(Population, Communities),
        expand(NewPopulation, Communities),
        ga(N, NewPopulation, FinalSociety):
ga(N, Population, FinalSociety):-
        N \= 0,
        bagof(Child,
            reproduce(Population, Population, Child),
            NewGeneration),
        N1 is N-1,
        ga(N1, NewGeneration, FinalSociety):


reproduce([Parent1|_], Population, Child):-
        pick_one_mate(Population, Parent2),
        generate_children(Parent1,Parent2,Child):
reproduce([_|Rest], Population, Child):-
        reproduce(Rest, Population, Child):


generate_children(Parent1,Parent2,Fitness-Child):-
        how_many_children_list(L),
        expand(_, L),
        gen_child( Parent1, Parent2, TempChild),
        mutation(TempChild, Child),
        evaluate(Child, Fitness).
```

/* meta-directives to allow population split */

```
    :- prune(split(Population,_)) if
        ga_parameter(emigration_after,ST),
        length(Population,L),
        L < ST.
    :- prune(reproduce(Population,_,_)) if
        ga_parameter(emigration_after,ST),
        length(Population,L),
        L >= ST.
```

/* meta-directives to control fitness */

```
    :-lemmapattern(evaluate(Child,Fitness), update, success) if
        lemma(evaluate(_,BestFitness)),
        better(Fitness,BestFitness).
    :-prune(ga(_,Population,_)) if
        average(Population,Fitness),
        lemma(evaluate(_,Best)),
        out_of_range(Fitness,Best).
```

Solving Optimisation Problems in the Aurora Or-parallel Prolog System

Péter Szeredi*

IQSOFT (SZKI Intelligent Software Ltd.)
Iskola u. 10,
H-1011 Budapest, Hungary
E-mail: szeredi@iqsoft.hu

Abstract

Aurora is a prototype or-parallel implementation of Prolog for shared memory multiprocessors. It supports the full Prolog language, thus being able to execute existing Prolog programs without any change. There are, however, several application areas where the simple built-in control of Prolog execution hinders efficient exploitation of or-parallelism.

In this paper we discuss the area of optimisation problems, a typical application area of this kind. The efficiency of an optimum search can be dramatically improved by replacing the exhaustive depth-first search of Prolog by more sophisticated control, e.g. the branch-and-bound algorithm or the minimax algorithm with alpha-beta pruning. We develop a generalised optimum search algorithm, covering both the branch-and-bound and the minimax approach, which can be executed efficiently on an or-parallel Prolog system such as Aurora. We define appropriate language extensions for Prolog—in the form of new higher order predicates—to provide a user interface for the general optimum search, describe our experimental implementation and present example application schemes.

Keywords: Logic Programming, Programming Methodology, Parallel Execution, Optimum Search.

1 Introduction

Aurora is a prototype or-parallel implementation of Prolog for shared memory multiprocessors [6]. It provides support for the full Prolog language, contains graphics tracing facilities, and gives a choice of several scheduling algorithms [3, 4, 2]. Aurora has been developed in the context of the informal "Gigalips" collaboration, incorporating Argonne National Laboratory (Illinois, USA), University of Bristol (UK) and SICS - the Swedish Institute of Computer Science. SZKI Intelligent Software Ltd (IQSOFT, Budapest, Hungary) joined the Gigalips consortium in 1990.

---

*Part of the work reported here has been carried out while the author was at the Department of Computer Science, University of Bristol, U.K.

One of the major outstanding problems in the context of parallel execution of Prolog is the question of non-declarative language primitives. These primitives, e.g. the built in predicates for modification of the internal data base, are quite often used in large applications. As these predicates involve side effects, they are normally executed in strict left-to-right order. The basic reason for this is the need to preserve the sequential semantics, i.e. compatibility with the sequential Prolog. Such restrictions on the execution order, however, involve significant overheads and consequent degradation of parallel performance.

There are two main directions for the investigation of this problem. First, one can look at using the unrestricted, "cavalier" versions of the side effect predicates. This opens up a whole range of new problems: from the question of synchronization of possibly interfering side effects, to the ultimate issue of ensuring that the parallel execution produces the required answers. Since one is using the non-logical features of Prolog here, it is natural that the problems encountered are similar to those of imperative parallel languages. We have explored some of these issues in [12].

Another approach, that can be taken, is to investigate why these non-logical features are used in the first place. One can try to identify typical subproblems which normally require dynamic data base handling in Prolog. Having done this, one can then define appropriate higher order language extensions to encapsulate the given subproblem and thus avoid the need for explicit use of such non-logical predicates. A typical example already present in the standard Prolog is the 'setof' predicate: this built-in predicate collects all solutions of a subgoal, a task which otherwise could only be done using dynamic data base handling.

In this paper we attempt to pursue the second path of action for the application area of optimum search problems. Efficient optimum search techniques, such as the branch-and-bound algorithm and the minimax algorithm with alpha-beta pruning, require sophisticated communication between branches of the search tree. Rather than to rely on dynamic data base handling to solve this problem, we propose the introduction of appropriate higher order predicates. We develop a general optimum search algorithm to be used in the implementation of these higher order predicates, which covers both the branch-and-bound and the minimax algorithm, and which can be executed efficiently on an or-parallel Prolog system such as Aurora.

Our presentation can be divided into the following parts:

- We define the *abstract domain*, i.e. the abstract search tree with appropriate annotations, suitable for describing the general optimum search technique.

- We develop a *parallel algorithm* in the context of the above framework.

- We define appropriate *language extensions* for Prolog, in the form of new built-in predicates, with the help of which the above algorithm can be embedded within a parallel Prolog system.

- We develop an experimental Aurora *implementation* of the language extensions using the parallel algorithm.

- We examine *application schemes* and *example applications* using the language extensions and their implementation.

Sections 2-6 of the paper deal with the above five topics, Section 7 discusses related and future work, while Section 8 summarises the conclusions.

2 The Abstract Domain

The abstract representation of the optimum search space is viewed as a tree with certain annotations. Leaf nodes have either a (numerical) value associated with them, or are marked as failure nodes. The root node and certain other non-leaf nodes are called *optimum nodes*. These nodes are annotated with either a *min* or a *max* symbol, indicating that the minimal (maximal) value of the given subtree should be calculated. Some non-leaf nodes can be annotated with constraints of form *<relational-op> Limit*, where *Limit* is a number, and *<relational-op>* is one of the comparison operators $<$, $\leq$, $>$ or $\geq$. Constraints express some domain related knowledge about values associated with nodes, as explained below.

We will use the term *value node* for the non-failure leaf nodes and the optimum nodes together. We define a value function, which assigns a numerical value to each value node. For a leaf node, the value is the one given as the annotation. For a max (min) node, the value is the maximum (minimum) of the values of all the value nodes directly below the given node.

A node annotated with a constraint *<relational-op> Limit* expresses the validity of the following fact:

> For each of the value nodes directly below the constraint node their value V satisfies V *<relational-op> Limit*.

The goal of the optimum search is to find the value of the root node.

The notion of search tree presented here is more general than that required by the branch-and-bound and minimax algorithms. The branch-and-bound algorithm uses a search tree with only a single optimum node (the root) and several constraint nodes below. The minimax algorithm applies to trees where there are several layers of alternating optimum nodes but there are no constraint nodes.

We introduce a further type of annotation in the search tree to cover some aspects of scheduling: each node can have a numeric priority assigned to it. This priority value can be used to control a best-first type search.

3 The Parallel Algorithm

We envisage several processing agents (workers) exploring the search tree in parallel, in a way analogous to the SRI model [13]. The workers traverse the tree according to some exhaustive search strategy (e.g. depth-first or best-first) and maintain a "best-so-far" value in each optimum node.

We introduce the notion of *neutral interval*, generalising the alpha and beta values used in the alpha-beta pruning algorithm. A neutral interval, characterised by a constraint of form *<relational-op> Limit* can be associated with a particular node if the following condition is satisfied:

The value of the root node will not be affected if we replace the value of a (value) node directly below the given node, which falls into the neutral interval, by another value falling into the neutral interval.

As the workers traverse the tree they assign neutral intervals to constraint and optimum nodes. When a constraint node is processed, the complement of the constraint interval is assigned to the node as a neutral interval. The precondition for this neutral interval to be valid is trivially satisfied, as there can be no value nodes directly below the given constraint node, that have a value falling into the neutral interval[1].

In a similar way, a neutral interval $\leq B$ ($\geq B$) can be associated with each max (min) node, which has a best-so-far value B.

An important property of neutral intervals is that they are inherited by descendant nodes, i.e. if a neutral interval is associated with a node, then it can be associated with any descendant of the node as well. This can be easily proven using the continuity property of intervals, as outlined below.

The only non-trivial case of inheritance is the one when a neutral interval is associated with the parent P of an optimum node N. To prove that the same neutral interval can be associated with node N, let us consider the effect of changing the value of a node directly below N within the given neutral interval (say the value is changed from V_1 to V_2, where both V_1 and V_2 are within the neutral interval). A simple examination of cases shows that if the old value of N or the new value of N is outside the closed interval bounded by V_1 and V_2, then the value of N (and consequently the value of the root) could not have changed. This means that if the value of N changes, it changes within the closed interval bounded by V_1 and V_2, that is within the given neutral interval. Using the premise that this neutral interval is associated with node P, we can conclude that the value of the root is unchanged in this case as well. This finishes the proof that the given neutral interval is inherited by the child node N.

There are basically two types of neutral intervals, ones containing $+\infty$ and the ones containing $-\infty$. Two intervals of the same type can always be replaced by the bigger one. This, together with the inheritance property, means that the worker can keep two actual neutral intervals as part of the search status, when the tree is being traversed (which is very similar to the alpha and beta values being kept up to date during the search).

The neutral intervals can be used to prune the search tree. Let us first consider a simplified universe of discussion, assuming that each constraint node has at least one value node below it. When a worker reaches a node the constraint of which is subsumed by a currently valid neutral interval, then the tree below the constraint node does not have to be explored, and a single solution with an arbitrary value within the neutral interval can be assumed[2]. Optimum nodes act as special constraint nodes in this respect: a max (min) node with a best-so-far value B is equivalent to a constraint $\geq B$ ($\leq B$).

A further optimisation can be made at optimum nodes. When a worker starts to explore a max (min) node with a neutral interval of form $\leq B$ ($\geq B$), then the initial best-so-far value can be established as B. Note that the workers still have to keep track of the fact whether there were any solutions at all within a particular optimum search, so that no false solutions are produced.

---

[1] Note that because of the inheritance of neutral intervals this seemingly trivial fact can be utilised for pruning subtrees below the constraint node (see later).

[2] This is the point where we use the assumption that there is a value node below each constraint node.

A crucial problem in the parallel execution of such optimum search programs is the propagation of neutral intervals. Let us consider the following situation: a worker is updating the best-so-far value of a max node while another worker is exploring a branch below this node. Updating this best-so-far value to B also means that the neutral interval, applicable to all nodes below, can now be extended to $\leq B$. There are two basic techniques for handling such a situation:

- The worker below is notified about the new neutral interval, i.e. the information on changes is propagated downwards.

- The downwards propagation is avoided at the expense of each worker scanning the tree upwards every time it wants to make use of the neutral interval (e.g. for pruning).

Reynolds and Kefalas [7] have used the second approach in their proposed extension of the Brave system. A serious drawback of this approach is, however, that it slows down the exploration, even if only a single worker happens to be working on a subtree. Therefore the first approach seems to be preferable, i.e. the worker updating a best-so-far value in an optimum node should notify all the workers below the given node about the new neutral interval.

So far we have assumed that each constraint node has at least one value node below it. Let us now expand the domain of discussion to include trees where this condition is not enforced. If we extend the range of values that can be associated with nodes to include the infinite values $-\infty$ and $+\infty$, then each failure node can be viewed as a proper value node, with the actual value being

- $-\infty$ if the optimum node immediately above is a max node,

- $+\infty$ if the optimum node immediately above is a min node.

The notion of constraint can have two interpretations in this extended framework. One can consider *strong* constraints, which actually guarantee the presence of a (finite) value node below; and *weak* constraints which may still hold if there is no proper value node in the subtree below. The implicit constraints generated by optimum nodes are obviously of the strong type. On the other hand, not all constraints can be assumed to be strong, as e.g. the constraints used in the case of the branch and bound algorithm applied to the traveling salesman problem are of the weak type.

A weak constraint can be used for pruning only in one of the two kinds of optimum searches. For example, a weak constraint $\geq B$ occurring in a maximum search expresses the fact that the contribution of the current subtree to the maximum search will either be a value $\geq B$, or $-\infty$. This means that such a constraint can not be used to prune the subtree, as it can not guarantee that all values will be part of a neutral interval $\geq C$. On the other hand the same weak constraint occurring in a minimum search will be equivalent to a strong constraint, and thus can safely be used for pruning, as the "failure" value $+\infty$ is actually part of the constraint interval $\geq B$.

4 Language Extensions

We propose new higher level predicates to be introduced to encapsulate the algorithm described in the previous section. The optimum search is generalised to allow arbitrary Prolog terms, and an arbitrary ordering relation *LessEq* is used instead of numbers and numerical comparison. The optimum search returns a pair of terms *Key-Info*, where the *Key* is used for ordering and *Info* can contain some additional information. To simplify the user interface, our experimental implementation assumes all (user-supplied) constraints to be weak.

The proposed new built-in predicates are the following:

maxof(+*LessEq*, ?*Key-Info*, +*Goal*, ?*Max*)
minof(+*LessEq*, ?*Key-Info*, +*Goal*, ?*Min*)

> *Max*(*Min*) is a *Key-Info* such that *Goal* is provable, and *Key* is the largest (smallest), according to the binary relation *LessEq*, among these *Key-Info* pairs. *LessEq* can be an arbitrary binary predicate, either user-defined or built-in, that defines a complete ordering relation.

bestof(+*Dir*, +*LessEq*, ?*Template*, +*Goal*, ?*Value*)

> *Dir* can be either max or min. bestof(max, ...) is equivalent to maxof(...) and bestof(min, ...) is equivalent to minof(...).

constraint(+*Term1*, +*LessEq*, +*Term2*)

> *Term1* is known to be less or equal to *Term2* according to the binary relation *LessEq*. This means that all solutions of the current branch will satisfy the given condition. One of *Term1* and *Term2* is normally a *Key* of a maxof, minof or bestof, in which case the constraint can be used for pruning.

priority(+*Priority*)

> Priority should be an integer. This call declares that the current branch of execution is of priority *Priority*. Several calls of the priority predicate can be issued on a branch, and the list of these priorities (earlier ones first), ordered lexicographically, will be used when comparing branches.

5 Implementation

We have designed an experimental implementation of the language primitives described in the previous section, within the current Aurora system itself. This uses a simplified version of the proposed algorithm, as it does not implement the propagation of neutral intervals. The implementation applies the best-first search strategy according to the user-supplied priority declarations and uses pruning based on the constraint declarations. This section gives a brief description of the experimental implementation.

Introduction of new control features is normally done via interpretation. We have decided to avoid the extra complexity and overheads of interpretation at the expense of requiring the application program to encapsulate the parts of the program using the new control features within a meta-predicate called task. A call of task has the following form:

task(*Goal, NewContext* - *OldContext*)

Here *Goal* is normally a conjunction, which begins with calls of the control predicates priority and constraint. The invocation of task should always be the last subgoal in the surrounding bestof. If the *Goal* in task contains an embedded call to bestof, this should be the last subgoal in the conjunction, to make the minimax algorithm applicable.

The second argument of task is required for passing the control information on surrounding tasks and optimum searches. Similarly, the bestof (and maxof/minof) predicates acquire an additional last argument of the same structure. We use the form *NewContext* - *OldContext* to indicate that the role of this argument is similar to a difference list. The *OldContext* variable links the given call with the surrounding bestof or task invocation (i.e. it is the same variable as the *NewContext* variable in the extra argument of the surrounding control call). Similarly the *NewContext* variable is normally passed to the *Goal* argument, for use in embedded task or bestof invocations.

In the next section we will show an example of a program augmented with the additional arguments required by our experimental implementation (the branch-and-bound algorithm in Figure 2).

The execution of an application in this experimental implementation is carried out as follows. If there are no calls of task embedded in a bestof, then the optimum search is performed in a fairly straightforward way: a best-so-far value is maintained in the Prolog database which is updated each time a solution is reached.

When an invocation of task is reached within the bestof predicate, first the constraints are processed: if a constraint indicates that the subtree in question will not modify the best-so-far value (i.e. the constraint is subsumed by the currently applicable neutral interval), then the task call fails immediately. Otherwise the goal of the task, paired with information on the constraint and context, is asserted into the Prolog database and the execution fails as well. When all the subtasks have been created and the exploration of the bestof subtree finishes, a best-first scheduling algorithm is entered: the subtask with the highest priority is selected and its goal is started. Such a subtask may give rise to further bestof and/or task calls, which are processed in a similar way.

For the sake of such nested task structure the best-first scheduling is implemented by building a copy of the search tree in the Prolog database, but with the branches ordered according to the user supplied priorities (in descending order). This tree is then used for scheduling (finding the highest priority task), as well as for pruning.

Pruning may be required when a leaf node of the optimum search is reached and the best-so-far value is updated. Following this update the internal tree is scanned and every task, which has become unnecessary according to its constraint, is deleted.

The experimental implementation is operational in a sequential environment, parallel debugging and detailed performance evaluation is yet to be done. A more detailed description of the implementation can be found in [11].

6 Applications

Two larger test programs were developed to help in debugging the implementation: a program for playing the game of kalah, using alpha-beta pruning, which is based on a version presented by Sterling and Shapiro [10]; and a program for the traveling salesman problem based on the branch-and-bound technique as described in [1].

This section presents the general program schemes of these test programs, namely the branch-and-bound and alpha-beta pruning schemes. We also give the top level code for the traveling salesman problem, using the branch and bound algorithm.

6.1 The Branch-and-Bound Algorithm

We describe a general program scheme for the branch-and-bound algorithm. We assume that the nodes of the search tree are represented by (arbitrary) Prolog terms. We expect the following predicates to be supplied by the lower layer of the application:

child_of(*Parent*, *Child*) Node *Child* is a child of node *Parent*.

leaf_value(*Leaf*, *Value*) Node *Leaf* is a leaf node, with *Value* being the value associated with it.

node_bound(*Node*, *Bound*) All leaf nodes below the (non-leaf) node *Node* are known to have a value greater or equal to *Bound*.

Figure 1 shows the top layer of the branch-and-bound scheme based on the above lower-level predicates.

```
% Leaf is the leaf below node with the minimal Value
branch_and_bound(Node, Leaf, Value):-
   bestof(min, =<, V-L,
           leaf_below(Node, L, V),
           Value-Leaf).

% Node has a Leaf descendant with value Value
leaf_below(Node, Node, Value):-
   leaf_value(Node, Value).
leaf_below(Node, Leaf, Value):-
   child_of(Node, Child),
       node_bound(Child, Bound),
       Priority is -Bound,
       constraint(Bound, =<, Value),
       priority(Priority),
   leaf_below(Child, Leaf, Value).
```

Figure 1: THE GENERAL SCHEME FOR THE BRANCH-AND-BOUND ALGORITHM

The program of Figure 1 can be invoked using the following call:

   branch_and_bound(Root, Leaf, Value)

Here Root is the root of the tree to be searched, Leaf will be instantiated to the leaf within the subtree which has the minimal value, while Value will become the corresponding value.

The program uses a single bestof call which relies on the recursive predicate

```
leaf_below(Node, Leaf, Value)
```

This predicate simply enumerates all the Leaf nodes and corresponding **Values** below **Node**. The logic of this predicate is very simple: either we are at a leaf node (first clause), in which case we retrieve its value, or we pick up any child of the node and recursively enumerate all the descendants of that child (second clause). This logic is complemented with the calls providing the appropriate control (shown with a deeper tabulation): calculating a lower bound for the relevant subtree (node_bound), calculating the Priority to be the negated value of Bound (so that the subtrees where the bound is lower have higher priority), and notifying the system about the bound (constraint) and the priority for the best-first search (priority).

```
% Leaf is the leaf below node with the minimal Value
branch_and_bound(Node, Leaf, Value):-
   bestof(min, =<, V-L,
          leaf_below(Node, L, V      , Ctxt
                    ),
          Value-Leaf                 , Ctxt-_
       ).

% Node has a Leaf descendant with value Value
leaf_below(Node, Node, Value         , _
          ):-
   leaf_value(Node, Value).
leaf_below(Node, Leaf, Value          , Ctxt
          ):-
   child_of(Node, Child),
      node_bound(Child, Bound),
      Priority is -Bound,
                                    task((
      constraint(Bound, =<, Value),
      priority(Priority),
   leaf_below(Child, Leaf, Value      , NCtxt
            )                       ), NCtxt-Ctxt)
```

Figure 2: THE AUGMENTED FORM OF THE BRANCH-AND-BOUND SCHEME

The augmented form of the program in Figure 1, suitable for execution by the experimental implementation is shown in Figure 2. The additional arguments and the call of task is shown at the far right of the figure, so that the left hand side is an exact copy of Figure 1 (except for the layout).

6.2 The Alpha-Beta Pruning Algorithm

We now proceed to describe a similar scheme for the minimax algorithm with alpha-beta pruning (Figure 3). Again we allow the nodes of the game tree to be represented by arbitrary Prolog terms. The topology of the tree and the values associated with nodes are expected through predicates of the same form as for the branch-and-bound algorithm (child_of(*Parent, Child*) and leaf_value(*Leaf, Value*)). We require two additional auxiliary predicates:

node_priority(*Node, Prio*) *Prio* is the priority of node *Node*.

absolute_min_max(*Min, Max*) *Min* and *Max* are the absolute minimum and maximum values for the whole of the game tree[3].

```
% Node of type Type (min or max) has the value
% Value, produced by Child.
alpha_beta(Node, Type, Child, Value):-
   bestof(Type, =<, V-C,
          child_value(Node, Type, V, C),
          Value-Child).

% Node of type Type has a Child with Value.
child_value(Node, Type, Value, Child):-
      absolute_min_max(Min, Max),
      constraint(Min, =<, Value),
      constraint(Value, =<, Max),
   child_of(Node, Child),
   opposite(Type, OppType),
   node_value(Child, OppType, Value).

% Node of type Type has Value.
node_value(Node, _, Value):-
   leaf_value(Node, Value).
node_value(Node, Type, Value):-
      node_priority(Node, Priority),
      priority(Priority),
   bestof(Type, =<, V-null,
             child_value(Node, Type, V, _),
             Value-null).

opposite(max,min).
opposite(min,max).
```

Figure 3: THE MINIMAX ALGORITHM WITH ALPHA-BETA PRUNING

---

[3]Note that the scheme is still usable if no such absolute bounds are available—one just has to delete those parts of the program, which deal with the constraints based on the absolute bounds.

A typical invocation of the minimax scheme is the following:

```
alpha_beta(Node, max, Child, Value)
```

Here Node represents a node of the game tree, and max indicates that this is a maximum node. The call will return the Child with the maximal Value, from among all children of Node.

The alpha_beta predicate is defined in terms of a bestof search over all Child-Value pairs enumerated by the child_value predicate. This predicate, in its turn, issues appropriate constraint directives, enumerates the children (child_of), and invokes node_value for every child. The node_value predicate has two clauses, the first is applicable in the case of leaf nodes, while the second invokes the opposite bestof over child_value recursively, after having informed the system about the priority applicable to the given subtree.

Note that the algorithm presented in Figure 3 calculates the optimum with respect to the complete game tree. It is fairly easy, however, to incorporate an appropriate depth limit, as usually done in game playing algorithms, by a simple modification of this scheme.

6.3 The Traveling Salesman Problem

We now present a variant of the general branch-and-bound scheme described in Section 6.1 for the case of the traveling salesman problem.

The traveling salesman problem involves finding a complete circle of minimal total weight in a graph with weighted edges. Following the algorithm described in [1], we build a binary search tree that enumerates all possible circles. We select an arbitrary edge of the graph and divide the search space into two disjoint parts: those including the given edge and those excluding it. The choice between these two parts is represented by a node of the search tree. We then continue this process by selecting another suitable edge within each part and subdividing the search space, until each part will consist of exactly one circle.

The nodes of this binary search tree will have to incorporate information on including or excluding edges of the graph. We have decided to couple this information with the description of the graph itself: each node of the search tree is represented by a term containing a list of edges that have been decided to be included in the circle, as well as the list of yet undecided edges. Information on an edge includes the weight.

There is a simple algorithm for obtaining a lower bound for the total weight of all possible circles within a subtree of our search tree: for each vertex of the graph consider the two lowest cost edges that are still allowed, sum their weights, divide by 2, and calculate the sum of this for all vertices. As it happens, it is fairly straightforward to extend the algorithm of calculating this lower bound to also return an arbitrary edge of the graph which is still undecided (i.e. both its inclusion and its exclusion is possible). That is why we have selected the following auxiliary predicates to be used in the program for the traveling salesman problem:

lower_bound(State, Bound, UndEdge) Calculate the Bound lower bound for the State node of the search tree and return an undecided edge in UndEdge (or none if none is found — this means the State describes a unique circle of cost equal to Bound).

include_or_exclude(State, Edge, NewState) NewState is the state obtained by either including Edge in State, or excluding Edge from State.

route_equivalent(FinalState, Route) Route is the unique circular route corresponding to FinalState.

Figure 4 shows the top layer of our solution for the traveling salesman problem using the above auxiliary predicates.

```
trav_salesman(State, Route, Cost):-
   bestof(min, =<, C-F,
      final_refinement_of(State, F, C),
      Cost-FinalState
         ),
   route_equivalent(FinalState, Route).

final_refinement_of(State, FState, Cost):-
   lower_bound(State, Bound, UndEdge),
   final_refinement_of(UndEdge, State, Bound, FState, Cost).

final_refinement_of(none, State, Bound, State, Bound):-
   !.
final_refinement_of(Edge, State, _, FState, Cost):-
   include_or_exclude(State, Edge, NState),
   lower_bound(NState, Bound, NEdge),
   Priority is -Bound,
   constraint(Bound, =<, Cost),
   priority(Priority),
   final_refinement_of(NEdge, NState, Bound, FState, Cost).
```

Figure 4: THE TRAVELING SALESMAN ALGORITHM

The structure of the traveling salesman program of Figure 4 is very similar to the one presented in Figure 1. Note that we could have actually used that algorithm by providing definitions for the child_of, leaf_value and node_bound predicates of Figure 1 in terms of the above predicates, at the expense of repeated execution of some calculations.

7 Related and Further Work

An important issue is the relation of our work to the mainstream of research in constraint logic programming (CLP). In current CLP frameworks (as e.g. in the one described by van Hentenryck in [5]) the constraints arising in optimum search algorithms are handled by special built-in predicates. The reason behind this is that the generation of constraints is implicit in an optimum search, as the applicable constraint depends on the best-so-far value. We believe that by replacing such special predicates with the bestof construct, our extended algorithm can be smoothly integrated into a general CLP system.

Another aspect of comparison may be the type of parallelism. Current CLP systems address the issues of and-parallel execution of conjunctive goals as e.g. in the CLP framework described by Saraswat [9]. Our approach complements this by discussing issues of exploiting or-parallelism. Combination of the two types of parallelism can lead to much improved performance as shown by existing and-or-parallel systems, such as Andorra [8].

The problems of or-parallel execution of optimum search problems have been addressed by Reynolds and Kefalas [7] in the framework of their meta-Brave system. They introduce a special database for storing partial results or *lemmas*, with a restricted set of update operators. They describe programs implementing the minimax and branch-and-bound algorithms within this framework. They do not, however, address the problem of providing a uniform approach for both optimisation algorithms. Another serious drawback of this scheme is that pruning requires active participation of the processing agent to be pruned: e.g. in the minimax algorithm each processing agent has to check all its ancestor nodes, whether they make further processing of the given branch unnecessary.

We plan to continue our work on the implementation of the bestof predicate by rewriting the current implementation to support proper propagation of constraints. In longer term we plan to integrate the optimum search predicates into the lower level implementation of Aurora, providing an efficient test-bench for applications.

Finally it may be interesting to mention a more theoretical point, raised by D.H.D. Warren. Using the bestof predicate one can implement both firstof and oneof, the predicates for finding the first (leftmost) solution and any solution of a goal, respectively[4].

The definition of the oneof predicate in terms of bestof is shown in Figure 5.

```
oneof(Goal):-
   bestof(min, =<, Key-[],
          oneof(Goal, Key), _).

oneof(Goal, Key):-
   constraint(Key, >=, 1),
   call(Goal),
   Key = 1.
```

Figure 5: THE oneof PREDICATE EXPRESSED IN TERMS OF bestof

The implementation of firstof in terms of bestof is more complex, as it requires the program in question to be modified. The essence of the modification is that a composite Key is returned along each solution, indicating the position of the solution in the search space.

This means that the described optimum search algorithm provides a very general form of pruning, which encapsulates the "ordinary" Prolog cut operator, its symmetric version, the commit, as well as the more sophisticated pruning operations discussed earlier. It may be interesting to explore the implications of this observation, possibly aiming at a more uniform discussion of pruning within logic programming.

---

[4]The firstof and oneof predicates are in turn equivalent to the cut and commit pruning operators.

8 Conclusions

The design and the implementation of the `bestof` predicate has several implications. First, we have developed a new higher order extension to Prolog, which is general enough to encapsulate two important search control techniques: the branch-and-bound and alpha-beta pruning algorithms. The `bestof` predicate makes it possible to describe programs requiring such control techniques, in terms of higher level control primitives such as constraints and priority annotations. On the other hand we gained important experience by implementing the new predicates on the top of Aurora system. We believe that this experience can be utilised later, in a more efficient, lower level implementation as well.

We view the development of the `bestof` predicate as a first step towards a more general goal: identifying those application areas and special algorithms where the simple control of Prolog is hindering efficient parallel execution, and designing appropriate higher order predicates that encapsulate these algorithms. We believe that the gains of this work will be twofold: reducing the need for non-declarative language components as well as developing efficient parallel implementations of such higher order primitives.

9 Acknowledgements

The author would like to thank his colleagues in the Gigalips project at Argonne National Laboratory, the University of Bristol, the Swedish Institute of Computer Science and IQSOFT. Special thanks are due to David H. D. Warren for continous encouragement and help in this work.

This work was supported by the ESPRIT project 2025 "EDS", and the Hungarian-U.S. Science and Technology Joint Fund in cooperation with the Hungarian National Committee for Technical Development and the U.S. Department of Energy under project J.F. No. 031/90.

References

[1] Alfred V. Aho, John E. Hopcroft, and Jeffrey D. Ullman. *Data Structures and Algorithms.* Addison-Wesley, 1983.

[2] Anthony Beaumont, S Muthu Raman, Péter Szeredi, and David H D Warren. Flexible Scheduling of Or-Parallelism in Aurora: The Bristol Scheduler. In *PARLE91: Conference on Parallel Architectures and Languages Europe.* Springer Verlag, June 1991.

[3] Ralph Butler, Terry Disz, Ewing Lusk, Robert Olson, Ross Overbeek, and Rick Stevens. Scheduling OR-parallelism: an Argonne perspective. In *Logic Programming: Proceedings of the Fifth International Conference*, pages 1590–1605. The MIT Press, August 1988.

[4] Alan Calderwood and Péter Szeredi. Scheduling or-parallelism in Aurora – the Manchester scheduler. In *Logic Programming: Proceedings of the Sixth International Conference*, pages 419–435. The MIT Press, June 1989.

[5] Pascal van Hentenryck. *Constraint Satisfaction in Logic programming*. The MIT Press, 1989.

[6] Ewing Lusk, David H. D. Warren, Seif Haridi, et al. The Aurora or-parallel Prolog system. *New Generation Computing*, 7(2,3):243–271, 1990.

[7] T. J. Reynold and P. Kefalas. OR-parallel Prolog and search problems in AI applications. In *Logic Programming: Proceedings of the Seventh International Conference*, pages 340–354. The MIT Press, 1990.

[8] V. Santos Costa, D. H. D. Warren, and R. Yang. The Andorra-I Engine: A parallel implementation of the Basic Andorra model. In *Logic Programming: Proceedings of the Eighth International Conference*. The MIT Press, 1991.

[9] Vijay A. Saraswat. *Concurrent Constraint Programming Languages*. PhD thesis, Carnegie-Mellon University, January 1989.

[10] Leon Sterling and Ehud Shapiro. *The Art of Prolog*. The MIT Press, 1986.

[11] Péter Szeredi. Design and implementation of Prolog language extensions for or-parallel systems. Technical Report, SZKI IQSOFT and University of Bristol, December 1990.

[12] Péter Szeredi. Using dynamic predicates in an or-parallel Prolog system. In *Logic Programming: Proceedings of the 1991 International Logic Programming Symposium*. The MIT Press, October 1991.

[13] David H. D. Warren. The SRI model for or-parallel execution of Prolog—abstract design and implementation issues. In *Proceedings of the 1987 Symposium on Logic Programming*, pages 92–102, 1987.

καππα: A Kernel Andorra Prolog

Parallel Architecture Design

Remco Moolenaar, Henk Van Acker and Bart Demoen[1]

e-mail: {remco, henk, bimbart}@cs.kuleuven.ac.be

Abstract:

This paper describes the design of a parallel implementation for Kernel Andorra Prolog (KAP) named καππα. The main features of καππα are AND/OR parallelism, committed choice guard evaluation combined with don't know nondeterminism and constraint operations on variables. The design is based on the Warren Abstract Machine with some important extensions. One of the main problems involving AND/OR parallel systems is the efficient handling of variables. We have adopted the PEPSys hashing scheme with additional mechanisms for handling guard blocking and waiting. A καππα computation is divided into a number of steps. Every step contains a deterministic phase and a nondeterministic phase. The deterministic phase is executed in a normal Prolog-like way. The nondeterministic phase prunes the tree or divides the tree into a number of OR-branches, which share a common part of the tree. Each OR-branch is executed in the usual Prolog-like manner.

Keywords: AND/OR parallelism, Andorra, Kernel Andorra Prolog.

1. Introduction

In recent years, different solutions have been proposed for exploiting parallelism in logic programs. These can be divided in a number of classes:

a) Committed choice languages [3],[13],[15].

b) OR-parallel Prolog [1],[4],[17].

c) Independent AND-parallel Prolog [9],[10].

d) Independent AND/Full OR-parallel Prolog [6],[12],[20].

They all have one major drawback: not all inherent parallelism is exploited.

In [8] an AND/OR computation model is proposed for the Kernel Andorra Prolog language, which subsumes languages like Prolog, GHC and Atomic Herbrand, and exploits all the inherent parallelism.

---

1. KU Leuven, Department of Computer Science, Celestijnenlaan 200A, B-3001 Heverlee, Belgium

This paper describes an efficient implementation of the KAP computation model.

The rest of the paper is organized as follows: section 2 introduces the basic principles of Kernel Andorra Prolog; the major design problems are sketched in section 3; section 4 explains the binding scheme used for καππα; section 5 describes the execution mechanism of καππα; and in section 6 conclusions are presented.

2. Kernel Andorra Prolog computation model.

Kernel Andorra Prolog combines don't care nondeterminism by means of cut and commit guarded clauses, and don't know nondeterminism by means of wait guarded clauses. It subsumes Prolog as well as the class of committed choice languages. KAP defines a generic language system by providing several blocking operations on the constraint operations.

KAP computation proceeds in successive phases of deterministic computation and nondeterministic steps. The philosophy is that all deterministic steps can be performed in parallel and that guessing (nondeterminism) is only allowed in specific circumstances. Indeed, the don't care nondeterminism (in terms of KAP: indeterminism) can induce incompleteness whereas the don't know nondeterminism can lead to unnecessary multiplication of work.

[8] defines a formal model of the KAP computation, on which our implementation will be based. We give here only a condensed overview of the model, [8] can be consulted for a more detailed presentation. The KAP computation tree is represented by 'boxes'. The top of the tree can contain several layers of or-boxes. An or-box represents a globally disjunctive computation. Hence every son of an or-box is available for OR-parallel execution. An or-box consists of a series of and-boxes or or-boxes.

An and-box contains a sequence of local goals, a set of variables which are local to this and-box and a list of constraints on external variables. These constraints have emerged from the computations local to the and-box, and are kept locally, until they can be published by deterministic promotion.

The local goals in an and-box can be atomic goals or choice-boxes. An atomic goal is either a constraint goal which is not yet resolved, a built-in goal, or a user-defined goal which is not yet expanded to a choice-box by local forking.

A choice-box represents local computation for clause selection. A choice-box contains a series of guarded goals which are not yet promoted, and which represent the candidate clauses for the goal out of which the choice-box was created. A guarded goal consists of an and-box or an or-box corresponding to the local computation within the guard, a guard operator (wait, cut or commit), and a sequence of atomic goals representing the body of the clause.

Deterministic promotion can occur when only one guarded goal is left in a choice-box, and its guard is completed. This means that all the goals of the and-box corresponding to the guard are resolved and there are no other candidate clauses left. The guard and-box then contains the constraint list resulting from the evaluation of the guard. The atomic goals of the body of the guarded goal are inserted in the father and-box of the choice, the constraints of the guard and-box on variables local to the father and-box are applied, and the other constraints of the guard and-box are added to the constraint list of the father and-box.

If a box is stable, this means that all deterministic computation within the box has been done, and the computation outside this box cannot reactivate any deterministic computation within the box, then the tree beneath the stable box is available for guessing. There are two possibilities for guessing. If a choice-box corresponds to a wait guarded clause, the guarded goals with totally resolved guards can give rise to a global fork – i.e. an or-box – with respect to the closest surrounding and-box. This is called nondeterministic promotion. If on the other hand a choice-box corresponds to a commit-guarded or cut-guarded clause, a clause with totally resolved guard can give rise to pruning of other alternatives in the choice-box. This is called indeterministic promotion.

Every constraint is wrapped in a primitive constraint operation which expresses the blocking behavior of the constraint. We will only consider equality constraints. Ask-constraints are not allowed to instantiate any variable. Tell_0-constraints block until they do not instantiate any external variable of the and-box in which they appear. Tell_1-constraints are not allowed to instantiate variables external to the closest parent and-box of the and-box in which they appear. Tell_ω-constraints are allowed to instantiate any variable and hence never block. Finally, $\text{Tell}_{(1/l)}$-constraints may instantiate only variables local to the and-boxes within the closest surrounding pruning choice-box.

3. Major design problems

3.1 Or-parallelism

Kernel Andorra Prolog exploits OR-parallelism by nondeterministic promotion of wait guarded clauses. This leads to the well known problem of multiple assignment of variables shared between processes working on different OR-branches of the same tree. In καππα this problem also occurs at local forking with choice-boxes (see next chapters). Several solutions to this problem have been reported by Ali [1], Crammond [4], D.H.D. Warren [17][18], D.S. Warren [19] and Westphal et al.[20].

3.2 And-parallelism

KAP also allows to exploit every available AND-parallelism. The classical problem of conflicting bindings by processes in different branches of a conjunction is no problem in KAP, as the constraints are kept local and are only imposed at deterministic promotion. If at that time a conflicting binding would be created, the conjunction must fail.

KAP however creates other problems as a result of AND-parallelism. The theoretical model defines that the constraints are kept local to each and-box. An implementation will have to provide a mechanism to mimic this. The problem then is how a processor will know of the (deterministic) instantiation of a variable it uses, by another process operating in a distant, but conjunctive, part of the tree.

Theoretically this is not a problem: the processor will know of the binding when it promotes to the place where the variable was originally created, and where the deterministic - or unconditional - binding is stored. In practice however, such an unconditional binding should be known earlier by a process using the bound variable, because a binding can result in more pruning, early failure, or reactivation of blocked constraint operations. This is complicated because at every level of and-boxes a process could create a constraint for a variable, which should be visible to all the underlying and-boxes. It is not feasible to browse through the constraints of all the enclosing and-boxes up to the and-box where the variable is created, when accessing a variable.

In the class of committed choice languages, the similar problem of suspension upon variables is solved by attaching to the variable a suspension list with all the processes waiting on its instantiation.

3.3 Locality of Variables

In KAP variables are local to an and-box. In order to correctly execute the constraint operations one has to know which and-box a variable is local to: the current and-box, the father and-box of the current, or an and-box external to the father and-box. This problem is complicated because during promotion of guarded clauses, the variables local to the promoted clause become local to the closest surrounding and-box. So, the notion of locality of a variable must be dynamic.

3.4 Task switches

The constraint operations such as Ask, $Tell_0$ and $Tell_1$ can make the guard of a clause block. Later on, a guard evaluation should be reactivated upon instantiation of the blocked variable. This problem is well known for committed choice languages. Because of this blocking we expect that at local forking and the subsequent guard evaluation, frequent switches will occur between the candidate clauses, and even between different parts of the tree. Also at successful evaluation of a wait-guard, a switch will occur to the other candidate clauses to check whether these evaluate successfully as well. Therefore we optimized our design for task switching. As Gupta & Jayaraman [7] show, we will have to pay for this in the efficiency of task creation and/or the variable access and binding time. Suspending and reactivation of processes introduce also the problem of scheduling.

3.5 Stability detection

A problem which is very specific for KAP is to decide when guessing may occur. Theoretically, guessing is allowed if the tree undergoing the guess is stable. This means that all possible deterministic rewrite rules within the tree are finished, and that no computation outside the tree can reactivate any deterministic rewrites inside the tree. For implementational simplicity, one could say that only the whole computation tree can get stable. However, this will introduce a serious bottleneck, because in that case all computation has to die out first, then one or more guesses can be performed, and after that, deterministic computation can hopefully restart. It is obvious that an implementation should behave similarly to the theoretical computation.

4. The binding scheme

In this section the binding scheme for our implementation will be presented. Our scheme is an extended version of the PEPSys hashing scheme [20]. We considered other binding methods, but they are not very suitable for a Kernel Andorra Prolog implementation. First we will discuss the other binding methods, secondly we describe the principles of the PEPSys hashing scheme, and thirdly, we present our extensions to this scheme.

4.1 Discussion of the considered binding schemes

Binding arrays.

The binding array method [19],[18] induces overhead for task switching. When switching from a starting node to a goal node, the bindings that were made along the path from the common ancestral node to the starting node must be removed from the binding array and the new bindings along the path from the common ancestral node to the goal node must be installed in the binding array. As we already indicated, we expect frequent task switches, so this method would induce considerable overhead.

Moreover the binding array method is not very suitable for AND-parallel execution: when two workers are operating along different paths below a common ancestral and-parallel node, conflicting offsets in the binding array for local variables can arise. This gives serious problems if these local variables must be communicated from one worker to the other via a common global variable. A different solution would be to make the binding array shared between workers with a common ancestral and-parallel node. This however gives serious race conditions for the binding array.

Stack copying.

Stack copying methods such as the Muse approach [1] also suffer from serious overhead at task switching. Applying such an approach would require intelligent scheduling strategies and compile time analysis in order to favor coarse grain parallelism and to avoid shallow switching between blocking flat guards – or building a mechanism to avoid stack copying at shallow switching.

4.2 The PEPSys hashing scheme

In this chapter we will sketch briefly the basic principles of the PEPSys binding scheme. This scheme is based on a couple of simple binding rules:

1) The binding of a variable can be done in place, iff the variable is created by the current process.
2) Otherwise, the binding of a variable will be saved in a hash-window local to the current process.
3) If the binding of a variable was made before a branch split, this binding is valid for all the branches after the split.
4) Otherwise, the ascending hash-windows (which are all descendants of the process, that created the variable) are checked for a valid binding of the variable. If no valid binding is found, the variable is unbound for this process.

To be able to check whether a binding is valid or not, some extra work must be done:
- Every binding of a variable is tagged with the current OR-branch level (OBL).
- Every new process starts with a OBL of zero, and increments the OBL every time a new branch-point is created.
A binding is valid, if the binding OBL is smaller than the OBL of the branch split (see Figure 1).

4.3 Extensions to the PEPSys hashing scheme

The main difference between parallel Prolog and Kernel Andorra Prolog is the use of blocking constraints in KAP. This means that before a variable gets a binding, its activation condition must be satisfied, otherwise the current process is blocked.

59

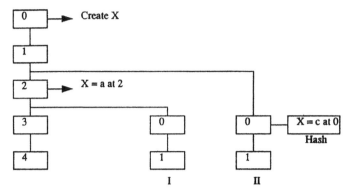

Figure 1: The binding X = a is valid for split branch I, whereas it is invalid for
split branch II. Split branch II has to use its own hash window for a binding.

The satisfiability of an activation condition depends on the locality of a variable. Therefore we need to know the creation time of a variable and compare it with the creation time of the current box. This induces extra overhead on the binding scheme; not only do we need to record the binding time of a variable, we need to record its creation time as well. This could be solved in two different ways.

The naive approach: instead of using one cell per variable (for the binding time), an extra cell is inserted to record the creation time of the variable. This approach is clearly easy to implement, but induces some extra space overhead.

The intelligent approach: the reference chain, after the creation of an unbound variable, has a minimal length of one. The end of this chain points to the variable on the heap, the start of this chain is kept in a register or environment variable. Our approach uses this chain in the following way: the binding time, of a variable, is recorded on the heap, that is, at the end of the chain; the creation time is recorded at the start of the chain.

This second, intelligent approach induces some extra space overhead when creating a structure on the heap with one or more new unbound variables. For these new variables a reference chain with a length of one is created. The start of the chain is saved in the structure, the end of the chain is saved on the first free heap cell after the structure. One additional improvement, compared to the naive approach, is the possibility to test whether an activation condition of a variable is satisfied or not, without dereferencing the variable.

Instead of using the OR-branch level tag, we use a timestamp mechanism to identify bindings made in different branches. This mechanism ensures that branches originating from the same root start their timestamps at the same value. The reason for this is, that it simplifies the test for the satisfiability of the activation condition. This can be explained using the satisfiability test for the $Tell_1$ activation condition:

Using OR-branch level (OBL):

(Local(Var) and Var.OBL >= CurrentBranchPoint.OBL - 1) or

(not Local(Var) and CurrentBranchPoint.OBL = 0 and Var.OBL = SplitOBL)

where Local(Var) means: Variable Var is created by the current process; SplitOBL is the OBL of
the branch point where the current branch originated.

Using timestamps:

    Var.Time >= BranchPoint.Time - 1

The computation model, including branch point handling and the use of timestamps, will be described in detail in the next section.

5. The Καππα execution model

In this section the καππα execution model for Kernel Andorra Prolog is described. Our model is based on the well-known Warren Abstract Machine [16] for sequential Prolog. It uses the local stack and heap as the WAM but these are completely modified; there is no trail.

First we will describe the use of the WAM in a parallel model; second, the memory organization of καππα; third, the description of the deterministic phase in καππα; and last, the nondeterministic phase of our model.

5.1. The parallel Warren Abstract Machine

The Warren Abstract Machine is an efficient implementation method for sequential Prolog, but it also has some nice properties that can be used in a parallel implementation. For instance, an environment consists of a number of value cells and a continuation that points to work still to be done. This is used to support AND-parallelism in our model. The only difference is that the continuation is not the continuation of the last selected clause (with an environment), but the continuation in the current selected clause (see Figure 2). The value cells in an environment can be seen as the parameters for the right branch of an AND-fork.

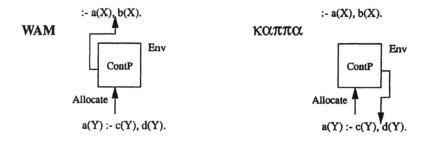

Figure 2: Using continuation in WAM and καππα

Another property of the WAM, that can be used in a parallel implementation, is the use of a choice point. The WAM choice point has all the ingredients to serve as an OR-branch: there is a pointer to extra work (L: the address of the next clause) and a number of value cells (A1 through An) containing the arguments for this procedure.

The reason for using a WAM like model is a direct consequence of our major design goal: optimize for speed in the deterministic phase. This will be further described in a following chapter.

5.2. *Memory organization of* καππα

In this chapter we will describe the memory organization of the καππα model. It is an adaptation of the WAM three stack scheme (heap, stack and trail).

Every processor has its own local stack and heap. Communication between processes or processors is established through message passing (in a shared-memory multiprocessor this could be simulated or become redundant depending on the message type).

The heap is used in a normal WAM like way, containing structures, constants and variables. Every value cell contains a timestamp, a tag and a value.

The stack contains a number of process blocks:

Branch point: is created when more than one clause could be selected (see WAM choice point).

AND-branch: is created when more than one goal could be selected (AND parallelism). This block contains the arguments for the next AND-branch (see WAM environment).

OR-branch: this block replaces a branch point when this branch point is selected for nondeterministic promotion (OR parallelism).

The καππα system does not use a trail to record nonlocal bindings, instead it uses binding lists. Every branch point records the bindings made during its activation in its own binding list. After a failure the binding lists are used to undo bindings (in the hash or in local memory). During promotion of a guard, the binding list is used to update the timestamps of the local variables (which must be local for the parent branch point after promotion) and to notify other AND-branches of a possible binding of a shared variable (in a following chapter we will explain this in more detail).

The branch point

The branch point is created every time a procedure is entered with more than one candidate clause. It contains the following cells:

• The creation timestamp.
• The depth of this branch point.
• The status of its execution.
• The arguments (A1...An) for this procedure.
• A pointer to the current AND-branch.
• Pointers to the father and child branch point.
• A pointer to the next alternative clause for this procedure.
• A pointer to a binding list on the heap.
• The number of guards active for this branch point[1].
• A pointer to a list of guards that are waiting for promotion.
• A pointer to a process list holding all the processes that are executing a branch from this branch point.

A guard is allowed to promote deterministically, if the number of active guards is one and there are no more candidate clauses left (the pointer to the next alternative clause is NIL). The list of waiting guards holds a single waiting guard, which is allowed to promote. Such a guard waiting block contains: the registers X1...Xn, AB, OB, BP, D, HT and P (see later), and a pointer to a binding list.

---

1. Active guards are guards that are being executed or are waiting for promotion.

The AND-branch

At the beginning of a new clause with more than one goal, an AND-branch is created. It holds the following cells:

- The status of its execution (Running, Finished, Waiting for completion, or Failed).
- The variables that are used for more than one goal (shared variables).
- A pointer (the continuation pointer) to the next instruction after a call statement.
- A pointer to the current branch point.
- Two pointers to the next and previous AND-branch.
- A pointer to a process list holding all the processes that used this AND-branch to grab work.

The continuation pointer used here is not the same as used in the WAM (see Figure 2): it points to the next goal in the clause where this AND-branch was created. This means that the continuation pointer, used after finishing a clause, is found in the current AND-branch and not in a register (see WAM CP register).

The OR-branch

After a branch point is selected for nondeterministic promotion, it is replaced by an OR-branch with a new timestamp. This new timestamp is used to separate the tree created before the OR-branch and the tree created after the OR-branch. This is important, because the branch points created before the OR-branch cannot be updated or removed. The reason for this is, that these branch points are shared between all the branches created by the OR-branch, for example (using $Tell_\omega$ constraint operation):

    :- generate(X), test(X).

    generate(X) :- X = 1 wait true.
    generate(X) :- X = 2 wait true.

    test(X) :- X > 1, X ≤ 3 wait true.
    test(X) :- X > 5, X ≤ 7 wait true.

The branch point created for **generate** is selected for nondeterministic promotion. The two guards for the **test** predicate are blocked and are waiting for a binding of X. The tree created for **test** is shared between the two branches of **generate**. To allow one of these branches to update or remove a branch of a shared tree, the part of the tree that is modified is copied from the original tree and the timestamps of this new tree are updated. The complete shared tree is not copied after creation of the OR-branch. If, for example, the guards of the **test** predicate have deeply nested predicates, the copying of the complete tree is superfluous, because of a possible early failure.

The καππα register set

The καππα model uses some registers to control the execution. Every processor has its own set of registers. The following registers are used:

P	Program pointer.
AB	Current AND-branch on the local stack.
OB	Current OR-branch.
BP	Current branch point.
T	Timestamp of the current branch.
D	Depth of the current branch.
HT	Pointer to the current hashtable.
H	Pointer to the top of the heap.
S	Structure pointer (see WAM).
WV	Pointer to a list of processes waiting for a binding of a variable.

X1...Argument / temporary variables.

5.3. The deterministic execution phase

One of the major design goals is to optimize the deterministic phase for speed. This means that the execution of abstract instructions like **call**, **execute** and **proceed** must have a similar behavior as in the WAM.

To illustrate the working of καππα, the most important abstract instructions are described, including the basic operations of the binding scheme.

fork N	Allocate a new AND-branch on the top of the stack. This instruction is the first instruction in a clause with more than one goal. It allocates space for an AND-branch containing N shared variables. The space must be completely allocated, because the execution can be stopped (e.g., due to a block on a variable) before a call instruction is applied. Register **AB** points to this AND-branch.
join	This is the instruction that precedes the final instruction of a clause with more than one goal. If the process list of the current AND-branch is empty (this means that this clause was executed sequentially), the AND-branch is discarded and register **AB** is set to the previous pointer from this AND-branch. Otherwise, the status of the current AND-branch is set to **SCHEDULED**, meaning that this AND-branch is no longer available to grab work from, but has to wait for other processes to finish.
call **Proc, N**	The size of an AND-branch is updated (if possible) to hold N shared variables. The program pointer is saved in the CP-cell of the current AND-branch. Register **D** and **T** are incremented. Execution proceeds at the address pointed to by **Proc**.
execute **Proc**	This is the last instruction of a clause. Register **D** is incremented. Execution proceeds at the address pointed to by **Proc**.
proceed	This is the last instruction of a clause. If the current AND-branch is created after the current branch point and the current AND-branch was grabbed from another process, then notify this parent process of the completion of this branch and update the bindings. If the current AND-branch has work left, it is used; otherwise the stack is searched for available work. If there is no work left, then other processes are asked for work.

wait / commit / cut   This instruction marks the end of the guard. If register **D** is not equal to the depth of the current branch point (the guard was promoted before its execution started), execution continues and **D** is decremented; else a guard waiting block is allocated and inserted in the guard waiting list of the current branch point.

Coding of clauses, using the instructions described above, looks like this (using the Tell_ω constraint operation):

    quicksort(InList, SortList, Rest) :- Inlist = [], SortList = Rest wait true.
    quicksort(InList, SortList, Rest) :-
            InList = [X | InListRest] wait
            partition(InListRest, X, Larger, Smaller),
            quicksort(Larger, SortList, [X | SortListRest]),
            quicksort(Smaller, SortListRest, Rest).

quicksort:	try_me_else	qs2
	getw_nil	A1
	wait	
	getw_value	A2, A3
	proceed	
qs2:	trust_me_else	fail
	fork	6
	getw_list	A1
	unify_variable	Y6
	unify_variable	A1
	get_variable	Y5, A2
	get_variable	Y3, A3
	wait	
	put_value	Y6, A2
	put_variable	Y4, A3
	put_variable	Y1, A4
	call	partition/4, 6
	put_value	Y4, A1
	put_value	Y5, A2
	put_list	A3
	unify_value	Y6
	unify_variable	Y2
	call	quicksort/3, 3
	put_value	Y1, A1
	put_value	Y2, A2
	put_value	Y3, A3
	join	
	execute	quicksort/3

The following instructions are internal operations. They are described as abstract instructions.

schedule **BP**   The branch point **BP** that is selected to be scheduled to another process is send (or copied) to become the root of this new process. A process block, containing all the necessary information to identify the new process, is inserted in the process list of the original branch point **BP**. The next / previous pointer and the pointer to the binding list in the new branch point are set to NIL. An initial hash block is created for the new process, containing the timestamp of **BP** and its process ID. The pointer to the next alternative clause is set to NIL[1]. Register **P** is set to the address of the selected branch.

schedule **AB**   The branch point belonging to **AB** is scheduled (see **schedule BP**, but without insertion of a process block). The original AND-branch **AB** is copied to the new process. A process block, containing all the necessary information to identify the new process, is inserted in the process list of the original AND-branch **AB** and this AND-branch is locked[2] to make it temporarily unusable. The next / previous pointer in the new AND-branch is set to NIL. Register **P** is set to the continuation pointer of the new AND-branch. This continuation is set to NIL.

promote **BP**   If another process grabbed the promoted branch, then notify the other process[3] (this involves sending the parent branch point of **BP** to the other process, which will become its new root) and insert process block in the parent branch point. Otherwise, if there is a guard waiting block (GWB) for **BP** then **restart GWB**. Otherwise, start execution of last guard (which is thus promoted before its execution starts). In all cases, remove **BP** and insert its binding list in the parent branch point. If the current AND-branch **AB** is created after **BP** then set the timestamps of the bindings made for the shared variables equal to the timestamp of the parent branch point of **BP**. If other processes used this AND-branch, then broadcast these updated bindings to the other processes[4].

restart **PR**   The status of the process **PR** is restored. This means: copy its binding list into the restarted branch point, restore all saved registers and restart execution.

block **Var**   Create guard waiting block and insert it in the current branch point. If this variable **Var** is a nonlocal variable, then put a reference to the guard waiting block in the

---

1. This means that after an early failure of this branch, a complete rescheduling for an alternative clause is performed, if the original branch point has such a clause. A real implementation could optimize this, by asking for a new branch. The address of the next clause is then copied from the original branch point, instead of the complete branch point.
2. The original AND-branch **AB** is unlocked after the first **call** instruction is executed in the new process. The continuation pointer in **AB** is set to the instruction after this **call**.
3. This process will execute **promote BP** for its own local branch point.
4. Special care must be taken for bindings containing structures with embedded local variables. These variables must be updated during promotion, or recognized during structure unification (The creation time of an embedded variable is greater than the creation time of the surrounding structure. During unification, the creation time of this variable is set equal to the creation time of the structure).

hash. Otherwise, insert **Var** and a reference to this block in the waiting variable list pointed to by the **WV** register.

fail   If the previous pointer in the current branch point is equal to NIL then notify the original branch (which will perform a **local fail** for this branch) else **local fail**.

local fail   If the current AND-branch is created after the current branch point, all the processes from the process list of this AND-branch are notified of the failure of this branch. If this process is saved in a guard waiting block, it is removed from its branch point, otherwise all the bindings are recovered using the binding list of the current branch point. Another branch is chosen.

value X   If X is not local for this process then return **nonlocal_value** X; otherwise return the value saved in local memory.

nonlocal_value X   This instruction is described in Pascal-like notation:

if HaveHashValue(X) **then**
    return HashValue(X)
else
    if X.Tag <> REFERENCE **and** BindTime(X) < SplitTime(X) **then**
        return X
    else
    begin
        SearchHash := Hash.Father
        while SearchHash.Time > CreationTime(X) **do**
        begin
            if HaveHashValue(X) **and** BindTime(X) < Hash.Time **then**
                return HashValue(X)
            else
                SearchHash := SearchHash.Father
        end
        return UNBOUND
    end

The creation time of the hash (Hash.Time) is equal to the timestamp of the branch that was grabbed from another process.

bind X, Value   The bindingtime of X is set to T. If X is not local for this process, the new binding of X (**Value**) is saved in the hash; otherwise **Value** is saved on the heap. X is inserted in the binding list of the current branch point.

5.4. *The nondeterministic execution phase*

The nondeterministic execution phase is entered after the deterministic phase has finished (that is, after all the processors stopped execution). The nondeterministic phase is then executed as follows: ·

• All the processors search in their own local stack for branch points that match the following criteria:

- If a branch point is waiting for indeterministic promotion or pruning (cut or commit guard) and this branch point has the lowest timestamp of all branch points that are waiting for indeterministic promotion or pruning, this branch point is the favored branch point for this processor.
- Otherwise, if there are no branch points waiting for indeterministic promotion or pruning, the branch point that is waiting for nondeterministic promotion (wait guard) and has the highest timestamp of all branch points that are waiting for nondeterministic promotion, is the favored branch point for this processor.

- If there are any favored branch points that are waiting for indeterministic promotion or pruning, the branch point that has the lowest timestamp is selected for indeterministic promotion or pruning. Otherwise, the branch point that has the highest timestamp is selected for nondeterministic promotion.

- If a branch point is selected for indeterministic promotion or pruning, remove all the pruned branches from this branch point (this could involve pruning of branches on a number of different processors) and notify the process that owns the branch point that this branch point can be reactivated. Quit the nondeterministic phase.

- Every waiting guard of the branch point that is selected for nondeterministic promotion gets its own copy of this branch point. The original branch point is replaced by an OR-branch, containing a list of pointers to all these copied branch points. The timestamps of the new OR-branch and the copied branch points are updated.

- Restart the deterministic phase.

Notice that pruning will be performed as high as possible in the tree, in order to prune as much as possible, and that nondeterministic promotion will be done as low as possible in the tree in order to limit multiplication of work.

The tree that was created before the OR-branch is shared between the new branches. This means that when a part if this shared tree must be updated or removed, it has to be copied to the process that wants to update or remove this tree.

When there is only one branch left in this OR-branch, a normal deterministic promotion is performed for the remaining branch.

6. Conclusions and future work.

We presented a design for a parallel implementation of Kernel Andorra Prolog. As stated in [8], several instantiations of the KAP language exist, and each could have an optimized implementation. If, for instance, the $Tell_\omega$ is the only constraint operator, thus simulating a Prolog like execution model, all internal operations involved in blocking of variables and restarting of branch points waiting for a variable can be removed. The removal of redundant internal operations can be applied to every instantiation of KAP. Our design can thus be used as a framework to optimize instantiations of KAP.

The main advantage of κα∏πα (and of Kernel Andorra Prolog) is, that it is able to exploit all the inherent parallelism offered by the language. This means that an instantiation of κα∏πα that has a Prolog like behavior, acts like an efficient full AND, full OR parallel implementation of Prolog.

Another advantage of κα∏πα, is that the design is independent of the underlying hardware architecture, allowing it to massively exploit all the inherent parallelism.

We are now working on a real implementation of καππα, which will give us the proof of the efficiency and practical usability of the initial καππα design. First, we will implement a rough version of καππα to get some notion on the overhead of internal operations and possible bottlenecks. Later on, a real optimized version of καππα will be implemented. We expect that this version will perform (for sequential execution of local branches) approximately two to three times slower than sequential Prolog implementations.

Acknowledgments

The authors wish to thank Danny De Schreye and Patrick Weemeeuw for their comments, and the 'Diensten voor de Programmatie van Wetenschapsbeleid' for support by project RFO/AI/02.

References

[1]   Khayri A. M. Ali, Roland Karlsson, "The Muse Or-Parallel Prolog Model and its Performance", in *Proceedings of the 1990 North American Conference on Logic Programming*, pp757-776, MIT Press, 1990.

[2]   Reem Bahgat, Steve Gregory, "Pandora: Non-deterministic Parallel Logic Programming", in *Proceedings of the Sixth International Conference on Logic Programming*, pp471-486, MIT Press,1989.

[3]   K. L. Clark & S. Gregory, "PARLOG: Parallel Programming in Logic", in *Concurrent Prolog: Collected Papers* ed. E. Shapiro, pp84-139, MIT Press, 1987

[4]   Jim Crammond, "A Comparative Study of Unification Algorithms for OR-Parallel Execution of Logic Languages", *IEEE Transactions on Computers*, vol. C-34, no. 10, pp911-917, IEEE Computer Society, October 1985.

[5]   Jim Crammond, *Implementation of committed choice logic languages on shared memory multiprocessors*, PhD thesis, Dept. of Computer Science, Heriot-Watt University, Edinburgh, May 1988.

[6]   Gopal Gupta and Bharat Jayaraman, "Compiled And-Or Parallelism on Shared Memory Multiprocessors", in *Proceedings of the North American Conference on Logic Programming, Cleveland*, pp 332-349, MIT Press, 1989.

[7]   Gopal Gupta and Bharat Jayaraman, "On Criteria for Or-Parallel Execution Models of Logic Programs", in *Proceedings of the 1990 North American Conference on Logic Programming*, pp737-756, MIT Press, 1990.

[8]   Seif Haridi and Sverker Janson, "Kernel Andorra Prolog and its Computation Model", in *Logic Programming, Proceedings of the Seventh International Conference*, pp 31-48, The MIT Press, 1990.

[9]   Manuel V. Hermenegildo, *An Abstract Machine Based Execution Model for Computer Architecture Design and Efficient Implementation of Logic Programs in Parallel*, PhD thesis, Department of Computer Sciences, The University of Texas at Austin, TR-86-20, August 1986.

[10]   Yow-Jian Lin, Vipin Kumar, "AND-parallel execution of Logic Programs on a Shared Memory Multiprocessor: A Summary of Results", in *Proceedings of the Fifth International Conference and Symposium on Logic Programming*, pp1123-1141, MIT Press, 1988.

[11]   Ewing Lusk, Ralph Butler, Terrence Disz, Robert Olson, Ross Overbeek, Rick Stevens, David H. D. Warren, Alan Calderwood, Peter Szeredi, Seif Haridi, Per Brand, Mats Carlsson, Andrzej

Ciepielewski, Bogumil Hausman, "The Aurora Or-parallel Prolog System", in *Proceedings of the International Conference on Fifth Generation Computer Systems*, pp 819-830, ICOT, Tokyo, 1988.

[12] B. Ramkumar, L. V. Kale, "Compiled Execution of the Reduce-OR Process Model on Multiprocessors", in *Proceedings of the North American Conference on Logic Programming*, pp313-331, MIT Press, 1989.

[13] Ehud Shapiro, "Concurrent Prolog: A Progress Report", in *Concurrent Prolog: collected papers*, ed. E. Shapiro, pp157-187, MIT Press, 1987.

[14] Ehud Shapiro, "The Family of Concurrent Logic Programming Languages", *ACM Computing Surveys*, vol. 21, no 3, pp 413-510, ACM Press, New York, September 1989.

[15] Kazunori Ueda, "Guarded Horn Clauses", in *Concurrent Prolog, collected papers*, ed. E. Shapiro, pp 140-156, MIT Press, 1987.

[16] David H.D. Warren, "An abstract Prolog instruction set", Technical Report no 309, SRI International, Menlo Park, 1983.

[17] David H. D. Warren, "Or-Parallel Execution Models of Prolog", in *TAPSOFT'87: Proceedings of the International Joint Conference on Theory and Practice of Software Development, Pisa, Italy*, pp 244-259, Springer-Verlag, 1987.

[18] David H. D. Warren, "The SRI model for or-parallel execution of Prolog - abstract design and implementation issues", in *Proceedings of the 1987 Symposium on Logic Programming*, pp 92-102, IEEE Computer Society Press, 1987.

[19] D. S. Warren, "Efficient Prolog Memory Management for Flexible Control Strategies", in *The 1984 International Symposium on Logic Programming*, pp198-202, IEEE, 1984.

[20] Harald Westphal, Philippe Robert, Jacques Chassin de Kergommeaux and Jean-Claude Syre, "The PEPSys Model: Combining Backtracking, AND- and OR-parallelism", in *Proceedings of the 4th Symposium on Logic Programming*, pp 436-448, IEEE, 1987.

A Flexible Scheduler for the Andorra-I System[*]

Inês de Castro Dutra[†]

Department of Computer Science

University of Bristol

Bristol BS8 1TR

e-mail: ines@compsci.bristol.ac.uk

Abstract

A flexible scheduler for distributing and- and or- parallel work in the Andorra-I system is presented. The scheduler allows workers to move freely between teams. Its strategy is based on estimates of and- and or- parallelism available in the execution tree. Preliminary results show that in most cases we can reach or surpass the best performance of Andorra-I running with any fixed team configuration. Since the teams are configured dynamically and automatically, the user does not need to be concerned with choosing an appropriate configuration. Further work is being done to improve the scheduler by using data obtained from compile-time analysis.

Keywords: And/Or-parallelism, Multiprocessors, Scheduling.

1. Introduction

There are two main sources of parallelism in logic programming, namely or- and and-parallelism. Or- parallelism is exploited when several alternative clauses for a goal are executed in parallel. And- parallelism is exploited when we execute two or more goals of the same clause simultaneously. Exploitation of full or- and and- parallelism is limited by the number of physical processors available in a system. And- parallelism is also limited by the interdependence among goals in a clause.

One very interesting way of exploiting and- parallelism in logic programs is used in Andorra-I [18, 19], where **determinate** goals are executed first and concurrently, according to the *Andorra Principle* [26]. Determinate goals are the ones that match at most one clause in a program. This way Andorra-I exploits dependent and- and independent determinate and- parallelism. Eager execution of determinate goals also results in a reduced search space, because unnecessary choicepoints are eliminated.

The Andorra-I parallel logic programming system exploits not only dependent and-parallelism, but also or- parallelism as in Aurora [16]. The system is composed of an engine, responsible for the execution of the Andorra-I programs [28, 29, 20], and a scheduler, whose main function is to find new tasks for the engine. A processing element that performs computation in the system is called a *worker*. Workers are divided into *teams* and cooperate with each other in order to share available and- work. Each team has a

---

[*]Research supported by CNPq, Brasilian Research Foundation under grant 202270/89.0

master, which is responsible for creating new choicepoints and *slaves* that are managed by their master. Teams of workers cooperate to share or- work.

The earlier status of the Andorra-I system was such that the organisation of teams could not be changed dynamically. The teams were of fixed size, the workers could not move from one team to another, and only master workers could grab or- work. This organisation of the system, although acceptable for some applications, is too rigid for a large number of applications where the degree of and- and or- work varies along the course of the execution. In such applications, the available parallelism is not completely exploited, if we have fixed the configuration of teams a priori.

Motivated by this limitation, we have designed a flexible scheduler and have implemented a simple version. The results obtained are shown in section 2.2. Although these results are better than those produced by Andorra-I with a fixed team configuration, we feel that the top-scheduler has some limitations, as discussed in section 3. This in turn led us to investigate other more intelligent strategies based on information provided by global analysis.

In the next section we discuss the top-scheduler strategy and show results obtained so far. In section 3 we discuss some issues and ways of enhancing the current strategy. In the last section we discuss alternatives of implementing more intelligent algorithms which will be investigated in the future.

2.   The Top-Scheduler

The current design of the flexible scheduler takes account of the fact that there already exist distinct schedulers to deal with and- and or- work. The novel part of the flexible scheduler, therefore consists of a *top-scheduler* which is responsible for making decisions when a worker does not find either and- or or- work. The or-scheduler is responsible for finding or- work, i.e. an unexplored alternative in the tree. Any Aurora or-scheduler [2, 21, 5, 3, 8] can be plugged into the system through the Aurora scheduler interface [7, 22, 23]. The and-scheduler is responsible for finding and- work, which corresponds to a goal in the run queue (list of goals not yet executed) of a worker in the same team.

Earlier schedulers were designed based on software engineering principles of having a clear and distinct interface between engine and scheduler. The top-scheduler was also designed via its interface functions. As a first step, the interactions between the top-, and-, and or- schedulers and the engine were identified and formed the basis of the interface functions. Details about the top-scheduler interface and its implementation can be found in [10].

In the subsequent sections we discuss the top-scheduler strategy and show the results obtained so far.

2.1.   The Top-scheduler Strategy

In Andorra-I, as described in the previous section, a worker can be a master or a slave of some team. In a flexible scheme we allow migration of workers from one team to another. A master can move to another team and become a slave when it runs out of or- work. A slave can move from its team to another whenever no and- work is found inside its team. It can also become a master of a new team.

The main goals of the top-scheduler are (a) to decide when an idle worker will change its type (master/slave) and (b) to choose the best team for a slave, while considering the cost of exchanging workers between teams. In order to avoid workers exchanging teams very often, we maintain a counter that registers the number of times a worker calls the top-scheduler without changing teams. As regards (a), the decision to change the type of a worker is based on a relation (*greatness factor*) between the current amount of and- and or- work available in the tree. Since we do not have sufficient information about the degree of parallelism in the application, this relation is tuned to adjust to the amount of parallelism available in the application. In fact, it represents the weight between and- and or- work. The best team is the one with more amount of and- work per worker (the one that has greatest *load*).

```
MASTER CALLS TOP-SCHEDULER:          SLAVE CALLS TOP-SCHEDULER:

Begin                                Begin
  calculate the amount of or-work;     calculate the load of the teams;
  calculate the amount of and-work;    If ( there is a team with
  ratio = and-work/or-work;                greatest load )
  If ( ratio > greatness factor )      move worker to the
     master becomes slave;                 best team;
     calculate the load of teams;     Else
     move new slave to                   calculate the amount of or-work;
        the best team;                   calculate the amount of and-work;
End.                                     ratio = or-work/and-work;
                                         If ( ratio > greatness factor )
                                            slave becomes master;
                                            new team is created;
                                  End.
```
Figure 1: Top-scheduler strategy

The basic algorithm that implements the strategy is shown in Figure 1. The amount of or-work is provided by the or-scheduler and corresponds to the number of live nodes (choicepoints that still have alternative clauses to be expanded) in the or-branch of a master worker. The amount of and-work is provided by the and-scheduler and corresponds to the total number of goals in a run queue. The load of a team is the quotient $\frac{run\ queue\ size}{team\ size}$. The *greatness* factor, as mentioned before, is varied according to the degree of and- and or- parallelism available in the application.

The worker cycle with respect to finding work is shown in Figure 2. The top-scheduler can be called from the or-scheduler when no or- work is found for a master worker. In this case, the top-scheduler has two alternatives: (a) let the master worker continue to look for or- work; or (b) make the master a slave and move it to the *best* current team. The top-scheduler can also be called by the and-scheduler if no local and- work (in the same team) is found for a slave worker. In this case, it has three alternatives: (a) let the slave worker continue to look for local and- work; (b) move this slave from its current team to another better team (the *best* currently available); (c) make the slave a master of a new

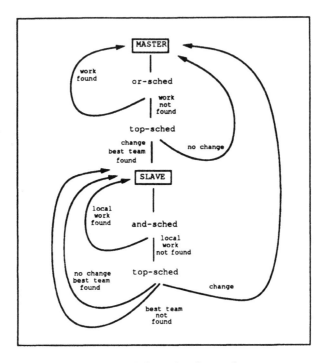

Figure 2: Life cycle of a worker

team.

2.2.   Preliminary Results

In Andorra-I with fixed teams, the team configuration must be specified from the beginning. The system can behave badly if, because of lack of knowledge about the quantity of
parallelism available in the application, the user cannot configure the right team. Moreover, for irregular applications where the type of parallelism varies during execution, the
system can still behave badly whatever initial configuration is selected. When designing
the top-scheduler, we thus expected to reach the best speedups achieved by Andorra-I for
programs with either and- parallelism or or-parallelism, and better or comparable results
for examples that mix both kinds of parallelism.

Table 1 shows the speedups obtained by Andorra-I when using fixed teams and the
flexible scheduler. The data related to the flexible scheduler shown in table 1 are the
results obtained by giving priority to and-work with a *greatness* factor of 3. This factor
was chosen as a starting point to measure the relation between and- and or- work as we
do not yet know what is an optimal relation. Best and Worst speedups were obtained
from 10 runs of the programs. For the version with fixed teams the Best and Worst
speedups were taken, respectively, from the best and worst times obtained among all
possible combination of workers. So, for example, **cross6**, had its best speedup running
with 2 masters and 2 slaves, whilst it had its worst speedup running with 4 masters. All
the examples run with the flexible scheduler started from one team of 4 workers.

Class	Pgm	Sp.fix.teams		Aver.	config	Sp.flex.sch.		Aver.
		Best	Worst		best sp.	Best	Worst	
artif. pgms.	and	3.04	0.99	2.015	1M 3S	3.08	2.64	2.860
	or	3.60	1.04	2.320	4M	3.76	3.53	3.645
	and/or	2.02	1.16	1.590	3M 1S	2.21	2.04	2.125
	or/and	3.20	2.33	2.765	3M 1S	3.30	2.49	2.895
	mixed	2.18	1.26	1.720	4M	2.01	1.74	1.875
and	fib	3.29	0.98	2.135	3S 1M	3.26	2.80	3.030
	mergesort	2.87	1.02	1.945	3S 1M	2.85	2.34	2.595
	nrv50	2.14	0.94	1.540	3S 1M	2.28	2.00	2.140
	nrv150	2.94	0.97	1.955	3S 1M	3.20	2.92	3.060
and>or	bqu	1.76	1.00	1.380	3S 1M	1.77	1.30	1.535
	scanner	1.92	1.25	1.585	3S 1M	1.88	1.51	1.695
and=or	cross6	1.93	1.38	1.655	2S 2M	2.03	1.56	1.795
	sets	2.99	2.11	2.550	2S 2M	2.94	2.39	2.665
or>and	db_conery	1.33	0.80	1.065	1S 3M	1.67	1.17	1.420
	qu_vitor	3.73	1.33	2.530	4M	3.88	3.80	3.840
	qu_reem	3.21	1.78	2.495	4M	3.50	3.28	3.390
	money	3.65	1.23	2.440	4M	3.75	3.70	3.725
	houses	3.31	1.54	2.425	4M	3.34	3.04	3.190
	qu_evan	3.81	0.87	1.840	4M	3.75	3.75	3.750
	map	3.35	0.95	2.150	4M	2.63	2.54	2.585
	rem_par	3.16	1.02	2.090	4M	2.66	2.45	2.555
or>>and	mutest	3.20	0.93	2.065	4M	3.12	2.89	3.005
	plan	2.70	1.15	1.925	4M	2.23	1.83	2.030

Table 1 - Speedups - FT x NFT (4 workers)

The first column of Table 1 represents the class of the applications. The first group (artificial programs) consists of well behaved artificial examples used to study the strategy of the top-scheduler. From this group program **and** only has and- parallelism and does not create any choicepoints, program **or** has no and- parallelism and creates a single choicepoint in the beginning. Program **and/or** has two phases. The first one has only and-parallelism and the second one creates a choicepoint. Program **or/and** has an or- parallel phase followed by an and- parallel phase. Finally, program **mixed** combines everything. The other programs are more realistic and are classified according to the degree of and- and or- parallelism available. The columns named "Aver." represent the average speedups and show that overall the results produced by Andorra-I under the top-scheduler strategy are much better than those obtained with a fixed configuration of teams.

We chose to run the examples, at first, using 4 workers, but each example has a least number of processors with which it should reach the theoretical or approximate expected speedup. If we consider an infinite number of processors, it is not difficult to find the best theoretical speedup. But if we limit the number of processors, it is yet not clear (a) what is the least number of processors we should use to obtain the maximum speedup; and (b) if we have a number of processors below the least number, what would be the best speedup for that number of processors. For the small examples of table 1, it is relatively easy to find the expected speedups for programs and and or running with 4 workers (which is approximately 4.0), but for complicated shapes of trees, this is a hard task.

For program and, as expected, Andorra-I running under the top-scheduler strategy produces speedups similar to the ones obtained by running Andorra-I with a fixed team of 1 master and 3 slaves. For program or, the result shown was also expected, because the speedup using the flexible scheduler should be comparable to Andorra-I running with a fixed team of 4 masters. We conclude that there is not much initial overhead of arranging the workers in 4 teams, given that we started with just one team of 4 workers.

For the mixed examples, Andorra-I running under the top-scheduler strategy behaved better or comparable to the version with fixed configuration of teams. Interestingly, program mixed shows slightly better speedup when using fixed teams. We observe similar results for some of the "real" examples. As discussed later, instant snapshots of the system may mislead the top-scheduler and sometimes it may make wrong decisions.

For the more realistic examples with just and- parallelism, Andorra-I with flexible scheduler behaves akin to Andorra-I with fixed teams, as expected.

In contrast, for the examples that have a balanced combination of and- and or- work, the top-scheduler performance depends strongly on its luck about deciding to change workers from one team to another. As an example, the program sets produced better speedups when the top-scheduler gave priority to or-work and the greatness factor was 0 (which means that the workers were allowed to change their types for any ratio between and- and or- work).

For the examples with more or- than and- parallelism, we can observe that as the amount of or- work in the program increases (following down the table), Andorra-I under the top-scheduler produces speedups worse than Andorra-I running with fixed teams. We believe that this is a consequence of the current strategy of giving priority to and-work. More tests are being made to confirm this.

In most cases, we can reach the best speedups for Andorra-I with fixed team size and, as expected, we can get better performance for the examples that have mixed parallelism and that can benefit from the current top-scheduler strategy. Obviously the worst performance using non fixed teams is always much better than the worst performance using fixed teams, because we can always find a fixed team configuration that makes the system behave badly. Additionally, from the point of view of the user it is much nicer to have a system where the programmer does not need to worry about the number of masters/slaves that should be used to run an application.

Figure 3 compare speedups obtained by varying the number of processors for program sets, which has a balanced combination of and- and or- parallelism. In order to obtain the best speedups for fixed teams it was necessary to use different combination of masters and slaves. For the flexible scheduler and 4 workers the result was obtained by running the strategy that gives priority to or-work and uses a greatness factor of 0 (this was the best result obtained after running sets and varying the greatness parameter to values 0, 10, 20, 50, 100, 1000). All other speedups were obtained by running the strategy that gives priority to and-work and uses a greatness factor of 3. Other results show that when we

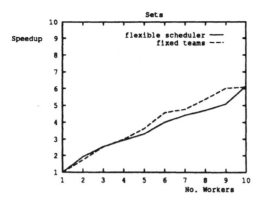

Figure 3: Speedups achieved by running the **sets** program

change the priority of giving work and the greatness factor we can benefit more from the parallelism available in the program, although this is not a regular behaviour according to the data collected so far.

3. Issues in Flexible Scheduling

We believe that the strategy we use to move workers from one team to another is still rather crude, although it produces results comparable to the best obtained using Andorra-I with fixed teams. In some examples, the performance could be better if decisions were not just based on immediate information about the program execution. For instance, two instants of the system configuration for the crossword puzzle problem were taken: time of decision (instant 1) and time of leaving the top-scheduler (instant 2). The following figure appeared:

	and_richness value	or_richness value
instant 1:	0	1
instant 2:	17	2

Based on the values at instant 1, the top-scheduler decided to create a new team because and_richness was equal to zero and there were alternatives left in the tree. But, despite the fact that **cross6** performed better under the flexible scheduler strategy, this decision was not the best, because at instant 2 and_richness was much greater than or_richness. Obviously, this decision could be in fact the right one if we knew beforehand the degree of determinacy of the goals in the run queues and the task sizes below these goals in the tree.

Sometimes the and-richness can mislead the top-scheduler (causing an "illusive" effect), because the run queues can contain many non determinate goals.

In addition, other issues should be taken into account in order to improve the performance of the system. For example, what should be the decision if there is no immediate and-work in the execution tree (which means and-richness equal to zero), and if the amount of or-work is equal to zero? How many processors should be used to achieve the maximum possible speedup without degrading the performance? What if the amount of and- and or- work are the same? How to use measure of the overheads of moving workers from one team to another?

Further work is being done in order to modify the Andorra-I preprocessor [19] and collect data that we think is important to improve the flexible scheduler: size of the paths below the goals in the run queues, type of goals in the run queues (totally determinate, totally non-determinate or with a probability of becoming determinate) and a rough approximation of the amount of parallelism below the goals estimated by $\frac{total\ number\ of\ nodes}{longest\ path}$, where *total number of nodes* is the number of nodes necessary to execute the goal sequentially, and *longest path* is the size of the longest branch below the goal by counting determinate reductions that can be done in parallel as only one node.

4. Future Topics

The problems with the current strategy mentioned show that a more intelligent strategy should be adopted to distribute and- and or- work. In order to do that, we assume that it is possible to obtain useful information (like priorities for execution of goals, *speculativeness* in the scope of cuts and commits, task granularity, degree of determinacy, graph of the program, rough amount of and- and or- work) from global analysis. Some work in the literature has shown that this task is feasible [9, 24, 4, 19, 11, 25, 27]. We are therefore going to concentrate on scheduler strategies that can use the mentioned information. We will be considering decentralised dynamic (adaptive) load balancing strategy, since the **exact** shapes of the search trees of logic programs are unpredictable.

Scheduling schemes [17] can have two policies: *supply-driven* or *demand-driven*. A supply-driven policy determines whether to accept a task whenever a new task becomes available. The latter allocates a processing element (worker) to a task, whenever the policy allocation notices that the worker is lightly loaded. A demand-driven policy is simpler and involves less overhead to workers as they are not interrupted by the scheduler. Also a policy can be *pre-emptive* or *non-preemptive*, which means that a worker can suspend or continue some task voluntarily and start another task.

Our approach will be to use a demand-driven and (perhaps) a pre-emptive scheduler which will navigate through the tree looking for *better* tasks. The guiding principle will be based on a rough graph of the computation tree (presumably the theoretical execution tree), the degree of determinacy of the goals, the priority of execution of the goals and the load of each processor. Given the graph of the computation tree, we have information about the longest path, that in a system to find all solutions, is particularly important because it gives us the least possible time to find all solutions in parallel. With information about the degree of determinacy of a goal we can measure the granularity of the tasks below that goal. We assume a pre-emptive policy as we intend to use priorities to schedule work. This way, if the worker is executing some speculative work (because there was no useful piece of work available) and some useful work appears in the tree, the scheduler can suspend the active worker and switch it to the useful piece of work. Our main objective will be to maintain the height close to that of the theoretical tree whenever possible and to avoid frequent task switching.

Example (1):

1) f(X,Y) :- p(X), q(Y).   6) p1(X) :- g1(X).
2) f(X,Y) :- p1(X), q1(Y).   7) q1(X) :- g2(X).
3) p(1).   8) g1(a).
4) p(2).   9) g2(b).
5) q(2).

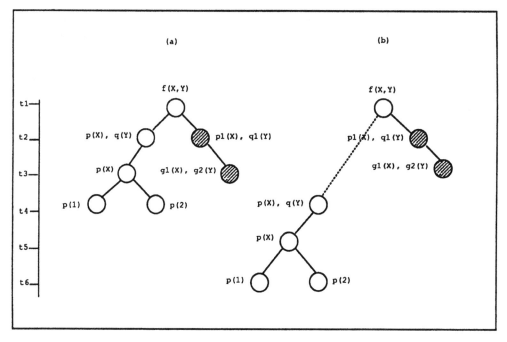

Figure 4: Different trees to execute Example (1) in parallel

Consider the simple trees in Figure 4 based on Example 1. Assume that the execution follows the Andorra computation rule. In Fig 4.(a), the theoretical speedup is $\frac{9}{3}$, i.e. $\frac{\text{number of nodes}}{\text{longest path}}$. The minimum number of steps to compute all solutions assuming an unbounded number of processors is 3. If we assume a limited number of processors, it does not matter if we execute the two and- goals of one of the dense nodes (shaded) shown in Figure 4 sequentially, because the length of the computation to calculate all the solutions will remain the same and consequently the speedup will remain the same. But if we choose to concentrate all the processors on the right branch (executing and- work), we will increase the length of the computation, transforming the tree of Figure 4.(a) to the tree of Figure 4.(b). The speedup in this case drops to $\frac{9}{5}$.

Our goal is to avoid this kind of situation by allocating the workers fairly to the tasks in the tree.

We can conceive the following four approaches to implement the scheduler strategies. At first, we are going to focus on the first one, as it is simpler and can be immediately applied to Andorra-I. The others are being investigated and should be considered long term research.

1. Traditional Approach

As discussed before, given the theoretical graph of the program (as in Figure 4, for instance), obtained through global analysis, write algorithms that try to keep the speedup as close as possible to the theoretical one (which is governed by the height of the longest path in the theoretical tree), without compromising the cost of task switching. The graph of the program is obtained according to the most general query and contains information about the size of paths, degree of determinacy and priorities of goals. The goal with less priority is the most speculative. We consider to reach or to approximate the size of the longest path because we are concerned about finding all-solutions and in this case the longest path is responsible for the overall speedup of the system. Some experiments can be done in order to build an algorithm to find a first solution. In this case, we should take into account the size of the shortest path.

2. Self organising network

Given the initial theoretical graph of the program, obtained through global analysis, map processors and tasks into nodes of an artificial neural network (ANN) ([6, 12, 1]).

For instance, consider example 1 again. For this example we have three branches to be executed, each one with a task size. Each possible combination of task/processor can be mapped as a node of the ANN, so if we have P processors and T branches, we will have $P \times T$ nodes in the network. The weight between any two nodes $N_{i,t}$ and $N_{i,q}$ in the same row, i.e. every connection between pairs of nodes that assign the same task to different processors, will be represented by -W (where +W represents the strongest connection) [13]. Whilst the load and the portions of the tree are being modified during the execution, new configurations will be calculated. The weight -W should be calculated from the cost of task switching and priority of execution of tasks.

Some researchers have been using neural networks to solve dynamic load balancing problems in distributed systems.

3. Simulated Annealing

Simulated Annealing is an algorithm based on a probabilistic decision of accepting states of computations. It basically consists of two nested loops. The outermost loop governs the number of iterations and checks if the computation is "stable". The innermost loop calculates new states and decides if this state should be output or not based on a probabilistic function. Simulated annealing is also applied to neural networks in order to find global minimum (maximum) of a computation. Ioannidis et al [14] used this algorithm to optimise logical queries, but it is accepted that this can not be the best approach because the algorithm is very slow to converge.

4. Branch and Bound algorithms

This approach was used by Lipovsky et al [15] to guide the scheduling of or- tasks in a computer architecture dedicated to databases. A heuristic function based on the likelihood of a branch failure is used to guide the search in an or-tree and it is based on a probabilistic model. The scheme is such that the bounds are in two categories: local and global. Local bounds ("weak") are updated during a "session" (sequence of user's queries) and global bounds ("strong") are updated between sessions. Bounds to the start session are taken from the global data. No consideration is made about guiding the search to the and-tree. Moreover all bounds are calculated at runtime. We could generate the starting bound values from global analysis, and adjust them during local and global bounds updates, extending the model to deal with the and-portions of the tree.

5. Conclusion

Our main objective in designing a flexible scheduler for Andorra-I is to allow the system to distribute work among the processors, in such a way that we have several teams when the application demands or-parallelism, and few teams with many workers if the application demands and-parallelism. The results in Table 1 show that we can achieve this goal and get performance close or better than the best produced by Andorra-I with fixed configuration of teams, without having to decide what configuration to use in advance. We believe that much can be gained if we use additional information to guide the top-scheduler strategy. Especially to prevent the "illusion" effect mentioned before, that misleads the top-scheduler when making decisions.

We believe that the problem of task scheduling in and-or trees of logic programming systems can be represented by a mathematical model that makes the task scheduling independent of the model or its implementation. It is sufficient that we identify the parameters involved in task scheduling and relate them in such a way that we can exploit the available and- and or- parallelism optimally.

Acknowledgements

I would very much like to thank David Warren for the discussions and ideas about parallelism and scheduling in logic programming. Also thanks to Rong Yang, Tony Beaumont and Vítor Santos Costa for giving me support for the implementation. I would also like to thank David, Rong, Vítor, Sanjay Raina, Gopal Gupta and Raed Sindaha for reading and correcting earlier drafts of this work.

References

[1] Valmir C. Barbosa and Priscila M. V. Lima. On the Distributed Parallel Simulation of Hopfield's Neural Networks. *Software–Practice and Experience*, 20(10):967–983, October 1990.

[2] Anthony Beaumont, S. Muthu Raman, and Péter Szeredi. *Flexible Scheduling of Or-Parallelism in Aurora: The Bristol Scheduler*. Technical Report to be published, University of Bristol, Computer Science Department, October 1990.

[3] Per Brand. Wavefront scheduling. 1988. Internal Report, Gigalips Project.

[4] Maurice Bruynooghe. A Practical Framework for the Abstract Interpretation of Logic Programs. *Journal of Logic Programming*, 10(2):91–124, February 1991.

[5] Ralph Butler, Terry Disz, Ewing Lusk, Robert Olson, Ross Overbeek, and Rick Stevens. Scheduling OR-parallelism: an Argonne perspective. In *Proceedings of the Fifth International Conference on Logic Programming*, pages 1590–1605, MIT Press, August 1988.

[6] Felipe M. G. França. A Self-Organising Updating Network. In *International Conference on Artificial Neural Networks, ICANN 91, Helsinki*, 1991.

[7] Alan Calderwood. Aurora—description of scheduler interfaces. January 1988. Internal Report, Gigalips Project.

[8] Alan Calderwood and Péter Szeredi. Scheduling or-parallelism in Aurora – the Manchester scheduler. In *Proceedings of the Sixth International Conference on Logic Programming*, pages 419–435, MIT Press, June 1989.

[9] Saumya K. Debray, Nai-Wei Lin, and Manuel Hermenegildo. Task granularity analysis in logic programs. In *Proceedings of the ACM SIGPLAN'90 Conference on Programming Language Design and Implementation*, pages 174–188, June 1990.

[10] Inês de Castro Dutra. Design of a Flexible Scheduler for Andorra-I. January 1991. Internal Report, ESPRIT Project 2471, PEPMA.

[11] Bogumił Hausman. *Pruning and Speculative Work in OR-Parallel PROLOG*. PhD thesis, The Royal Institute of Technology, Stockholm, 1990.

[12] J. J. Hopfield. Neural Networks and Physical Systems with Emergent Collective Computational Abilities. *Proc. Natl. Acad. Sci., USA*, 79:2554–2558, April 1982.

[13] Hung Khei Huang and Valmir Carneiro Barbosa. *Static Task Allocation in Heterogeneous Distributed Systems*. Technical Report ES-149/88, Federal University of Rio de Janeiro, COPPE/Sistemas, 1988.

[14] Yannis E. Ioannidis and Eugene Wong. Query Optimization by Simulated Annealing. In *SIGMOD - Proceedings of the 1987 International Conference on Management of Data*, pages 9–22, ACM, 1987.

[15] G. J. Lipovsky and M. V. Hermenegildo. B–LOG: A Branch and Bound Methodology for the Parallel Execution of Logic Programs. In *Proceedings of the 1985 International Symposium on Logic Programming*, pages 560–567, IEEE, 1985.

[16] Ewing Lusk, David H. D. Warren, Seif Haridi, et al. The Aurora or-parallel Prolog system. *New Generation Computing*, 7(2,3):243–271, 1990.

[17] Douglas Pase and Peter Borgwardt. *Load Balancing Heuristics and Networks Topologies for Distributed Evaluation of Prolog*. Technical Report, Imperial College, Department of Computer Science. Available as TR: Parallel Logic Programming 57, Parlog Group.

[18] V. Santos Costa, D. H. D. Warren, and R. Yang. The Andorra-I Engine: A parallel implementation of the Basic Andorra model. In *Logic Programming: Proceedings of the 8th International Conference*, MIT Press, 1991.

[19] V. Santos Costa, D. H. D. Warren, and R. Yang. The Andorra-I Preprocessor: Supporting full Prolog on the Basic Andorra model. In *Logic Programming: Proceedings of the 8th International Conference*, MIT Press, 1991.

[20] Vítor Santos Costa and Rong Yang. *Andorra-I User's Guide and reference manual.* Technical Report, University of Bristol, Computer Science Department, Sept 1990. Internal Report, Gigalips Project.

[21] Raed Sindaha. Scheduling speculative work in the Aurora or-parallel Prolog system. March 1990. Internal Report, Gigalips Project, University of Bristol.

[22] Péter Szeredi and Mats Carlsson. *The Engine–Scheduler Interface in the Aurora Or–Parallel Prolog System.* Technical Report TR-90-09, University of Bristol, Computer Science Department, April 1990.

[23] Péter Szeredi, Mats Carlsson, and Rong Yang. Interfacing engines and schedulers in or-parallel prolog systems. In *PARLE91: Conference on Parallel Architectures and Languages Europe*, Springer Verlag, June 1991.

[24] Evan Tick. Compile Time Granularity Analysis for Parallel Logic Programming Systems. In *International Conference on Fifth Generation Computer Systems 1988*, ICOT, 1988.

[25] David H. D. Warren. Oct 90. Personal Communication.

[26] David H. D. Warren. The Andorra model. March 1988. Presented at Gigalips Project workshop, University of Manchester.

[27] R. Warren, M. Hermenegildo, and S. Debray. On the practicality of global flow analysis of logic programs. In *Proceedings of the Fifth International Conference on Logic Programming*, MIT Press, August 1988.

[28] Rong Yang. Programming in Andorra-I. August 1988. Internal Report, Gigalips Project.

[29] Rong Yang. Solving simple substitution ciphers in Andorra-I. In *Proceedings of the Sixth International Conference on Logic Programming*, pages 113–128, MIT Press, June 1989.

The Pandora Abstract Machine: An Extension of JAM

Reem Bahgat

Department of Computer Science, City University

Northampton Square, London EC1V 0HB, England

e-mail: reem@cs.city.ac.uk

Abstract

Combining stream and-parallelism and don't-know non-determinism in a unified logic programming language introduces new difficulties which affect both the language design and implementation. Nevertheless, recent work suggests that it may be feasible to tackle these problems. A language called Pandora was recently introduced, which extends Parlog with a deadlock handling mechanism and a "lazy" form of don't-know non-determinism. In this paper, we present an abstract machine for Pandora targetted towards a shared memory multi-processor architecture. It is based on the JAM: an abstract machine for committed-choice languages, and modifies it to support features of Pandora that are not in Parlog.

1. Introduction

Most of the logic programming languages that have been seriously implemented and used to date fall into one of two categories: (a) variants of Prolog, and (b) the concurrent committed-choice languages, such as Parlog [4]. The basic distinction is that Prolog features don't-know non-determinism; the concurrent languages provide dependent or stream and-parallelism but are based on committed-choice non-determinism.

Combining don't-know non-determinism and stream and-parallelism into a single language introduces new difficulties which affect both the language design and implementation. Nevertheless, several attempts are being made to tackle the problem of their combination, and to integrate them into a single language. One such language is Pandora, which is a member of the Andorra Prolog family [5]. Pandora extends Parlog with a powerful deadlock handling mechanism and a "lazy" form of don't-know non-determinism.

In this paper, we propose an abstract machine for Pandora targetted towards a shared memory multi-processor architecture. It is based on the JAM abstract machine for committed-choice languages [3], and modifies it to support features of Pandora that are not in Parlog. Some of the well established techniques for efficiently implementing don't-know non-determinism in Prolog-like languages are borrowed, and new techniques are introduced to solve the problems emerging from the integration.

An overview of the Pandora language is given in the rest of this section. Then, the data areas, data structures, and basic operations of the Pandora abstract machine are introduced. Finally, a summary of results and conclusions are presented. This paper assumes some familiarity with the Parlog language as well as the WAM [8] and JAM implementations.

1.1. Pandora

Pandora [1] is a parallel logic programming language combining both stream and-parallelism and a "lazy" form of don't-know non-determinism. There are two kinds of relation in a Pandora program: don't-care relations and don't-know relations. A Pandora conjunction may contain goals for both kinds of relation. A *don't-care relation* is defined as a normal flat Parlog procedure [4], and its goal may suspend on input arguments similar to a Parlog goal. A *don't-know relation* is defined by an undeclared procedure comprising a sequence of (guarded) clauses, each of the form:

p(T1, T2, ..., Tn) :- D: B.

D is a *det-guard*: a conjunction of goals (possibly empty) for certain primitives, including at least unification (=); we also allow other primitives such as <, >, =<, >=. **B**, the clause body, is any Pandora conjunction.

A pandora computation alternates between two phases: the and-parallel phase and the deadlock phase. During the *and-parallel phase*, all goals in a parallel conjunction are evaluated concurrently. A goal for a don't-care relation may suspend on input matching, that is a goal is delayed if its arguments are insufficiently instantiated to match the clause head arguments. A goal for a don't-know relation P is reduced provided it is *deterministic*, i.e. if and only if at least k-1 clauses are non-candidates, where k is the number of clauses in P's procedure. A *non-candidate clause* for a goal is a clause which has false (unsatisfiable) head unification and/or a det-guard.

If the computation deadlocks, a *deadlock phase* is started. The default deadlock breaking mechanism in Pandora is to select an arbitrary goal for a don't-know relation and to create a choice point for it; a new and-parallel phase is then started for each or-branch. Alternatively, the user can optionally define the deadlock handler Pandora relation, deadlock_handler/4, in the program. If the computation deadlocks and deadlock_handler/4 is defined, a goal for it is invoked whose input argument is a list of ground terms representing the suspended goals. The deadlock handler relation provides a powerful way to handle deadlock in a manner suited to the particular application. One way in which it can be used is in combination with the non-deterministic fork, to implement a heuristic search. This is a way to reduce the search space by intelligently selecting a don't-know non-deterministic goal to execute, when several are possible. More generally, the deadlock handler relation can be utilized to manipulate suspended goals at the time of deadlock in a more flexible manner.

Redundant goals can be removed, new goals can be added, and a group of goals can be replaced by a simpler group. For a full definition of the Pandora deadlock handler, the reader may refer to [1].

In addition to the parallel conjunction operator ',', Pandora goals can be conjoined with the sequential conjunction operator '&'. Assume the following conjunction of goals:

G1 , G2 & G3 , G4 & G5

This indicates that G1 and G2 are first evaluated concurrently until they both terminate successfully. Then, the evaluation of G3 and G4 is begun. G5 is evaluated when all the other goals in the conjunction have succeeded.

2.   The Pandora Abstract Machine (PAM)

The Pandora abstract machine (PAM) is the core of a parallel implementation of the Pandora language. The instruction set of PAM is an extension of the JAM instruction set [3]. A don't-care relation is compiled to a sequence of instructions from the JAM instruction set. A don't-know relation is compiled to two sequences of instructions: the determinacy code and the non-determinacy code. The *determinacy code* for a don't-know relation is used in the and-parallel phase to reduce a deterministic goal and to suspend a non-deterministic goal until it becomes deterministic. The sequence of instructions in a determinacy code is also a subset of the JAM instruction set except for the first instruction which indicates a pointer to the non-determinacy code of the same relation. The *non-determinacy code* is used in the deadlock phase to non-deterministically reduce a goal and to create a choice point for it; its instructions are WAM-like instructions [8].

PAM is based on a process-oriented execution model. There are two kinds of processes: don't-care processes and don't-know processes, corresponding to the two kinds of relation in a Pandora program. A process is responsible for reducing a goal using a candidate clause for it and spawning child processes to evaluate the goals in the body of the clause.

PAM is designed for a shared memory multi-processor architecture. A processor in PAM is either a master or a slave. There is only one master processor; the others are slaves. Each processor has its own set of data structures which are accessed by the other processors. The shared memory is divided by data areas and each data area is then divided into blocks; one for each processor. The main data structures are: the process stack, the argument stack, the heap, the run queue, the code area, the deadlock list, the choice-point stack, and the trail. The first five data structures are borrowed from the JAM implementation and they play the same role as in JAM. Namely:

- Process Stack contains "process structures" which are fixed sized data structures containing the necessary information to execute a (goal) process.

- Argument Stack contains goal arguments and environments, i.e. the variable sized parts of a process. Environments store variables that occur before and after a sequential conjunction in a clause.

- Heap   contains structured terms, lists and variables created during program execution, referenced from the arguments and environments on the argument stack.

- Run Queue   contains runnable processes that are waiting for idle processors to execute them.

- Code Area   contains instructions and data comprising the compiled form of the program. This includes the definition of the clauses as well as the determinacy code for the don't-know relations.

Additionally, new data structures are introduced to support don't-know non-determinism in a Pandora computation by backtracking, as well as the Pandora deadlock handler capabilities. Moreover, the integration of don't-know non-determinism with stream and-parallelism introduces a number of new implementation issues; we discuss the more important ones below.

2.1. The Deadlock List

In order to be able to manipulate suspended goals in the deadlock phase, each processor maintains a *deadlock list*. The union of all processors' deadlock lists forms a distributed data structure by which suspended processes can be accessed in the deadlock phase.

When processes suspend on an unbound variable, a *suspension list* attached to that variable is formed. It is a linked list which starts at the variable itself. Instead of adding each suspended process to the deadlock list, an optimization is employed: when a process is the first to suspend on a variable, the processor executing it adds a pointer to that variable at the end of its deadlock list. Other suspensions on the same variable do not affect the deadlock list. As a result, each element in the deadlock list represents a list of processes that are suspended on the same variable.

If a pointer to a variable is added to the deadlock list and before creating a choice point the variable gets bound, then the pointer can be deallocated ([1] explains how to remove such elements from the deadlock list).

2.2. The Choice-Point Stack

The *choice-point stack* is a stack of choice-point structures in the order of their creation. This stack together with the argument stack correspond to the WAM stack. A choice point may be created during the deadlock phase for a (don't-know relation goal) process. Each processor has its own choice-point stack. In a *choice-point structure*, the tops of the processor's data structures are saved; their values are different for different processors. Choice-point structures are pushed on all processors' stacks at the same time during the deadlock phase (explained later in Section 2.5), and they all represent one choice point for a suspended process. Two additional fields are only added to the choice-point structure in the master's stack; a pointer to the process structure for which the choice point is created, and a pointer to the code for the next clause to try in the don't-know procedure should the current clause fail.

2.3. The Trail

As in WAM, a binding to a variable is called *unconditional* if the variable is created after the last choice point, otherwise, it is *conditional*. The *trail* contains the necessary information to undo conditional bindings when the computation backtracks.

An unbound variable might be pointing to a suspension list; its value may be conditionally updated by either instantiating the variable or adding a new process to its suspension list. When backtracking, the variable should point back to its original suspension list that existed before the creation of the most recent choice point. As a result, trailing a variable saves its old value as well as its address. Not only a variable can be bound conditionally, but process fields in a process structure may also be conditionally updated and, hence, require trailing.

The following issues should be considered when trailing: (a) several processes may suspend on a variable after the most recent choice point, each of them updates the variable's suspension list but only the variable's value when the choice point was created needs to be recovered before trying the next clause. Similarly, a process field can be updated several times between two consecutive choice points; (b) in WAM, a simple address comparison is performed to check whether a variable's binding is conditional or unconditional. If the variable's address is less than the choice point, i.e. the variable was created before the choice point, then the binding is conditional; otherwise, it is unconditional. In a multi-processor implementation, if the variable is not owned by the processor that is binding it then an address comparison requires checking the addresses of other processors' areas. This test is even more expensive when updating process fields because processes tend to migrate a lot among processors while variables are usually instantiated by their own processors.

In point (a) above, trailing multiple bindings for a variable (or a process field) after the most recent choice point inefficiently consumes time and memory. It also requires keeping the order of bindings that might be saved in different processors' trails, and undoing them in the reverse order so that to finally recover the original value of the variable (or process field).

In order to overcome the above problems, we define a new concept: *a data object's age*, which corresponds to the variable's physical address in WAM. Unlike its physical address, a data object's age should be modifiable so that only the first binding of the object after a choice point is *conditional*; other bindings before creating a new choice point are considered *unconditional* and thus do not require trailing.

A new global register, **choice-point count**, is also introduced. It reflects the current number of choice point structures on a choice-point stack. The value of **choice-point count** is tested by all processors but is only modified by the master. It is incremented every time a new choice point is created, and decremented whenever a choice point is removed.

In a process structure, an extra field, **Age**, is added to denote the *process' age*. When a process is created, the **Age** field is initialized to the value of **choice-point count** at that time. If a process field is to be updated and the process' **Age** is equal to the current value of **choice-point count**, it is an *unconditional* update. If **Age** is less than **choice-point count**, then the update is *conditional* and should be trailed.

In order to trail a process structure, the processor first examines the **Age** field to check if a conditional update is taking place. If **Age** is less than **choice-point count**, a lock is set which prevents other processors from trailing the process. Once locked, the test for the process' age is repeated in case another processor has trailed the process before the lock was obtained. Then, the whole process structure is trailed, the value of **Age** is modified to be equal to **choice-point count**, the field in the process structure is (conditionally) updated, and the lock is released. Other updates to any of the process fields before creating a new choice point will be considered unconditional. The result is trailing a process structure at most once between two consecutive choice points.

Trailing the whole process structure is justified by the following facts:

(a) Once a process is created, most of the fields in the process structure can be modified during its lifetime whether by the processor executing it or the processors executing its children.

(b) Pandora is designed for applications in which the main theme of computation is don't-care non-deterministic while don't-know non-determinism is required lazily as the last solution to deadlock situations. In such applications, most of the process structure's fields are expected to be updated, and thus trailed, during the same and-parallel phase.

(c) trailing a field by itself when it is to be conditionally updated requires an extra space to save the age of each field instead of having only one field indicating the age of the whole process.

An extra advantage of trailing the whole process structure is the ability to re-use the structure of a terminated process for a newly created one even if its physical address in the process stack is less than the most recent choice point. However, we are currently investigating other means of trailing process fields.

When a variable is created, it is tagged as unbound while its value is initialized to be equal to the value of **choice-point count** at that time. This represents the *variable's age*. When a variable is pointing to a suspension list, the *variable's age* is denoted by the age of the most recent process in its suspension list. When an unbound variable is assigned a value or when a process suspends on it, its value is *conditionally* updated if the variable's age is less than the current value of **choice-point count**. Otherwise, the update is *unconditional*.

2.4. The Pandora Deadlock Handler

When the computation deadlocks, the master processor scans the deadlock lists of all processors and generates *Suspended_Processes*: a list of the processes that are still suspended on variable(s). then, the master processor loads its first argument register with the Suspended_Processes list and creates a process to evaluate a goal for the predefined $deadlock/1 relation, which the master executes itself.

If deadlock_handler/4 is not defined in the program, $deadlock/1 searches for a don't-know process in Suspended_Processes and sets a global register, **choice-point flag**, to point to that process.

If deadlock_handler/4 is defined, *Meta_Suspended*: a list of meta-level representation of Suspended_Processes is generated. Additionally, a dictionary, *Meta_Var_Dictionary*, of all the variables in the arguments of the suspended goals (i.e. the variables in the deadlock lists), together with their meta-level representation in Meta_Suspended, is generated. Then, $deadlock/1 creates a child (don't-care) process for deadlock_handler/4, whose input argument is Meta_Suspended, and suspends on children.

Failure of deadlock_handler/4 is the same as failure of any other (goal) process (explained in Section 2.6). If deadlock_handler/4 succeeds, the $deadlock/1 process resumes to inspect the bindings of deadlock_handler/4's output arguments.

$deadlock/1 may remove processes in Suspended_Processes. A process is removed by marking it to be dead. When a variable on which the process is suspended gets bound, the process will not be executed since it is dead. If new goals should be added to the conjunction of goals, Meta_Var_Dictionary is inspected and any meta-level representation of a variable in these goals is replaced by a reference to the corresponding variable. Then, $deadlock/1 spawns sibling processes for the new goals and terminates successfully.

Alternatively, a don't-know process may be selected for a non-deterministic execution; **choice-point flag** is then set to point to that process.

2.5. Scheduling

After the initialization of the PAM, each processor will be in one of three states: execute state, search state, and deadlock state. The state of a processor is denoted by its **status flag**. A processor is in *execute* state as long as it is executing a process. The processor enters the "scheduling algorithm" and changes its state to *search* state if it runs out of work or else if an event is signalled.

Events are occasions when all processors must synchronize and execute specific functions. Examples of events are: interrupts, garbage collection, and termination. If any process in the process tree fails or the root process succeeds, a *termination event* is signalled so that all processors terminate. A processor checks an **event flag** on each process reduction, that is a global register which is accessed by any processor. If the flag is set, the processor queues the current process on its own run queue and invokes the scheduling algorithm which, in turn, enters the event handler and executes the appropriate event(s).

If a running process terminates (and the parent cannot be continued) or suspends on variable(s), the processor enters the scheduling algorithm to search for work. It first examines its own run queue. If it is empty, the processor searches for work in other processors' run queues. If a process is found, it is loaded and the processor exits from the scheduling algorithm to execute the process, after changing its status back to execute state.

In order to take work from a run queue, the processor first examines the queue pointers to check if the queue is empty. If non-empty, a lock is set which prevents other processors from stealing a process. Once locked, the test for empty queue is repeated in case another processor has stolen the last process before the lock was obtained. Then, a process is taken from the queue and the lock is released.

If the master fails to find work, it enters a third processor state: *deadlock* state, and then waits for each slave to follow suit. If all processors enter deadlock state, then deadlock has occurred. Otherwise, if one of the slaves enters execute state instead, then the master re-enters search state and waits for all the slaves in deadlock state to undeadlock before proceeding to rescan the remote run queues. Slave processors cannot enter deadlock state unless the master has done so. Therefore, if the master is not deadlocked, the slave makes another scan of the remote run queues. Otherwise, the slave enters deadlock state and waits for the master's state to change.

When deadlock occurs **choice-point flag** is examined. If the flag is set to null, the master processor generates Suspended_Processes, as described in the previous section, and loads its first argument register with this list. It then creates a process to invoke $deadlock/1; thus it leaves the deadlock state and, so other processors re-enter the search state. The parent of the created process is the root process.

If the **choice-point flag** is non-null when examined, each processor pushes a new choice-point structure onto its choice-point stack. Then, a slave processor re-enters the search state while the master executes the process for which the choice point was created after incrementing **choice-point count** and resetting the **choice-point flag** to null. Figure 1 illustrates the PAM scheduler.

In order to non-deterministically execute the selected (don't-know relation goal) process, the process should be removed from the suspension list(s) on which it is suspended. Removing the actual process structure from the suspension list would require modifying the pointer to the process from the previous element in the list. Alternatively, a copy of the process structure with age equals to the current value of **choice-point count** is made to act as a *substitute* (don't-know relation goal) process while the original process is marked to be dead.

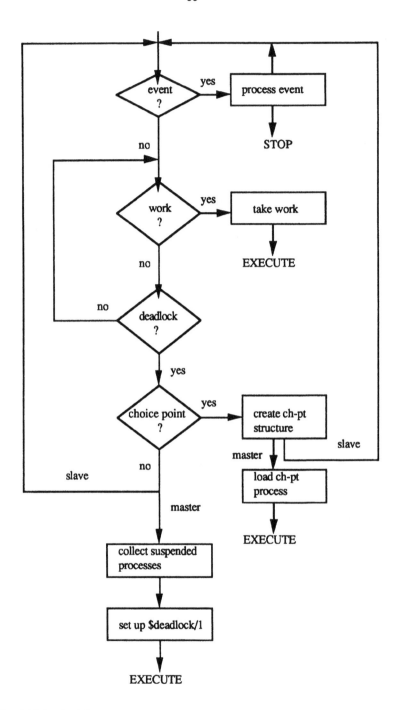

Fig 1. The PAM scheduler.

2.6. Failure and Backtracking

If a process fails to reduce its goal, a *failure event* is signalled. Then, each processor backtracks to the most recent choice point. Objects that are trailed are returned their old values from the trail, registers are reset to their values as saved in the choice point, and the run queue is emptied. An object does not need to be locked when restoring its value from a processor's trail since it is trailed only once after the most recent choice point.

After backtracking, a slave processor loops searching for work, while the master processor loads the process for which the choice point was created and executes it. If the clause being entered is the last clause to try for the goal, then the master decrements **choice-point count** by one before entering the clause (last clause optimization). Otherwise, the master updates the next clause field in the choice point structure to point to the clause following the one being entered.

3. Summary and Conclusions

This paper describes an abstract machine for Pandora as an extension of the JAM implementation. Three new data structures have been introduced: the choice-point stack, the trail, and the deadlock list. The choice-point stack and the trail support don't-know non-determinism in Pandora. They play the same role as their counter parts in a standard Prolog implementation such as the WAM. The deadlock list supports the Pandora deadlock-handler. It is used to collect the remaining suspended goal processes on deadlock. Instead of scanning the heap to collect the processes that are suspended on variables, the deadlock list points to variables with suspension lists. Thus, an element in the deadlock list represents a list of suspended processes.

A new concept has been defined, a "data object's age", to play the role of the physical address for a data object in the WAM. Unlike the physical address, a data object's age has to be modifiable to accommodate the multiple updates to the value of the data object between two consecutive choice points. It should also be independent of which processor the data object belongs to since a data object can be created by one processor in its own data structure and accessed by other processors. An extra benefit from the age concept is the decentralization of the trail and choice-point stack. Each processor has its own trail and choice-point stack which it manages. This has removed the necessity to lock the trail when adding (or removing) an item to (from) it and has minimized the periods when a processor remains idle.

The PAM machine is highly tuned towards executing committed-choice programs, i.e. programs that do not require the creation of choice points. The only overhead introduced by the PAM is a comparison operation for each binding to check whether it is conditional. Since all bindings in these programs are unconditional, no trailing is required and, hence, the overhead is expected to be low when compared to running the same programs on the JAM.

The implementation of the PAM abstract machine will be completed by August 1991. A distributed implementation of Pandora has been also designed [6]. For illustration purpose, Table 1 presents the run-time (in seconds) of several committed-choice programs on the Andorra-I system [2] with and without the comparison operation per each binding. Andorra-I is is a prototype implementation of the basic Andorra model which runs both or-parallelism and stream and-parallelism (closely following the JAM). The average overhead of the comparison operation on committed-choice programs, as shown in Table 1, is 1.65%. However, this percentage should be slightly higher when comparing the performance of the PAM with the JAM, since the JAM is a compiled system while Andorra-I is an interpreter (i.e. slightly slower).

Program Name	Andorra-I	Andorra-I + comparison	Overhead
fibonacci_15	1.53	1.54	0.6%
naive_reverse_150	3.61	3.7	2.5%
merge_sort_200	1.57	1.61	2.5%
boyer	6.05	6.11	1.0%

Table 1. The overhead of a comparison operation per each binding on committed-choice programs.

Pandora is a member of the Andorra Prolog family. However, there are various differences between the PAM implementation and the Andorra-I system. Namely: (a) don't-know non-determinism is implemented by backtracking in PAM while it is implemented by or-parallelism in Andorra-I; (b) PAM deals with two kinds of relation goals instead of one kind as in Andorra-I; (c) PAM supports the powerful Pandora deadlock handler; and finally (d) the order of goals in a conjunction is maintained by Andorra-I in order to create the choice point of the leftmost suspended goal while the order of goals in a parallel Pandora conjunction is irrelevant.

References

[1]   Bahgat, R.M.R. 1991. *Pandora: non-deterministic parallel logic programming.* PhD thesis, Dept of Computing, Imperial College, London University.

[2]   Costa, V.S.; Warren, D.H.D. and Yang, R. 1991. 'The Andorra-I engine: a parallel implementation of the basic Andorra model'. In *Proceedings of the eighth International Conference on Logic Programming*, Paris.

[3]   Crammond, J.A. 1990. 'The Abstract machine and implementation of parallel Parlog'. Research Report, Dept. of Computing, Imperial College, University of London.

[4]   Gregory, S. 1987. *Parallel logic programming in Parlog: the language and its implementation.* Reading, Massachusetts: Addison-Wesley.

[5]   Haridi, S. and Janson, S. 1990. 'Kernel Andorra Prolog and its computation model'. In *Proceedings of the seventh International Conference on Logic Programming*, Jerusalem, pp.31-46.

[6]   Leung, H-F. 1991. 'Distributed Implementation of Pandora'. Research Report, Dept. of Computing, Imperial College, London University.

[7]   Warren, D.H.D. 1983. 'An abstract Prolog instruction set'. Technical Note 309, SRI International, Menlo Park, CA. (October 1983).

Performance of Muse on the BBN Butterfly TC2000

Khayri A. M. Ali and Roland Karlsson

Swedish Institute of Computer Science, SICS

Box 1263, S-164 28 Kista, Sweden

khayri@sics.se and roland@sics.se

Shyam Mudambi

Department of Computer Science

Brandeis University

Waltham, MA 02254

srm@cs.brandeis.edu

Abstract

Muse is a simple and efficient approach to Or-parallel implementation of the full Prolog language. It is based on having multiple sequential Prolog engines, each with its local address space, and some shared memory space. It is currently implemented on a number of bus-based and switch-based multiprocessors.

The performance results of Muse on bus-based multiprocessor machines have been presented in previous papers. This paper discusses implementation and performance results of Muse on the BBN Butterfly TC2000. It also compares the Muse results with the corresponding results of the Aurora Or-parallel Prolog system. The results of Muse execution show that high real speedups can be achieved on Prolog programs that exhibit coarse-grained parallelism, the scheduling overhead being equivalent to around 8 – 26 Prolog procedure calls per task, and that for a large set of benchmarks the Muse system is faster than the Aurora system.

1 Introduction

A variety of approaches toward exploitation of parallelism in Prolog programs are under current investigation. Many of these deal with efficient implementation of Prolog on multiprocessor machines by exploiting either Or-parallelism or Independent And-parallelism or a combination of both. The Muse approach belongs to those that only exploit Or-parallelism [1].

The Muse approach is based on having several sequential Prolog engines, each with its local address space, and some shared memory space. It is currently implemented on a bus-based shared memory machine TP881V, from Tadpole Technology, with 4 (88100) processors, a bus-based machine with local/shared memory with 7 (68020) processors constructed at SICS, a bus-based shared memory S81, Sequent Symmetry, with 26 (i386) processors, and switch-based shared memory machines, BBN Butterfly I (GP1000) and II (TC2000), with 96 (68020) and 45 (88100) processors respectively. The sequential SICStus Prolog [8], a fast, portable system, has been adapted to support the Muse model of Or-parallelism. The extra overhead associated with this adaptation is very low in comparison with the other approaches. It is around 3% for TP881V, 5% for the constructed prototype and Sequent Symmetry, and 8% for the BBN Butterfly GP1000. The performance results of Muse on the BBN Butterfly TC2000 will be presented in this paper. The Muse implementation and its performance results on the other machines have been presented in [1, 2, 3, 4, 5].

The paper is organized as follows. Section 2 briefly describes the Muse approach. Section 3 discusses Muse implementation on the BBN Butterfly TC2000. Section 4 presents performance results of the Muse implementation on the Butterfly TC2000. Section 5 compares the Muse results with the corresponding results of another Or-parallel Prolog system, named Aurora. Section 6 concludes the paper.

2 Muse Approach

In Muse, Or-parallelism in a Prolog search tree is explored by a number of *workers* (processes or processors). A major problem introduced by Or-parallelism is that some variables may be simultaneously bound by workers exploring different branches of a Prolog search tree. The Muse execution model is based on having a number of sequential Prolog engines, each with its own local address space, and some global address space shared by all engines. Each sequential Prolog engine is a worker with its own WAM stacks. The stacks are not shared between workers. Thus, each worker has bindings associated with its current branch in its own copy of the stacks.

This simple solution allows the existing sequential Prolog technology to be used without loss of efficiency. But it requires copying data (stacks) from one worker to another when a worker runs out of work. In Muse, workers incrementally copy parts of the (WAM) stacks and also share nodes with each other when a worker runs out of work. The two workers involved in copying will only copy the differing parts between the two workers states. This reduces copying overhead. Nodes are shared between workers to allow dynamic load balancing, which reduces the frequency of copying.

A node on a Prolog search tree corresponds to a Prolog choicepoint. Nodes are either *shared* or *nonshared (private)*. These nodes divide the search tree into two regions: *shared* and *private*. Each shared node is accessible only to workers within the subtree rooted at the node. Private nodes are only accessible to the worker that created them.

Each worker can be in either engine mode or in scheduler mode. In engine mode, the worker works exactly like a sequential Prolog engine on private nodes, but is also able to respond to interrupt signals from other workers. In scheduler mode, the worker establishes the necessary coordination with other workers. The two main functions of the scheduler are to maintain the sequential semantics of Prolog and to match idle workers with the available work with minimal overhead. The main sources of overhead in the Muse model are copying a part of a worker state, making local nodes shareable, and grabbing a piece of work from a shared node.

The current implementation of Muse supports the full Prolog language with its standard semantics. It also supports asynchronous (parallel) side-effects and internal database predicates. A complete description of the Muse approach is found in [1, 3].

3   Muse on the BBN Butterfly TC2000

The Butterfly TC2000 is a multiprocessor machine capable of supporting up to 512 processors. The TC2000 is made up of two subsystems, the processor nodes and the butterfly switch, which connects all nodes. A processor node consists of the Motorola 88100 microprocessor with two 16k data and instruction caches, 4 MB of memory and a Processor Node Controller (PNC) that manages all references. The Butterfly switch is a multi-stage omega interconnection network. The peak bandwidth of the Butterfly switch is around 38 MBytes per second per path. In the TC2000 there is actually a three level memory hierarchy: cache memory, local memory and remote memory. Cache memory access is faster than local memory access which is faster than remote memory access. Unfortunately no support is provided for cache coherence of shared data. Hence by default shared data are not cached.

The main optimization of Muse for the BBN Butterfly was the creation of separate copies of the WAM code for each processor. The copies of the code were placed in non-shared memory, thus making them cachable. We have also tried to optimize the scheduler by reducing non-local busy waits and by optimal placement of memory. All the shared memory used is spread across all the nodes to avoid switch contention. We also identified and removed some hot spots. For example, data associated with a shared choicepoint can be simultaneously accessed by many workers (when looking for work), hence on the BBN Butterfly access to this data was serialized. Similarly data which are most frequently accessed by a single worker (such as the global registers associated with each worker) are stored in its local memory.

To reduce copying overheads, the local address space of each worker is mapped into a separate part of the global address space of the system. This enables the two workers involved in copying to copy parts of the WAM stacks in parallel. A cache coherence protocol for the WAM stack areas has also been implemented. The basic idea of this protocol is as follows. Every worker keeps track of all stack areas that it reads from any other worker during its last copying operation.

When a worker Q is going to copy data from another worker P on the next copying operation, Q invalidates those areas and P flushes its cache for those stack areas to be copied by Q before copying starts.

In the current Muse implementation, there is one extra cell associated with every choicepoint frame. These cells are accessible by the all workers. To simplify caching of the WAM stacks, we have saved those cells in a separate stack associated with every worker. This stack is not cachable.

4 Performance Results

In this section we discuss the performance of the Muse implementation on the BBN Butterfly TC2000 for a large set of benchmarks. The set of benchmarks used in this paper is the same set of benchmarks that has already been used for the evaluation of Or-parallel Prolog systems on bus-based multiprocessor architectures [1, 6, 7, 12]. We extend this set with some benchmarks that have been used for the Aurora Or-parallel Prolog system on the Butterfly machines [11]. The set of benchmarks used in this paper contains benchmarks with different characteristics. It is divided into four groups listed according to the amount of parallelism in each group: (*11-queens1, 11-queens2, semigroup*), (*8-queens1, 8-queens2, tina, salt-mustard*), (*parse2, parse4, parse5, db4, db5, house*), and (*parse1, parse3, farmer*). The four groups are referred to in the following sections as *GI, GII, GIII,* and *GIV* respectively. The group *GI* represents programs with the greatest amount of parallelism, and the group *GIV* represents programs with the lowest amount of parallelism. This set does not contain programs with major cuts. Programs with major cuts are evaluated in a longer version of this paper [5].

N-queens1 and *N-queens2* are two different N queens programs from ECRC. *semigroup* is a theorem proving program for studying the R-classes of a large semigroup from Argonne National Laboratory. *tina* is a holiday planning program from ECRC. *salt-mustard* is the "salt and mustard" puzzle from Argonne. *parse1 - parse5* are queries to the natural language parsing parts of Chat-80 by F. C. N. Pereira and D. H. D. Warren. *db4* and *db5* are the database searching parts of the fourth and fifth Chat-80 queries. *house* is the "who owns the zebra" puzzle from ECRC. *farmer* is the "farmer, wolf, goat/goose, cabbage/grain" puzzle from ECRC. All the benchmarks look for all solutions of the problem.

4.1 Timings and Speedups

Table 1 shows the runtimes (in seconds) from the execution of the set of benchmarks for Muse on the TC2000 machine. The runtimes given in this paper are the **mean values obtained from eight runs**. On the BBN Butterfly, mean values are more reliable than best values due

Benchmarks	Muse Workers					SICStus0.6
	1	10	20	30	32	
semigroup	1178.63	118.56(9.94)	60.06(19.6)	40.72(28.9)	38.35(30.7)	990.89(1.19)
11-queens1	225.23	22.78(9.89)	11.58(19.4)	7.88(28.6)	7.41(30.4)	190.87(1.18)
11-queens2	729.77	73.12(9.98)	36.92(19.8)	24.93(29.3)	23.43(31.1)	574.27(1.27)
• GI Σ	2133.63	214.46(9.95)	108.53(19.7)	73.52(29.0)	69.18(30.8)	1756.03(1.22)
8-queens1	1.79	0.21(8.52)	0.14(12.8)	0.13(13.8)	0.13(13.8)	1.48(1.21)
8-queens2	4.80	0.53(9.06)	0.31(15.5)	0.26(18.5)	0.25(19.2)	3.77(1.27)
tina	4.28	0.58(7.38)	0.39(11.0)	0.34(12.6)	0.34(12.6)	3.07(1.39)
salt-mustard	0.71	0.10(7.10)	0.08(8.88)	0.09(7.89)	0.10(7.10)	0.44(1.61)
∘ GII Σ	11.58	1.42(8.15)	0.91(12.7)	0.82(14.1)	0.81(14.3)	8.76(1.32)
parse2*20	1.82	0.80(2.27)	0.84(2.17)	0.85(2.14)	0.87(2.09)	1.43(1.27)
parse4*5	1.67	0.42(3.98)	0.43(3.88)	0.45(3.71)	0.47(3.55)	1.31(1.27)
parse5	1.18	0.24(4.92)	0.22(5.36)	0.24(4.92)	0.24(4.92)	0.93(1.27)
db4*10	0.68	0.20(3.40)	0.21(3.24)	0.21(3.24)	0.21(3.24)	0.53(1.28)
db5*10	0.83	0.23(3.61)	0.24(3.46)	0.25(3.32)	0.25(3.32)	0.64(1.30)
house*20	0.98	0.58(1.69)	0.61(1.61)	0.63(1.56)	0.63(1.56)	0.94(1.04)
⋄ GIII Σ	7.16	2.46(2.91)	2.54(2.82)	2.62(2.73)	2.65(2.70)	5.78(1.24)
parse1*20	0.48	0.40(1.20)	0.40(1.20)	0.41(1.17)	0.42(1.14)	0.38(1.26)
parse3*20	0.41	0.39(1.05)	0.41(1.00)	0.42(0.98)	0.42(0.98)	0.33(1.24)
farmer*100	0.83	1.01(0.82)	1.03(0.81)	1.07(0.78)	1.05(0.79)	0.66(1.26)
* GIV Σ	1.72	1.80(0.96)	1.83(0.94)	1.89(0.91)	1.88(0.91)	1.37(1.26)
Σ	2154.09	220.14(9.79)	113.83(18.9)	78.85(27.3)	74.53(28.9)	1771.94(1.22)

Table 1: Runtimes (in seconds) of Muse on TC2000.

to variations of timing results from one run to another. These variations are due mainly to switch contention and are highest in the smaller benchmarks.

In Table 1, times are shown for 1, 10, 20, 30, 32 workers with speedups given in parentheses. These speedups are relative to running times of Muse on one worker. The running times of SICStus0.6 on one TC2000 node, with their ratio to the running times on one Muse worker, are shown in the last column. For benchmarks with small runtimes the timings shown refer to repeated runs, the repetition factor being shown in the first column. Σ in the last row corresponds to the goal: (11-queens1, 11-queens2, semigroup, 8-queens1, 8-queens2, tina, salt-mustard, parse2*20, parse4*5, parse5, db4*10, db5*10, house*20, parse1*20, parse3*20, farmer*100). That is, the timings shown in the last row correspond to running the whole set of benchmarks as one benchmark. In all tables, the last row for each group of a set of benchmarks represents the whole group as one benchmark.

As shown in the last column of Table 1, on one worker, Muse is about 22% slower than

Benchmarks	Muse	SICStus0.6
GI	1829.03	1756.03(1.04)
GII	9.36	8.76(1.07)
GIII	6.19	5.78(1.07)
GIV	1.47	1.37(1.07)
Σ	1846.05	1771.94(1.04)

Table 2: Comparison of runtimes (in seconds) of 1 Muse worker (with Prolog tables cached) vs. SICStus0.6

SICStus0.6, the sequential Prolog system from which Muse is derived. This overhead is mainly due to maintaining the private load, checking some global flags by each Muse worker, and accessing the Prolog tables. In the SICStus system all code, data, and tables are cachable while in Muse the tables and shared data are not cachable. The global tables are partitioned into parts and each part resides in the local memory of one processor. In order to verify that it was the Prolog tables that caused the extra overhead, we compared the execution times of Muse with one worker (making the Prolog tables cachable) versus SICStus0.6 on the TC2000 (Table 2). We see that the overhead of Muse is between 4% to 7%, which is quite close to the overhead observed in Muse on the Sequent Symmetry. This overhead is higher for programs that access the global tables (e.g., predicate table, atom table etc) heavily. The *salt-mustard* (Table 1) has 61% overhead per worker, because it makes heavy use of meta calls, which require accessing the predicate table. The corresponding overhead in the other Or-parallel Prolog systems is much higher (see Section 5).

The performance results that Table 1 illustrates are encouraging: on 32 processors the average speedup factor is 30.8 for the *GI* programs, 14.3 for the group *GII*, 2.7 for the group *GIII*, and 0.91 for the group *GIV*. The speedup factor for the whole set of benchmarks on 32 processors is 28.9. The average real speedups on 32 processors, in comparison to SICStus on one TC2000 processor, are 25.4 for the *GI* programs, and 23.8 for the whole set of benchmarks (calculated from Table 1). For all programs in the group *GI*, increasing number of workers results in shorter runtimes. For programs in the groups *GII, GIII* and *GIV*, increasing number of workers beyond a certain limit results in no further improvement of running times. Actually, increasing number of workers results in slightly longer runtimes for the latter three groups. This degradation is due to the extra runtime scheduling overhead, which will be discussed in Section 4.2.

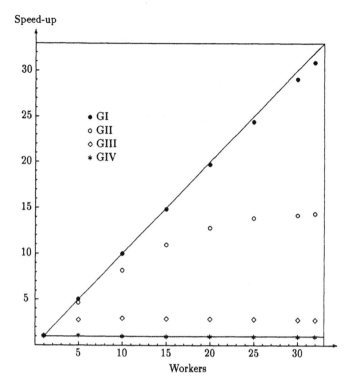

Figure 1: Speedups of Muse relative to 1 Muse worker on TC2000.

Figure 1 shows the speedup curves for the four groups of benchmarks: *GI*, *GII*, *GIII* and *GIV*. These curves correspond to speedups obtained from Table 1. We observe from Figure 1 that when the amount of parallelism was not enough for all workers in the system, the speedup curves level off and reach an almost constant value. This characteristic is very important for any parallel system (such as Muse) that dynamically schedules work at runtime.

4.2 Worker Activities and Scheduling Overhead

In this section, we present and discuss the time spent in the basic activities of a Muse worker on the TC2000 machine. A worker time is distributed over the following activities:

1. *Prolog:* time spent in executing Prolog, checking arrival of interrupt signals, and keeping the value of the private load up to date.

2. *Idle:* time spent in waiting for work to be generated when there is temporarily no work available in the system.

3. *Grabbing Work:* time spent in grabbing available work from shared nodes.

4. *Sharing:* time spent in making private nodes shared with other workers, in copying parts of the WAM stacks, in binding installation, and in synchronization with other workers while performing the sharing operation.

5. *Looking for work:* time spent in looking for a worker with private load.

6. *Others:* time spent in other activities like spin lock, signalling other workers either requesting sharing or performing commit/cut to a shared node, etc.

Table 3 shows the percent of time spent in each activity relative to the total time, for one selected benchmark from each group of the benchmarks. The last row of each table gives the scheduling overhead, which is the sum of all the activities excluding *Prolog* and *Idle*. The *11-queens2* is selected from *GI*, *8-queens2* from *GII*, *parse5* from *GIII*, and *farmer* from *GIV*. Results shown in Table 3 have been obtained from an instrumented system of Muse on the TC2000. The times obtained from an instrumented system are longer than those obtained from an uninstrumented system by around 13%. We believe that the percentage of time spent in each activity obtained from the instrumented system reflects what is happening in the uninstrumented system.

In all benchmarks, the *Prolog* percentage of time decreases and the *Idle* percentage of time increases as the number of workers is increased. This is because each benchmark has a limited amount of parallelism and increasing number of workers decreases the amount of work assigned to each worker. For *11-queens2*, a program with high Or-parallelism, the *Prolog* percentage decreases by 1.1% from 3 workers to 32 workers and the *Idle* percentage increases by 0.4% from 3 workers to 32 workers. The total percentage of scheduling overhead (activities 3 – 6) on 32 workers is only 0.7%.

For *8-queens2*, the scheduling overhead increases from 0.9% on 3 workers to 17% on 32 workers. The rate by which the *Prolog* percentage decreases and the *Idle* percentage increases (w.r.t. to the number of workers) is much higher in *8-queens2* than in *11-queens2*. This is due to the fact that *8-queens2* has much less parallelism.

For *parse5* on 32 workers, the *Prolog* percentage is only 20.8%, while the *Idle* percentage reaches 52.4%. This benchmark has a reasonable amount of parallelism up to 10 – 15 workers, but not beyond. The scheduling overhead is higher than in the previous two benchmarks (5.3% on 3 workers and around 26% on 10 or more workers). *parse5* contains finer grain parallelism than *8-queens2* and *11-queens2*.

For *farmer*, the amount of parallelism is only enough for 2 – 3 workers. The scheduling overhead reaches its maximum value (33.9%) on 3 workers and then decreases with an increasing number of workers. The reason for the decrease in the percentage of scheduling overhead is that adding more than 3 workers just increases the total *Idle* time in the system, which then dominates the total execution time.

Activity	Muse Workers								
	1	3	5	10	15	20	25	30	32

11-queens2

Activity	1	3	5	10	15	20	25	30	32
Prolog	100	100	99.9	99.8	99.7	99.5	99.4	98.9	98.9
Idle	0	0.0	0.0	0.1	0.1	0.2	0.2	0.3	0.4
Grabbing Work	0	0.0	0.0	0.1	0.1	0.2	0.2	0.3	0.3
Sharing Work	0	0.0	0.0	0.0	0.1	0.2	0.2	0.3	0.3
Looking for Work	0	0.0	0.0	0.0	0.0	0.0	0.0	0.1	0.1
Others	0	0.0	0.0	0.0	0.0	0.0	0.0	0.0	0.0
Sched. Overhead	0	0.0	0.0	0.1	0.2	0.4	0.4	0.7	0.7

8-queens2

Activity	1	3	5	10	15	20	25	30	32
Prolog	100	98.9	97.6	93.0	87.5	81.3	74.0	67.0	64.3
Idle	0	0.2	0.5	2.0	4.2	8.1	11.5	16.6	18.7
Grabbing Work	0	0.3	0.7	1.8	3.0	3.6	5.0	5.5	5.2
Sharing Work	0	0.5	0.9	2.3	3.9	5.1	6.3	7.7	8.0
Looking for Work	0	0.1	0.2	0.7	1.2	1.6	2.7	2.6	3.1
Others	0	0.0	0.0	0.2	0.3	0.3	0.4	0.7	0.7
Sched. Overhead	0	0.9	1.8	5.0	8.4	10.6	14.4	16.5	17.0

parse5

Activity	1	3	5	10	15	20	25	30	32
Prolog	100	93.9	84.6	60.6	46.5	34.0	27.5	22.4	20.8
Idle	0	0.8	2.1	13.3	21.3	30.5	41.0	48.4	52.4
Grabbing Work	0	1.8	2.9	3.4	3.9	3.9	3.5	3.3	3.0
Sharing Work	0	3.1	8.3	16.8	21.0	22.3	19.7	18.1	16.8
Looking for Work	0	0.4	2.0	5.7	6.9	8.7	7.8	7.2	6.4
Others	0	0.0	0.1	0.2	0.3	0.5	0.6	0.6	0.6
Sched. Overhead	0	5.3	13.3	26.1	32.1	35.4	31.6	29.2	26.8

farmer

Activity	1	3	5	10	15	20	25	30	32
Prolog	100	44.8	25.7	12.0	7.8	5.8	4.6	3.8	3.5
Idle	0	21.3	42.6	70.3	80.6	85.8	88.7	90.6	91.2
Grabbing Work	0	5.0	4.1	2.1	1.4	1.0	0.8	0.7	0.7
Sharing Work	0	21.5	20.6	11.4	7.5	5.4	4.3	3.7	3.5
Looking for Work	0	6.0	6.1	3.6	2.4	1.7	1.4	1.1	1.1
Others	0	1.3	1.0	0.6	0.4	0.2	0.2	0.2	0.2
Sched. Overhead	0	33.8	31.8	17.7	11.7	8.3	6.7	5.7	5.5

Table 3: Percent of time spent in basic activities of a Muse worker on TC2000.

Benchmark	Muse Workers								
	1	3	5	10	15	20	25	30	32
11-queens2	31410506	52004	20530	8412	3839	2712	2267	1463	1382
8-queens2	207778	980	618	174	124	91	66	61	58
parse5	39119	132	58	43	28	23	20	20	20
farmer	33486	16	11	11	11	11	11	11	11

Table 4: Task sizes for selected benchmarks on TC2000.

Benchmark	Muse Workers								
	1	3	5	10	15	20	25	30	32
11-queens2	0	10.8	10.2	9.0	9.2	9.8	10.2	10.7	11.4
8-queens2	0	9.0	11.9	9.3	11.8	11.9	12.9	14.9	15.4
parse5	0	7.5	9.1	18.5	19.3	24.0	22.9	26.0	25.8
farmer	0	12.1	13.6	16.2	16.4	16.0	16.2	16.5	17.0

Table 5: Scheduling overheads per task in terms of Prolog procedure calls.

In all benchmarks, the sharing overhead is the dominating part of the scheduling overhead. Sharing overhead ranges from 0.0% on the *11-queens2* to 22.3% on the *parse5*.

A possible explanation for the increase of overheads when increasing number of workers is shown in Table 4, which shows the effect of increasing number of workers on the average task sizes (expressed as the number of Prolog procedure calls per task). A task is a continuous piece of work executed by a worker.

In Table 4 the task size decreases as the the number of workers is increased until it reaches a constant value, 20 for *parse5* and 11 for *farmer*. The reason the task size is almost constant after a certain number of workers is that the Muse system supports a form of delayed release of work that tries to avoid a continuous decrease in task size as the number of workers is increased. Supporting such a mechanism is crucial in order to avoid a continuous high increase in scheduling overhead with an increasing number of workers. The idea of the delayed release mechanism supported in the Muse system is as follows. When a worker reaches a situation in which it has only one private parallel node, it will make its private load visible to the other workers only when that node is still alive after a certain number, k, of Prolog procedure calls. (A node on the Prolog tree can be either parallel or sequential. By default all nodes are parallel. Sequential nodes can be obtained by annotating the corresponding predicates.) The value of k is a constant value selected to be larger than the number of Prolog procedure calls equivalent to the scheduling overhead per task (see below).

Table 5 shows the scheduling overhead per task in terms of Prolog procedure calls for the four selected benchmarks. The scheduling overhead (all activities except *Prolog* and *Idle*) is equivalent to around 8 – 26 Prolog procedure calls per task. It is almost constant (around 10) for *11-queens2*, a program with coarse-grained parallelism. It is higher and increases with adding more workers for the other three, programs with finer grain parallelism. For *parse5*, the scheduling overhead per task is somewhat higher in comparison to the other benchmarks. *parse5* generates a search tree with two long branches and each branch has many short branches.

To conclude, the scheduling overhead per task of Muse for the selected four benchmarks on TC2000 ranges from 8 to 26 Prolog procedure calls per task. This value is affected by the relative speeds of the Prolog engine and the scheduler. For instance, the corresponding value for the Muse system on Sequent Symmetry is around 5 – 7 Prolog procedure calls per task. The time of a Prolog procedure call is between 23 to 30 microseconds on TC2000, and between 83 to 100 microseconds on Sequent Symmetry. The relative cost of scheduling overhead is higher on TC2000 than on Sequent Symmetry due to the relatively high ratio of processor speed to communication speed in the former. So, in order to avoid losing any gain obtained by exploiting parallelism, the Muse system on TC2000 should avoid letting the task sizes fall below 26 Prolog procedure calls. That is, the value of k should be larger than 26. Actually, all results presented in this paper correspond to k equal to 10.

We have also experimented with increasing k to 15, 25 and 30, the result being that some improvements were obtained for programs with very fine granularity (e.g. *farmer*).

5 Comparison with Aurora

In this section we compare the timing results of Muse with the corresponding results for Aurora with the Manchester scheduler [10]. Both Aurora and Muse are based on the same sequential Prolog, SICStus version 0.6, and are implemented on the same BBN Butterfly. The main difference between Muse and Aurora is that Aurora is based on another model for Or-parallel execution of Prolog, named the SRI model [13]. The idea of the SRI model is to extend the conventional WAM with a large binding array per worker and modify the trail to contain address-value pairs instead of just addresses. Each array is used by just one worker to store and access conditional bindings, i.e. bindings to variables which are potentially shareable. The WAM stacks are shared by all workers. The nodes of the search tree contain extra fields to enable workers to move around the tree. When a worker finishes a task, it moves over the tree to take another task. The worker starting a new task must partially reconstruct its array using the trail of the worker from which the task is taken.

Many optimizations have been made of the implementation of Aurora on the Butterfly machines. These optimizations are the same as the Muse optimizations, with the exception of caching the WAM stacks. In Aurora the WAM stacks are shared by the all workers while in Muse each worker has its own copy of the WAM stacks. Therefore, it is straightforward on Muse to make the WAM stack areas cachable whereas in Aurora it requires a complex cache coherence protocol to achieve this effect.

The Manchester scheduler for Aurora also tries to avoid a continuous decrease in task sizes with an increasing number of workers. The idea used by the Manchester scheduler is that each busy worker checks for the arrival of signals from other workers on every N Prolog procedure calls. The best value of N on TC2000 is 20. All Aurora timing results presented in this paper correspond to $N = 20$.

Table 6 shows the runtimes of Aurora with the Manchester scheduler on TC2000 for the set of benchmarks used in Table 1. It also shows in the last column the running times of SICStus0.6 on one TC2000 node, with their ratio to the running times on one Aurora worker.

Figure 2 shows the speedup curves of Aurora for the four groups of benchmarks: *GI, GII, GIII* and *GIV*. These curves correspond to speedups obtained from Table 6. Variations around the mean value are shown by a vertical line with two short horizontal lines at each end. Variations of less than 0.4 are not shown in both the Figures 1 and 2. (Variations on Muse are less than 0.4, thus they are not shown in Figure 1.) We observe from Figure 2 that the Aurora system with the Manchester scheduler is almost ideal for GI programs but not for the others.

The average real speedups on 32 processors, in comparison to SICStus on one TC2000 processor, are 17.6 for the *GI* programs, and 15.7 for the whole set of benchmarks (calculated from Table 6). The corresponding figures on Muse, calculated from Table 1, are 25.4 and 23.8 respectively. It can also be seen from Tables 1 and 6 that Muse is faster than Aurora in all benchmarks. The Muse system has even better speedups for hard benchmarks, i.e., benchmarks of groups *GII, GIII* and *GIV*. Those hard benchmarks are a good test of the schedulers. Table 7 shows the ratio of the running times on Aurora to the running times on Muse for each group and the whole set of benchmarks. Aurora timings are 39% to 171% longer than Muse timings.

Benchmarks	Aurora Workers					SICStus0.6
	1	10	20	30	32	
semigroup	1699.78	169.62(10.0)	87.03(19.5)	58.90(28.9)	54.68(31.1)	990.89(1.72)
11-queens1	369.14	36.92(10.00)	18.54(19.9)	12.47(29.6)	11.70(31.6)	190.87(1.93)
11-queens2	1044.49	105.38(9.91)	52.83(19.8)	35.37(29.5)	33.19(31.5)	574.27(1.82)
• GI Σ	3113.41	311.91(9.98)	158.38(19.7)	106.68(29.2)	99.55(31.3)	1756.03(1.77)
8-queens1	2.85	0.33(8.64)	0.21(13.6)	0.22(13.0)	0.23(12.4)	1.48(1.93)
8-queens2	6.97	0.76(9.17)	0.43(16.2)	0.35(19.9)	0.36(19.4)	3.77(1.85)
tina	6.33	0.83(7.63)	0.65(9.74)	0.88(7.19)	1.16(5.46)	3.07(2.06)
salt-mustard	1.47	0.19(7.74)	0.12(12.2)	0.12(12.2)	0.14(10.5)	0.44(3.34)
○ GII Σ	17.62	2.10(8.39)	1.40(12.6)	1.55(11.4)	1.81(9.73)	8.76(2.01)
parse2*20	2.46	1.30(1.89)	1.50(1.64)	1.74(1.41)	1.87(1.32)	1.43(1.72)
parse4*5	2.25	0.74(3.04)	0.81(2.78)	1.01(2.23)	1.08(2.08)	1.31(1.72)
parse5	1.59	0.46(3.46)	0.47(3.38)	0.54(2.94)	0.59(2.69)	0.93(1.71)
db4*10	0.91	0.28(3.25)	0.35(2.60)	0.55(1.65)	0.58(1.57)	0.53(1.72)
db5*10	1.11	0.30(3.70)	0.36(3.08)	0.54(2.06)	0.60(1.85)	0.64(1.73)
house*20	1.55	0.79(1.96)	1.12(1.38)	1.99(0.78)	2.63(0.59)	0.94(1.65)
◇ GIII Σ	9.87	3.86(2.56)	4.60(2.15)	6.24(1.58)	7.17(1.38)	5.78(1.71)
parse1*20	0.66	0.62(1.06)	0.73(0.90)	0.85(0.78)	0.84(0.79)	0.38(1.74)
parse3*20	0.57	0.62(0.92)	0.71(0.80)	0.70(0.81)	0.74(0.77)	0.33(1.73)
farmer*100	1.14	1.80(0.63)	2.14(0.53)	2.33(0.49)	2.37(0.48)	0.66(1.73)
∗ GIV Σ	2.37	3.03(0.78)	3.56(0.67)	3.80(0.62)	3.91(0.61)	1.37(1.73)
Σ	3143.27	320.92(9.79)	167.95(18.7)	118.47(26.5)	112.60(27.9)	1771.94(1.77)

Table 6: Runtimes (in seconds) of Aurora on TC2000.

Benchmarks	Workers				
	1	10	20	30	32
GI	1.46	1.45	1.46	1.45	1.44
GII	1.52	1.48	1.54	1.89	2.23
GIII	1.38	1.57	1.81	2.38	2.71
GIV	1.38	1.68	1.95	2.01	2.08
Σ	1.46	1.46	1.48	1.50	1.51

Table 7: Ratio of running times on Aurora to running times on Muse.

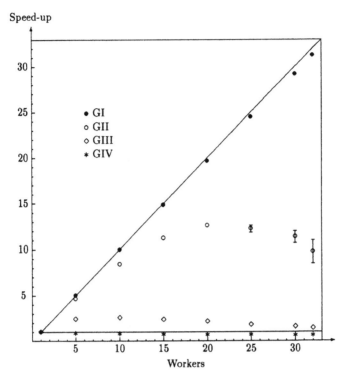

Figure 2: Speedups of Aurora relative to 1 Aurora worker.

6 Conclusions

The Muse implementation and its performance results on the BBN Butterfly TC2000 have been presented and discussed. A large set of benchmarks with different amount of parallelism have been used. The performance results of Muse have also been compared with the corresponding results of the Aurora Or-parallel Prolog system.

The results obtained for the Muse system are very encouraging: almost linear speedups (around 31 on 32 processors) for Prolog programs with coarse grain parallelism, and a speedup factor of almost 1 for programs with very low parallelism. The average real speedup on 32 TC2000 processors, in comparison to SICStus on one TC2000 processor, is 25.4 for the programs with coarse grain parallelism.

The extra overhead of Muse associated with adapting the sequential SICStus Prolog system to an Or-parallel implementation is around 22% on the TC2000. Most of this overhead is due to accessing the global Prolog tables, which are cachable in SICStus but not in Muse. (The global tables, in Muse and Aurora, are partitioned into parts and each part resides in the local memory of one processor.) The corresponding extra overhead per worker for the Aurora system on TC2000 is around 77%. One reason the overhead per worker is higher in Aurora (than in Muse) is that in Aurora the WAM stacks are shared by the all workers, and thus the stacks are not cachable. In Muse each worker has its own copy of the WAM stacks, thus it is straightforward to make the WAM stacks cachable. There is also the extra overhead of maintaining the binding arrays used in Aurora. For all benchmarks used in this paper, the Muse system is faster than the Aurora system. Aurora timings are 39% to 171% longer than Muse timings.

The delayed release mechanism supported by the Muse system avoids a continuous decrease in task sizes as the number of workers grows. Without such a mechanism the speedups can be lost as the number of workers is increased, due to the increasing overheads for scheduling work because of decreasing task sizes. The scheduling overhead of the Muse system on TC2000 for a set of benchmarks ranges between 8 to 26 Prolog procedure calls per task. The corresponding cost for Muse on Sequent Symmetry is around 5 – 7 Prolog procedure calls per task. The relative cost of scheduling overhead is higher on TC2000 than on Sequent Symmetry due to the relatively high ratio of processor speed to communication speed in the former. Thus, the task size should be controlled at runtime to be not less than 26 Prolog procedure calls on TC2000 in order to avoid performance degradation.

In the current Muse implementation, speculative and non-speculative work are scheduled equally. Speculative work is defined as work which is within the scope of a cut and therefore may never be done by the sequential implementation. In the near future we plan to support a scheduling scheme that gives lower priority of scheduling speculative work, using one of the schemes presented in [9]. The Muse group at SICS is collaborating with a group at BIM to extend the BIM sequential Prolog system to an Or-parallel implementation using the Muse approach. We believe that extending the BIM Prolog system will be as simple and efficient as extending the SICStus Prolog system.

7 Acknowledgments

We would like to thank the Argonne National Laboratory group for allowing us to use their Butterfly machines. Shyam Mudambi was supported by NSF grant CCR-8718989.

References

[1] Khayri A. M. Ali and Roland Karlsson. The Muse Approach to Or-Parallel Prolog. International Journal of Parallel Programming, pages 129–162, Vol. 19, No. 2, April 1990.

[2] Khayri A. M. Ali and Roland Karlsson. The Muse Or-Parallel Prolog Model and its Performance. In Proceedings of the 1990 North American Conference on Logic Programming, pages 757–776, MIT Press, October 1990.

[3] Khayri A. M. Ali and Roland Karlsson. Full Prolog and Scheduling Or-Parallelism in Muse. To appear in the International Journal of Parallel Programming, Vol. 19, No. 6, Dec. 1990.

[4] Khayri A. M. Ali and Roland Karlsson. Scheduling Or-Parallelism in Muse. In Proceedings of the 1991 International Conference on Logic Programming, Paris, June 1991.

[5] Khayri A. M. Ali, Roland Karlsson, and Shyam Mudambi. Performance of Muse on Switch-Based Multiprocessor Machines. Submitted to NGC Journal, 1991.

[6] Uri Baron, Jacques Chassin de Kergommeaux, Max Hailperin, Michael Ratcliffe, Philippe Ropert, Jean-Claude Syre, and Harald Westphal. The Parallel ECRC Prolog System PEP-Sys: An Overview and Evaluation Results. In Proceedings of the International Conference on Fifth Generation Computer Systems 1988, pages 841–850, ICOT, November 1988.

[7] Alan Calderwood and Péter Szeredi. Scheduling Or-parallelism in Aurora—the Manchester scheduler. In Proceedings of the sixth International Conference on Logic Programming, pages 419–435, MIT Press, June 1989.

[8] Mats Carlsson and Johan Widén. SICStus Prolog User's Manual. SICS Research Report R88007B, October 1988.

[9] Bogumil Hausman. Pruning and Speculative Work in OR-parallel Prolog. PhD thesis, Swedish Institute of Computer Science, SICS Dissertation Series 01 (SICS/D-90-9901), March 1990.

[10] Ewing Lusk, David H. D. Warren, Seif Haridi, et al. The Aurora Or-parallel Prolog System. New Generation Computing, 7(2,3): 243–271, 1990.

[11] Shyam Mudambi. Performance of Aurora on NUMA machines. In Proceedings of the 1991 International Conference on Logic Programming, Paris, June 1991.

[12] Péter Szeredi. Performance analysis of the Aurora Or-parallel Prolog System. In Proceedings of the 1989 North American Conference on Logic Programming, pages 713–732, MIT Press, March 1989.

[13] David H. D. Warren. The SRI Model for Or-parallel Execution of Prolog—Abstract Design and Implementation Issues. In Proceedings of the 1987 Symposium on Logic Programming, pages 92–102, 1987.

Scheduling Strategies and Speculative Work

Anthony Beaumont

Department of Computer Science, University of Bristol,
Bristol BS8 1TR, U.K.

Abstract

This paper gives a short report on the current state of our research into scheduling speculative tasks in the Aurora or-parallel Prolog system. A Speculative task is one that may be pruned by a cut or commit, rendering any work done on that task to be wasted. The use of pruning operators is commonplace in most Prolog applications so there is a need to schedule speculative tasks in a way that avoids wasted work.

Several schedulers have already been developed for the Aurora system but none of the current schedulers make any distinction between speculative and non-speculative work.

We show that by treating speculative work differently it is possible to obtain a significant improvement in performance as measured both by the reduction of wasted work and an improvement in speedups.

1   Introduction

Aurora is a prototype or-parallel implementation of the full Prolog language for shared-memory multiprocessors, currently running on Sequent and Encore machines. It has been developed in the framework of the Gigalips project, a collaborative effort between groups at Argonne National Laboratory, University of Bristol, and the Swedish Institute of Computer Science (SICS). A full description of Aurora can be found elsewhere [8].

Aurora is based on the SRI model [11] in which or-parallel execution of Prolog programs consists of the exploration of a search tree in parallel by a number of **workers**. A worker is defined as an abstract processing agent. During execution, a tree of **nodes** is created, each node containing a **task** which represents a new and unexplored branch of the tree. Workers will execute the tasks in parallel, each worker working on a single task until the work in that task is exhausted. Each worker is composed of a Prolog engine and a scheduler [10], the worker being controlled by the engine until either the worker comes to the end of its current task or it receives a message from another worker. The scheduler will take control in the cases when either the worker needs to find a new task or to process a message from another worker.

One of the aims of our work has been to compare the scheduling strategies used by previous Aurora schedulers with the approach taken by the Muse scheduler [1][2]. To this end we have developed a flexible scheduler in which we can easily implement different scheduling strategies and assess their strengths and weaknesses [3]. In section 2 we briefly discuss the approaches taken in the design of these schedulers and report some figures on the amount of task switching following from the different approaches to sharing tasks.

Sections 3 and 4 discuss how we identify speculative work and the implications speculative work has on scheduling.

Section 5 presents a program which models speculative work and gives some results showing the behaviour of several scheduling strategies as the amount of speculative work is changed.

Section 6 gives some results from some real Prolog applications containing speculative work.

2   Scheduling strategies

We have several different options when choosing how to match idle workers with available tasks. Previous schedulers for Aurora were designed with a fixed strategy based on the idea that workers would share only the topmost node on their branch (known as **topmost dispatching**). The reason behind this is that dividing the work at the top of the tree should allow each worker to work separately on its own local portion of the search tree. This strategy works well if the amount of work contained in each task is large, but if the the tasks are quickly exhausted, the workers must frequently perform a global search for a new task. We call this global search a **major task switch** and they represent a large scheduling overhead.

One way to reduce the number of expensive major task switches is to increase the number of tasks accessible to each worker by sharing many tasks instead of just one, an idea first used in the Muse scheduler. This is known as **bottom-most dispatching** because idle workers are given the bottom-most task of a partially explored branch. If that task is quickly exhausted then there are often several other tasks nearby which can be accessed by backtracking up the branch (**public backtracking**). We refer to this method of finding new tasks as **minor task switching** and these are considerably cheaper than performing a major task switch.

Both of these strategies have been implemented in the Bristol scheduler and compared in terms of the amount of task switching. We would predict that topmost dispatching will lead to more major task switches but relatively few minor task switches. Bottom-most dispatching however will create a much larger public region in the tree, leading to an increased amount of public backtracking. This kind of backtracking is more expensive than private backtracking and so the two approaches represent a trade off between the cost of increased major task switching against increased public backtracking. In order to assess the performance of each approach we have measured the amount of time each worker spends in task switching under each strategy. Figure 1 shows the percentage of time spent by each worker in task switching during a number of benchmark programs where we are finding all solutions.

The difference between the two strategies in respect of the average amount of time spent task switching is quite small, but over all the benchmark programs bottom-most dispatching generally leads to less time spent task switching.

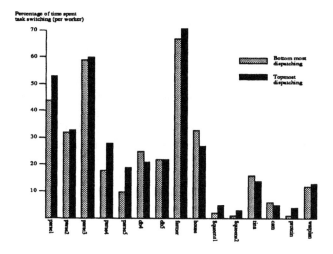

Figure 1: DATA ON TIME SPENT TASK SWITCHING

3 Speculative Work

We call a task **speculative** if it falls within the scope of a pruning operator and could be pruned. If we allow workers to begin work on such tasks, that work will be wasted if the task gets pruned. In a sequential Prolog system no wasted work will ever get done because the tree is searched from left to right. We do not wish to make all speculative work sequential since this is a large and valuable source of parallelism so we must take care to avoid highly speculative work and so reduce the amount of work which gets wasted. Before we discuss scheduling strategies to accomplish this we must take some time to look at how we detect the presence of speculative work and how if possible we can quickly remove it by making it non-speculative.

As pointed out by [5], speculative work can be made non-speculative either when all branches to its left fail without leading to a cut, or when a branch to its left executes a cut and prunes it. We should therefore aim to both increase the chances of being able to prune speculative work and also to do the pruning as soon as it becomes safe to do so. We look first at the cut and when it is safe for a cut to prune branches to its right in an or-parallel environment.

When cuts are encountered, we want to execute as much of the pruning as possible. We are only allowed to prune branches that will also be pruned by the action of any cuts to our left. Therefore a cut should suspend its pruning only if it could itself be pruned by a cut of smaller scope.

It has been proposed that branches executing a cut need not suspend at all, and that the worker could continue with the work after the pruning, leaving the completion of the pruning to be done when all branches to its left have failed. This has been implemented successfully in Muse, although it must be pointed out that, since there is no real suspension in Muse, a worker executing a cut would otherwise have to busy-wait on that branch until either it was pruned or the branches on its left failed. We feel that it is better for the cut to be suspended (since it is known to be speculative) and for the suspending worker to look for less speculative work in a system where that is possible.

Without any information about the presence and scope of cuts we would have to force all cuts to suspend until they are leftmost within the subtree rooted at the cut scope node. Hausman [6] describes algorithms to decorate the tree with information about the presence and scope of cuts, reporting that use of this information improves performance on some examples by up to 40% with an overhead of only 2% to maintain the information. This scheme has been implemented in the Bristol scheduler.

Returning to the subject of speculative work we can note that the further left a branch is within a speculative subtree, the lower the probability that one of the branches to its left will succeed in pruning it. Therefore we would want our scheduling algorithm to give priority to work on the left side of speculative subtrees.

A general strategy which we have proposed [3] would be to try to avoid scheduling workers on to areas of the computation which are speculative, however if only speculative work exists, we would want to avoid the highly speculative work and concentrate on the tasks to the left of that region.

We consider a speculative subtree to begin as soon as the first clause containing a cut is encountered. Within that subtree we do not make further distinctions based on the number of cuts present.

4 Scheduling speculative work

Two similar schemes are being developed at Bristol to implement a way of giving priority to less speculative work, our own and one by Sindaha [9]. In our scheme we allow idle workers to search speculative subtrees from left to right, and take the leftmost available task (**leftmost dispatching**) has been implemented in the Bristol scheduler. We combine this with bottom-most dispatching since deeper tasks on a particular branch are less speculative that higher ones. This method of finding work is quite expensive since the search involves locking to synchronise moving right through the tree and the scheduler is also required to maintain a record of the left to right order of workers in the tree. Sindaha's scheme aims to reduce these overheads. It reduces the cost of searching for tasks by linking the tips of each branch to form a datastructure similar to that used in the wavefront scheduler [4]. Work is found by traversing this list rather than searching the nodes of the tree.

The drawback of these schemes is that maintaining the left to right ordering and searching for work is more expensive than scheduling schemes which do not take account of speculative work. If the computation does not involve, or has very little, speculative work, these ways of scheduling tasks would not perform as well as those schedulers which took no account of speculative work. Therefore we suggest that the scheduler must be flexible enough to be able to use different criteria for scheduling tasks based on whether or not those tasks are speculative

The speculativeness of a particular task may change if branches appear or disappear to its left. A worker may take the least speculative task initially but it may become highly speculative if many branches appear to its left. Unless the task is exhausted the worker will not get a chance to reposition itself and move to a less speculative task. For this reason we have also investigated the effect of allowing the workers periodically to suspend a task in favour of a less speculative one to avoid them becoming stuck in highly speculative computations, what we call **voluntary suspension**.

5 Modelling speculative work

To get some insight into what can be gained by employing a leftmost dispatching algorithm we have tried to model speculative computation, using an example suggested by Kluźniak [7].

This program (Figure 2) generates permutations of a list and tests them to find if they match with a given, fully instantiated, goal pattern. The search space for, say,
permutation([1,2,3,4,5,6,7,8], P)
is uniformly filled with the permutations of [1,2,3,4,5,6,7,8], in lexicographic order. The position and size of a set of solutions can be specified by invoking
query([1,2,3,4,5,6,7,8], GP)
with an appropriate goal pattern GP.

```
%%%  permutation( + list, - its permutation )

permutation( [], [] ).

permutation( L, [ E | P ] ) :-
      delete( L, E, D ),
      permutation( D, P ).


%%%  delete( + non-empty list, - one of its elements, - remaining list )

delete( [ H | T ], H, T ).

delete( [ H | T ], E, [ H | L ] ) :-
      delete( T, E, L ).


%%%  find a permutation matching the goal

query( List, Goal ) :-
      permutation( List, Permuted ),
      Permuted = Goal,
      ! .
```

Figure 2: Modeling speculative work

We then measure the number of resolutions made by several workers and divide this by the number of resolutions made by one worker. This gives us an idea of how much wasted work has been done.

We map the performance of three scheduling strategies on speculative computation, by dividing the search tree into segments, each segment representing a subtree whose root is the branch giving the first element of the permuted list. We vary the amount of speculative work by moving the position of the goal pattern from left to right through the different segments, for example [3,1,2,4,5,6,7,8] is the leftmost solution in the third segment, and [2,8,7,6,5,4,3,1] is the rightmost solution in the second segment.

We get some idea of the amount of wasted work by dividing the number of resolutions done by 10 worker by the minimum number of resolutions necessary which is the number taken by a single worker, backtracking left to right through the tree. We compare the values of this ratio when allowing tasks to be scheduled according to the topmost, bottommost or leftmost strategies. At this point we do not use voluntary suspension.

Figure 3 shows that when the goal pattern is to the left of the search tree and the amount of speculative work is high, the deepest and topmost strategies are almost random in their performance, although typically they lead to around three times as much work as a single worker would do on the same computation. Leftmost dispatching performs quite consistently and is never much above 1.5 times as much work.

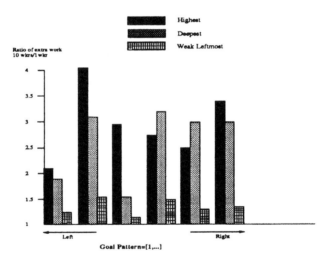

Figure 3: GOAL PATTERN POSITIONED IN THE LEFTMOST SEGMENT OF THE SEARCH TREE

Figure 4 shows shows the results from segment 2, in which leftmost dispatching performs most consistently and leads to very little wasted work. However, as the position of the solution is moved to the right in this segment both the topmost and deepest strategies cause an increased amount of wasted work. This reflects the fact that the solutions on the left of this segment can be found very quickly, giving less time for wasted work. However, there may be several workers working to the right of this segment and all the work done by them will be wasted. The longer it takes to find the solution, the more wasted work there will be.

By the time we get to the third segment, as shown in Figure 5, most workers will begin working to the left of the solution and it is easier to avoid wasted work, even without

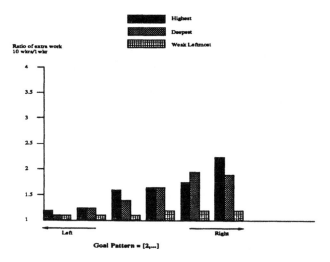

Figure 4: GOAL PATTERN POSITIONED IN THE SECOND SEGMENT OF THE SEARCH TREE

voluntary suspension. All three strategies give ratios of better then 1.5, although the most consistent is again the leftmost strategy.

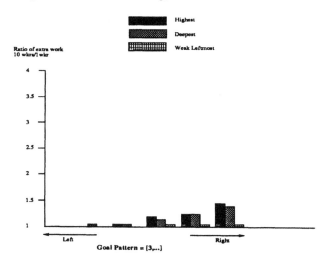

Figure 5: GOAL PATTERN POSITIONED IN THE THIRD SEGMENT OF THE SEARCH TREE

To the right of the the third segment all of the strategies manage to avoid wasted work most of the time.

When we look at the speedups (Table 1) we find that the leftmost strategy has an extra overhead associated with it giving between 10-20% worse performance than the other two strategies when doing the same amount of work.

To convert the better performance on avoiding wasted work into better speedups we clearly need to reduce the overheads of scheduling the leftmost work first. We hope that results from [9] will demonstrate this.

Goal Pattern	Topmost	Bottom-most	Leftmost
[1,3,5,6,4,2,7,8,9]	5.0	5.1	6.3
[1,3,7,6,4,2,5,8,9]	2.9	3.2	5.9
[1,5,3,6,4,2,7,8,9]	4.7	3.9	6.6
[1,5,7,6,4,2,3,8,9]	3.0	3.7	6.5
[1,7,3,6,4,2,5,8,9]	3.1	3.0	6.5
[1,7,5,6,4,2,3,8,9]	3.0	2.9	6.7
[2,4,6,5,3,1,7,8,9]	8.6	8.9	8.0
[2,4,8,5,3,1,7,6,9]	7.9	8.0	7.7
[2,6,4,5,3,1,7,8,9]	6.8	7.3	7.8
[2,6,8,5,3,1,7,4,9]	5.8	6.1	7.6
[2,8,4,5,3,1,7,6,9]	5.2	4.9	7.5
[2,8,6,5,3,1,7,4,9]	4.8	4.8	7.2
[3,1,5,6,4,2,7,8,9]	9.8	10.0	8.0
[3,1,7,6,4,2,5,8,9]	8.9	9.7	8.3
[3,5,1,6,4,2,7,8,9]	8.4	9.7	8.1
[3,5,7,6,4,2,1,8,9]	8.0	9.0	8.0
[3,7,1,6,4,2,5,8,9]	8.1	8.2	8.0
[3,7,5,6,4,2,1,8,9]	7.2	7.8	7.7
[5,1,3,6,4,2,7,8,9]	9.9	10.0	8.4
[5,1,7,6,4,2,3,8,9]	9.8	10.0	8.2
[5,3,1,6,4,2,7,8,9]	9.8	10.0	8.5
[5,3,7,6,4,2,1,8,9]	9.4	9.8	8.3
[5,7,1,6,4,2,3,8,9]	8.6	8.9	8.2
[5,7,3,6,4,2,1,8,9]	8.2	8.4	8.1
[7,1,3,6,4,2,5,8,9]	9.9	10.0	8.5
[7,1,5,6,4,2,3,8,9]	9.9	10.0	8.5
[7,3,1,6,4,2,5,8,9]	9.9	10.0	8.5
[7,3,5,6,4,2,1,8,9]	9.7	9.8	8.4
[7,5,1,6,4,2,3,8,9]	9.4	9.7	8.4
[7,5,3,6,4,2,1,8,9]	9.3	9.3	8.4

Table 1: SPEEDUPS USING 10 WORKERS FOR EACH GOAL PATTERN

Next we investigate whether or not the performance of bottom-most and leftmost scheduling could be improved by allowing workers to voluntarily suspend speculative tasks, and move to take work which is less speculative. Figure 6 shows that by combining bottom-most dispatching with voluntary suspension, and allowing workers to reposition leftwards, improves the performance considerably. This may be a useful combination of strategies because the initial distribution of work by bottom-most dispatching is much cheaper than leftmost dispatching and by allowing workers in highly speculative regions to suspend their tasks we can correct the mistakes that may be made if the original choice of task is not a good one. Figure 7 shows that the amount of wasted work leading from leftmost dispatching can also be reduced still further by employing voluntary suspension. When converted into speedups however, the performance does not improve much. This is because the voluntary suspension leads to more workers trying to share the tasks on the left of the search tree and this in turn reduces the amount of work available to each worker, leading to more task switching.

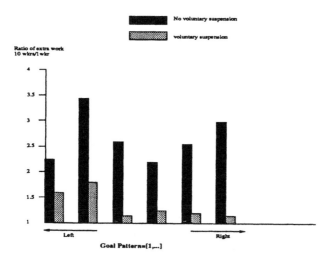

Figure 6: BOTTOM-MOST DISPATCHING WITH VOLUNTARY SUSPENSION

6 Some applications containing speculative work

From modelling speculative work we move to some real applications which contain speculative work.

We have investigated speedups obtained from different scheduling strategies on a number of applications, where we are only interested in finding the leftmost solution. The results are shown is Table 2 and they indicate that we can significantly improve the speedups obtained on these programs by using leftmost dispatching. Augmenting that strategy with voluntary suspension improves the speedups still further on most of the examples.

Figure 8 shows the amount of wasted work on four applications where again we are looking for the leftmost solution.

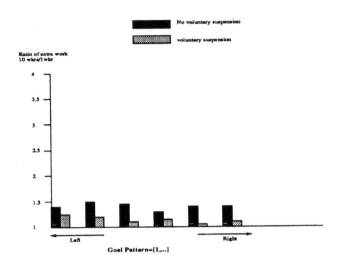

Figure 7: LEFTMOST DISPATCHING WITH VOLUNTARY SUSPENSION

Application	Aurora one worker	Dispatching strategy								
		Deepest			Leftmost			Leftmost+VS		
		Ave	Best	Worst	Ave	Best	Worst	Ave	Best	Worst
Protein	1	2.45	2.56	2.32	3.92	4.63	3.48	4.61	4.89	4.31
Puzzle	1	1.37	2.06	1.22	5.65	6.11	4.99	5.96	6.33	5.51
14Queens	1	1.84	2.01	1.56	1.81	1.91	1.70	4.70	5.30	4.31
Fly-pan	1	3.30	3.46	3.05	4.18	4.24	4.00	4.60	5.63	3.83
Warplan	1	1.11	1.15	1.01	1.52	1.59	1.46	1.46	1.52	1.40
Parse5*10	1	1.33	1.37	1.31	1.44	1.45	1.42	1.81	1.84	1.75
Average	1	1.90	2.11	1.74	3.09	3.32	2.84	3.86	4.25	3.52

Table 2: SPEEDUPS (AVE, BEST AND WORST FROM 6 RUNS) USING 10 WORKERS TO FIND THE FIRST SOLUTION

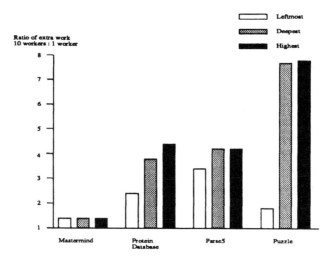

Figure 8: GRAPH COMPARING WORK DONE BY 10 WORKERS WITH WORK DONE BY 1 WORKER

7 Conclusions

Although our work in this area is not complete we are able to show that leftmost dispatching is an effective strategy if we are scheduling speculative tasks. This strategy is able to avoid wasted work and leads to better speedups. However, the overheads of using it are quite high due to the need for maintaining the left to right order within the tree and the synchronisation necessary during the search for work. Leftmost dispatching also tends to lead to the concentration of workers in one region of the tree which reduces the amount of work available to each worker and causes there to be more task switching. For these reasons we do not suggest leftmost dispatching as a general scheduling strategy but feel that it would be useful in combination with bottom-most dispatching which would distribute workers better on non-speculative work. We have also noted that the amount of wasted work in speculative computations can be reduced still further by allowing voluntary suspension. Our results from real applications show that leftmost dispatching with voluntary suspension gives better performance than both leftmost dispatching without voluntary suspension, and dispatching on deepest.

8 Acknowledgements

The author is indebted to other members of the Gigalips project for careful reading and invaluable comments on this paper.

This work was supported by ESPRIT projects 2471 ("PEPMA").

References

[1] Khayri Ali. *Or-parallel execution of Prolog on BC-Machine*. SICS Research Report, Swedish Institute of Computer Science, 1987.

[2] Khayri A. M. Ali and Roland Karlsson. The Muse or-parallel Prolog model and its performance. In *Proceedings of the North American Conference on Logic Programming*, MIT Press, October 1990.

[3] Anthony Beaumont, S Muthu Raman, Péter Szeredi, and David H D Warren. Flexible Scheduling of Or-Parallelism in Aurora: The Bristol Scheduler. In *PARLE91: Conference on Parallel Architectures and Languages Europe*, Springer Verlag, June 1991.

[4] Per Brand. Wavefront scheduling. 1988. Internal Report, Gigalips Project.

[5] Andrzej Ciepielewski. Personal communication. May 1991.

[6] Bogumił Hausman. *Pruning and Speculative Work in OR-Parallel PROLOG*. PhD thesis, The Royal Institute of Technology, Stockholm, 1990.

[7] Feliks Kluźniak. *Developing Applications for Aurora*. Technical Report TR-90-17, University of Bristol, Computer Science Department, August 1990.

[8] Ewing Lusk, David H. D. Warren, Seif Haridi, et al. The Aurora or-parallel Prolog system. *New Generation Computing*, 7(2,3):243–271, 1990.

[9] Raed Sindaha. Scheduling speculative work in the Aurora or-parallel Prolog system. March 1990. Internal Report, Gigalips Project, University of Bristol.

[10] Péter Szeredi, Mats Carlsson, and Rong Yang. Interfacing engines and schedulers in or-parallel prolog systems. In *PARLE91: Conference on Parallel Architectures and Languages Europe*, Springer Verlag, June 1991.

[11] David H. D. Warren. The SRI model for or-parallel execution of Prolog—abstract design and implementation issues. In *Proceedings of the 1987 Symposium on Logic Programming*, pages 92–102, 1987.

Performance of Competitive OR-Parallelism

Wolfgang Ertel

Institut für Informatik, Technische Universität München
Augustenstraße 46 Rgb., D-8000 München 2
email: ertel@informatik.tu-muenchen.de

Abstract

We present a very simple parallel execution model suitable for inference systems with nondeterministic choices (OR-branching points). All the parallel processors solve the same task without any communication. Their programs only differ in the initialization of the random number generator used for branch selection in depth first backtracking search. This model, called random competition, permits us to calculate analytically the parallel performance for arbitrary numbers of processors. This can be done exactly and without any experiments on a parallel machine. Finally, due to their simplicity, competition architectures are easy (and therefore low-priced) to build.

As an application of this systematic approach we compute speedup expressions for specific problem classes defined by their run-time distributions. The results vary from a speedup of 1 for linearly degenerate search trees up to clearly "superlinear" speedup for strongly imbalanced search trees. Moreover, we are able to give estimates for the potential degree of OR-parallelism inherent in the different problem classes. Such an estimate is very important for the design of particular parallel inference machines, since spedups strongly depend upon the application domain.

1   Introduction

Many parallel search procedures have been developed in the last few years. Implementations on parallel machines with a small number of processors show promising results. But how can these results be extrapolated to very high numbers of processors? This is an important question since for most of the combinatorial search problems in AI computation times increase exponentially or even worse with the problem size and currently only very small problems can be solved. Therefore, apart from heuristic techniques highly parallel architectures are of great importance in this field. Experiments on highly parallel machines are expensive and time consuming. Thus mathematical models of parallel architectures for inference in AI are necessary. Since most of these parallel architectures use sophisticated load balancing mechanisms or share data in a global memory, mathematical models of such systems are hard to derive.

A promising approach to qualitative performance models of parallel depth first search based on the term of isoefficiency is presented in [KR90]. In [Ali87] a parallel Prolog

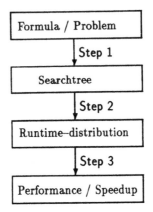

Figure 1: *Procedure for computing the competition performance. Step 3, the computation of the parallel speedup from sequential performance figures, is described in this paper.*

execution model with very loosely coupled sequential processors is described, but without any detailed performance analysis.

In the present paper we introduce an even more simple, non interacting, parallel search architecture called *random competition* for which we derive a statistical performance model. This model enables us to compute exact parallel performance figures for arbitrary high numbers of processors without any parallel experiments. A similar theoretical study for parallel Prolog, based on different classes of random trees was described in [JAM87]. Compared with this study, the present work emphasizes the interpretation of theoretical results and their application to particular inference systems and problem domains.

An important question in this context is: How high is the speedup of a specific random competitive search procedure when applied to a certain problem? To answer this question we propose a three step procedure (see Figure 1). In the first, and hardest, step, the structure of the search tree must be derived from the problem. From this search tree the frequency distribution of the run-time is computed in the second step.[1]

In the following (Section 3) we will focus on step three for computing parallel speedup figures from sequential run-time frequency distributions. In Section 4 this formalism is applied to some example distributions.

First, however, in Section 2 we introduce the parallel execution model.

2 The Competitive Parallel Execution Model

In many cases there exists a number of different algorithms[2] for solving a problem, where each algorithm consumes a different amount of time for execution. If it is known in advance

---

[1]Step 2 is currently under investigation, whereas step 1 is a goal of future research.

[2]Examples for different search algorithms are: depth first search with leftmost selection, depth first search with rightmost selection, breadth first search, $A*$ with different heuristic evaluation functions.

which algorithm is the best, only one processor is necessary to execute this algorithm. In many artificial intelligence applications, however, this is not known. In this case a gain in computation time is achieved if the different algorithms are executed competitively in parallel. We will show that the larger the difference between the minimal and the average run-time the larger the speedup of the competitive system will be.

In our competition model the task to be solved is not partitioned among the processors like in most other parallel architectures. Rather, each processor gets an identical copy of the whole problem. This works as follows (see Fig. 2):

1. **Startup phase**
   The host sends the whole task to all the worker processors.

2. **Working phase (Competitive Search)**
   On each of the worker processors runs a *different* program (algorithm) for solving the whole task.

3. **Termination**
   If a processor finds a solution for the task, or if he fails[3] to find a solution, he sends a message (with the solution in case of success) to the host. If the host receives such a message, he stops all the workers and outputs the result.[4]

In the rest of this paper we will neglect the time consumed by the startup and termination phases since for most problems of interest in parallel computing these times can be neglected as compared to the working time.

Obviously, during the whole working phase no communication between the processors is necessary. As a consequence no idle times occur and load is perfectly balanced all the time. Due to its simplicity, such a competitive system is very easy to implement on almost every parallel MIMD computer. The number of parallel processors is bounded by the number of different algorithms available for the given computation task.

A typical hardware for competition needs only a broadcasting medium connecting the host to all the workers, where every message (start message containing task, termination message containing the solution) from the host or a worker is sent to all the other processors.

The run-time T_k of the parallel system is the minimum of all the sequential run-times t_i $(i=1,...,k)$ of the k different algorithms.[5]

To define the speedup S of competition for a specific task we need a sequential run-time which we define as the mean value $\langle T_{seq} \rangle$ of the run-time for the different sequential

---

[3]A processor reports a fail to the host if he has found no solution after exploring the whole search tree.

[4]If the underlying hardware allows broadcasting, the workers can also be stopped by the message of the first terminating processor himself.

[5]Please note the difference between T_i and t_i. t_i stands for the sequential run-time of algorithm number i, whereas T_i denotes the run-time of the competitive parallel system with i parallel processors (i.e. i different algorithms).

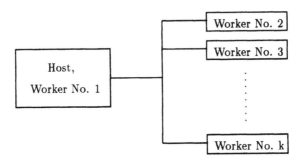

Figure 2: *A possible hardware architecture required for competition consists of $k + 1$ fast processors and a broadcasting medium connecting the host to the k worker processors.*

algorithms. With the definitions

$$\langle T_{seq} \rangle = \frac{1}{k} \cdot \sum_{i=1}^{k} t_i \qquad \text{and} \qquad T_k = \min\{t_1, \ldots, t_k\}$$

the speedup S evaluates to

$$S := \frac{\langle T_{seq} \rangle}{T_k} = \frac{\sum_{i=1}^{k} t_i}{k \cdot \min\{t_1, \ldots, t_k\}}$$

It is easy to see that

$$1 \leq S \leq \frac{1}{k} + \frac{(k-1) \cdot \max\{t_1, \ldots, t_k\}}{k \cdot \min\{t_1, \ldots, t_k\}}$$

holds. S is equal to the upper bound if one processor has a short time and all the others have the same long time. In this case the speedup with k processors can become much larger than k. This justifies the intuition that strongly scattering run-times are a prerequisite for good competitive performance. On the other hand, if all run-times are equal, the speedup equals one, since $k - 1$ of k processors do redundant work.

The requirement of strongly scattering run-times is often fulfilled for heuristic search algorithms (e.g. A^*) with a number of different possible heuristic evaluation functions and missing knowledge about which heuristic will perform best for a given task.

If there exist no or only a few heuristics for a given search task, the number of competitive parallel processors is very small. In this case random competition offers a much higher potential for parallelism.

2.1   Random Competition

The model described so far is adaptable to any kind of problem for which different algorithms exist. In the following we will specialize on combinatorial search problems, which also fall into this category. In particular we focus on such domains for which no good search guiding heuristics exist.[6] The search space of most search problems in the fields of planning, robotics, theorem proving, game theory and problem solving can be represented as OR-tree or AND-OR-tree, where different branches at a choice point stand for independent alternatives. If one of these independent alternatives is successful, none of the others need to be expanded.

In our model we use depth-first backtracking search. If the search tree is infinite, global bounds have to be imposed which in case of failure are iteratively increased ([Kor85]). At each choice point one of the open branches is selected at random. This sequential search procedure, which we call *random search*, is the same on all the processors. According to the general competition model described before, the task to be solved is the same for all the processors. The only difference between the programs running on the worker processors is the initialization of their random number generators which are used for random branch selection. The processor number can be used for this purpose, i.e. worker number i uses i as initial random number what produces different sequences of random numbers.[7] For determining the branch to be expanded the following modulo operation is applied on the integer random number

No. of selected branch = (random number *modulo* actual branching factor) + 1.

Since the programs running on the different processors are identical and no communication occurs during the working phase, this model is ideally suited for implementation on highly parallel SIMD machines with arbitrarily high numbers of processors. The number of processors is only restricted by the problem size as evaluated in Section 3.

The difference between this model and other OR-parallel models (e.g. [SL90], [KPB+89]) can be illustrated informally with the following scenario. Suppose a needle is lost in a big hay stack and ten persons together want to search this needle. One possibility to organize their search is to assign individuals to small parts of the stack which they treat exclusively. During the evolution of the search process it may become necessary to repartition the remaining stack from time to time if some searchers have no more work. The reason for this is that the hay stack (search space) is too large and complex to be partitioned it into equal parts before starting to explore it.

The other possibility is *not* to organize the search. Every searcher goes his own (random) way without being disturbed by the others. This method saves all the organization overhead, but redundant work is being done. The details about the efficiency of this method will be discussed in the following Section.

3 Analytical Computation of Performance

The goal of this Section is to compute with methods of elementary statistics an analytical expression for the speedup $S(k)$ of random competition with k parallel processors, which

---

[6]Even with heuristics a big part of the search space may remain which has to be searched by an uninformed algorithm.

[7]In terms of the general competitive model these different sequences of random numbers represent the required different search algorithms (strategies).

we define as

$$S(k) = \frac{\langle T_1 \rangle}{\langle T_k \rangle},$$

where $\langle T_k \rangle$ $_{(k=1,2,...)}$ stands for the mean value (expected value) of the run-time T_k with k processors. T_k is a stochastic variable with values $t \in I\!\!R^+$ and probability density $p_k(t)$. In order to obtain objective parallel speedup figures, $\langle T_k \rangle$ must be computed from a representative set of random search runs. If for $k = 1$ a single deterministic sequential search procedure is used, the only run-time which can be obtained may be by chance very short or very long, depending on the location of the solution(s) in the search space.[8] With statistic sampling of random-search runs this effect can be avoided. For such a set of samples $\langle T_k \rangle$ is defined as[9]

$$\langle T_k \rangle = \int_0^\infty p_k(t) \cdot t \ dt \tag{1}$$

where $p_k(t)$ stands for the probability density of the competitive parallel system with $k \geq 1$ processors. The probability for observing a sequential run-time in an infinitesimally small interval of width dt located at t is $p_1(t)dt$. The rest of this Section is devoted to compute $p_k(t)$ starting from the sequential run-times, i.e. from $p_1(t)$.

The basis for the performance analysis are sequential frequency distributions $n(t)$ for the run-time, which denote the number of times a run-time t occurs in a set of samples. An empirical frequency distribution of run-times obtained with the automated theorem prover SETHEO [LSBB91] is shown in Figure 3.

The probability for observing the (sequential) run-time t is

$$p_1(t) = \frac{1}{N} \cdot n(t), \quad \text{where} \quad N = \int_0^\infty n(t)dt. \tag{2}$$

The parallel probability density p_k is obtained from p_1 in three steps via the distribution functions $P_1(t)$ and $P_k(t)$. The probability $P_1(t)$ for the sequential algorithm to terminate in a time less or equal to t evaluates to

$$P_1(t) = \int_0^t p_1(t')dt' \tag{3}$$

Suppose we know this probability P_1. Since our k competitive processors are independent we can now apply the laws of probability and compute the probability $P_k(t)$ for our random competition system with k parallel processors to terminate in a time less or equal to t.

---

[8]In fact, many researchers wonder about very strongly scattering experimental speedup results, even if they do extensive sampling of parallel runs. The reason for this is that they do no sampling of sequential runs with a random selection function.

[9]In case of empirical data, which are discrete in time, it is better to define the expected values by summation over the possible times, where we get e.g. $\langle T_{seq} \rangle = \langle T_1 \rangle$. In the following, however, we aim at analytical computation of the speedup for (piecewise) continuous probability density functions.

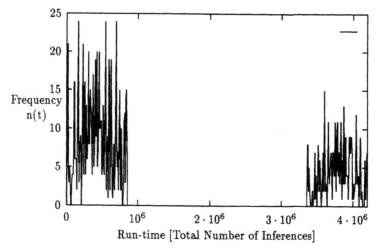

Figure 3: *Distribution of the search effort (tot. no. of inferences) of SETHEO applied to the theorem IP_1 ([Pfe88]) in random search mode. The graph splits into two clusters, separated by a region of times which were not observed ($n(t) = 0$). The total number of runs (samples) is 1402.*

$$P_1(t) \;=\; \text{Probability for one processor to terminate in a time } T_1 \leq t.$$

$$1 \,-\, P_1(t) \;=\; \text{Probability for one processor \textbf{not} to terminate in a time } T_1 \leq t.$$

$$(1 \,-\, P_1(t))^k \;=\; \text{Probability for k independent processors \textbf{not} to terminate in a time } T_k \leq t.\text{[10]}$$

$$1 \,-\, (1 \,-\, P_1(t))^k \;=\; \text{Probability for at least one of k independent processors to terminate in a time } T_k \leq t.\text{[11]}$$

As a consequence

$$P_k(t) \;=\; 1 \,-\, (1 \,-\, P_1(t))^k. \tag{4}$$

This formula is the key for the step from sequential to parallel performance figures. In order to calculate $\langle T \rangle_k$ with equation (1) we need the parallel probability density $p_k(t)$ which we obtain from

$$P_k(t) = \int_0^t p_k(t')dt' \tag{5}$$

as

$$p_k(t) \;=\; \frac{d}{dt}P_k(t) \tag{6}$$

$$=\; k \cdot (1 - P_1(t))^{k-1} \cdot \frac{d}{dt}P_1(t) \tag{7}$$

---

[10] Here we made use of the fact that $P(A \wedge B) = P(A) \cdot P(B)$ for independent events A and B.

[11] This derivation via the probabilities of the complement is much easier than the direct way where we would have to sum over all the different cases for one of k processors to terminate in a time $T \leq t$.

$$= k \cdot (1 - \int\limits_0^t p_1(t')dt')^{k-1} \cdot p_1(t) \qquad (8)$$

The last equation together with (2) enables us to compute the parallel probability density for every given sequential frequency distribution $n(t)$. If we use experimentally derived distributions which are given numerically, the integrals over t in the derived formulas change into sums over the discrete observed time values $t_1, \ldots, t_m$. In the next Section, however we will compute the speedup analytically for functionally given probability density functions. This is mathematically much easier by integration over continuous distributions, rather than by summation.

3.1 Maximum OR-Parallel Speedup

From an OR-parallel search algorithm one expects an increase of performance with increasing number of processors. For each problem, however, there exists an upper bound for the speedup since there is a lower bound for the parallel run-time $\langle T \rangle_k$ which is the same for all OR-parallel algorithms. This lower bound is equal to the shortest possible sequential run-time t_0 with random search. This case happens if one processor immediately without backtracking or communication finds a solution. Therefore

$$\lim_{k \to \infty} S(k) = \frac{\lim\limits_{k \to \infty} \langle T_1 \rangle}{\lim\limits_{k \to \infty} \langle T_k \rangle} \leq \frac{\int\limits_0^\infty p_1(t) t \, dt}{t_0} \qquad (9)$$

for all OR-parallel architectures. Now we show that for random competition this inequality becomes an equality. From equation (4) we get

$$\lim_{k \to \infty} P_k(t) = \begin{cases} 1 & \text{if } t > t_0 \\ 0 & \text{if } t \leq t_0 \end{cases} \qquad (10)$$

since $P_1(t) > 0$ iff $t > t_0$. Now we use equation (6) to compute $p_k(t)$. Although P_k is not differentiable at $t = t_0$ we can apply the theory of distributions and get $p_k(t) = \delta(t - t_0)$, where δ is the Dirac delta function. With (1) we get $\lim_{k \to \infty} \langle T \rangle_k = t_0$ which is the optimal possible OR-parallel execution time.

The reason for this optimal asymptotic result of competition is that no communication and idle times occur. Although this is a promising result, it is of minor practical interest since the efficiency $S(k)/k$ becomes very small for $k \to \infty$.

4 Particular Distributions

In this Section we compute the speedup for some mathematically treatable probability density functions. This allows us to make propositions about the asymptotic behaviour of the competitive system. With these results we are able to derive upper bounds for the degree of parallelism possible with any OR–parallel system.

4.1 Exponential Distribution

First we consider the exponential distribution $p_1(t) = \lambda \cdot e^{-\lambda t}$. Applying the formalism of Section 3, a simple computation yields linear speedup:

$$\langle T \rangle_k = \frac{1}{k \cdot \lambda} \quad \text{and} \quad \boxed{S(k) = k}$$

4.2 Twofold uniform distribution

In some of our theorem proving examples like that of Figure 3 we observed distributions with two separate clusters. This type of distribution is produced by search in trees consisting of two subtrees with different size and one solution in the smaller subtree.[12] As an approximation of this type of distribution we use the density function

$$p_1(t) = \begin{cases} \frac{1}{2a} & \text{if } l \le t \le l+a \\ 0 & \text{if } l+a < t < L-a \\ \frac{1}{2a} & \text{if } L-a \le t \le L \end{cases}$$

the graph of which is

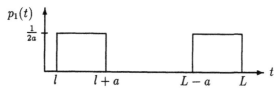

It consists of two separated uniform distributions with same height ($\frac{1}{2a}$) and same width a. The procedure of Section 3 results in (see [Ert90])

$$S(k) = \frac{(r+1)(k+1)2^{k-1}}{(k+1)(r-1)(1-2b) + 2^k(k+1+(r-1)2b)} \tag{11}$$

where $r = \frac{L}{l}$ and $b = \frac{a}{L-l}$.

Two graphs of this speedup expression for different values of the parameters r and b are shown in Figures 4 and 5. The whole spectrum from sublinear and bounded up to highly superlinear speedups is possible with competition, depending on the distribution of the run-times.

In the asymptotic limit ($k \to \infty$) we get the (not surprising) result

$$\lim_{k \to \infty} \langle T \rangle_k = l \quad \text{and} \quad \lim_{k \to \infty} S(k) = \frac{r+1}{2} = \frac{L+l}{2 \cdot l}$$

which could also directly be obtained from equation (9). This is the upper bound for every OR-parallel search procedure.

---

[12]This results from current work on step 2 of the procedure depicted in Figure 1.

If $b = 0$ (i.e. $a = 0$), the distribution consists of only two run-times l and L and $S(k)$ is

$$S(k, b = 0) = \frac{r+1}{2 \cdot [1 + (r-1) \cdot (1/2)^k]}$$

This equation shows that for large r (i.e. $L \gg l$) and small k the speedup grows exponentially as $S(k) \approx 2^{k-1}$. This superlinear behaviour of the speedup is due to the strongly imbalanced structure of search trees which causse the given run-time distribution for large r. Many researchers argue that significantly superlinear speedups like in these figures should not (can not) occur. In case of OR-parallel depth first search, however, parallelization introduces a breadth first component which is not present in the sequential algorithm. In many (not all) of these superlinear cases the use of breadth first search for computing $\langle T_1 \rangle$ would lower the speedup results below the line $S(k) = k$. An other way of eliminating this superlinear speedup behaviour – and thus a way of enhancing the underlying sequential algorithm – is to simulate (e.g. time-slice) the competitive search (or more general: parallel search) on a sequential computer. For such a simulation one should use that value of k for which the parallel efficiency $E(k) := S(k)/k$ is maximal. For our example distribution and $b = 0$, $k = 1000$ (see Fig. 4) the maximum of $E(k)$ lies at $k_{max} \approx 13$ and $E(13) = 34.3$. Thus, the sequential simulation with $k = 13$ is about 34 times faster than with $k = 1$. For $b = 0$, $k = 200$ we have $k_{max} \approx 10$ and $E(10) = 8.4$.

In case of $b = 1/2$ (single uniform distribution) we get

$$S(k) = \frac{(r+1)(k+1)}{2(r+k)} \tag{12}$$

and

$$\lim_{r \to \infty} S(k) = \frac{k+1}{2}$$

Figure 5 allows a comparison of competition with other OR-parallel architectures since $b = 1/2$ represents the uniform distribution which results from balanced search trees with constant branching factor and one solution. For large search problems r becomes very large and $S(k)$ therefore is nearly linear ($S(k) \approx (k+1)/2$) even for large numbers of processors.

Typical search problems which touch the limits of todays computers produce search trees with a size between 10^6 and 10^9 nodes to be explored. If we assume an exponential tree with 10^7 nodes and a constant branching factor of 10, we get $r = 1.11 \cdot 10^7/7 = 1.59 \cdot 10^6$. From equation (12) we obtain a speedup of 4969 with 10000 processors. This result is not optimal, but it is realistic since it is exact and the parallel implementation causes no overhead.

4.3   Application of Results to a Realistic Frequency Distribution

In Figure 6 the exact speedup curve for the experimental distribution of the IP_1 runs (Figure 3) is plotted. This has been obtained by applying the formalism of Section 3 (discrete variant) directly (numerically) to the distribution of Figure 3. As a main result

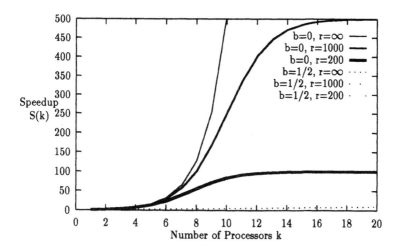

Figure 4: *Speedup figures of the simple distribution with only two different run-times (b = 0). The two graphs r = 200 and r = 1000 show a strongly superlinear behaviour for up to 15 processors and are bounded by the limits of $\frac{r+1}{2}$. The graph r = ∞, which represents the case that the shorter of the two run-times l is zero, grows exponentially with k.*

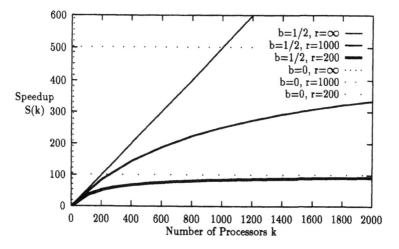

Figure 5: *Speedup figures of the uniform distribution (b = 1/2). If the shortest run-time is zero (r = ∞) the speedup behaves linear (S(k) = (k + 1)/2). Otherwise the graphs are sublinear and again bounded by $\frac{r+1}{2}$.*

one can see that the speedup is linear up to about 120 processors. This gives a good estimate for the size of a hardware architecture which is well suited for problems of this size and class. Performing such computations for a class of problems representative for a particular application domain is therefore very helpful in designing special purpose parallel hardware.

We are now ready to apply equation (11) to the experimental distribution of the IP_1 runs (Figure 3) with $r = 524$ and $b = 0.2$, i.e. to approximate the experimentally derived distribution by the analytically treatable twofold uniform distribution.[13] The resulting speedup curve is shown as the thin line in Figure 6.

Although the approximation of the distribution by a twofold uniform distribution is very rough, the speedup results are quite similar. The higher speedup of the exact curve is caused by the fact that the approximation enlarges the effective width (variance) of the two clusters what decreases the speedup. On the other hand, the asymptotic speedup value of the approximation ($S(\infty) = 262.5$ for $r = 524$, $b = 0.2$) is higher than that of the exact computation ($S(\infty) = 191.7$) since $\langle T_1 \rangle$ of the (symmetric) twofold uniform distribution is larger than that of the original (asymmetric) distribution.

Finally, we want to mention again, that the method described here requires no parallel experiments for computing the parallel performance. For parallelizing an inference system one needs the run-time frequency distribution of the sequential system which can be obtained from a representative set of sample runs. Given such a distribution, the described method computes the exact average speedup of the parallel random competition system for an arbitrary number of processors.

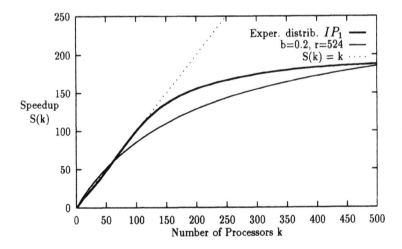

Figure 6: *Speedup figures for the experimental distribution of Figure 3. The exact numerically derived results (Label: Theorem IP_1) are compared with the approximation through a twofold uniform distribution.*

---

[13]From the data plotted in Figure 3 we extract: $l = 8000$, $L = 4192000$, $a = 836000$

5 Conclusion

We introduced random competition, a parallel search procedure which we analyzed with a statistical method. This provides a means for transforming sequential performance measurements into exact speedup values of the competitive parallel system.

The performance figures computed for some example distributions show that random competition is efficient (often superlinear) in case of imbalanced search trees, for which the variance of run-times is high. The general upper bound (which is the same for all OR-parallel systems) for the speedup together with the maximum of $S(k)/k$ provides the user of a search procedure or of an inference system with an estimate of the number of processors required for efficient parallel execution of problems in specific application domains. As part of our future work we are aiming at an extension of this method and its application to other parallel search procedures.

Finally, random competition is easy to implement on most parallel computers as well as on (large) local area networks since there is no communication between the processors.

References

[Ali87]   K. A. M. Ali. Or-parallel execution of PROLOG on a multi-sequential machine. *Int. Journal of Parallel Programming*, 15(3):189–214, 1987.

[Ert90]   W. Ertel. Random Competition: A Simple, but Efficient Method for Parallelizing Inference Systems. Technical Report TUM-I9050 (SFB 342/27/90 A), Technische Universität München, 1990.

[JAM87]   V. K. Janakiram, D. P. Agrawal, and R. Mehrotra. Randomized parallel algorithms for Prolog programs and backtracking applications. In *Int. Conf. on Parallel Processing*, pages 278 – 281, 1987.

[Kor85]   R. E. Korf. Depth-first iterative-deepening: An optimal admissible tree search. *Artificial Intelligence*, 27:97–109, 1985.

[KPB+89] F. Kurfeß, X. Pandolfi, Z. Belmesk, W. Ertel, R. Letz, and J. Schumann. PARTHEO and FP2: Design of a Parallel Inference Machine. In Ph. Treleaven, editor, *Parallel Computers: Object-Oriented, Functional, Logic*, chapter 9, pages 259–297. Wiley & Sons, Chichester, 1989.

[KR90]   Vipin Kumar and V. Nageshwara Rao. Scalable parallel formulations of depth-first search. In P.S. Gopalakrishnan Vipin Kumar and Laveen N. Kanal, editors, *Parallel Algorithmus for Maschine Intelligence and Vision*, pages 1–41. Springer Verlag, New York, 1990.

[LSBB91] R. Letz, J. Schumann, S. Bayerl, and W. Bibel. SETHEO, A High-Performance Theorem Prover. *to appear in Journal of Automated Reasoning*, 1991. available as Technical Report TUM-I9008 from Technical University Munich.

[Pfe88]   F. Pfenning. Single axioms in the implicational propositional calculus. In *9th Int. Conf. on Automated Deduction*, pages 710 – 713, Berlin, 1988. Springer.

[SL90]   J. K. Slaney and E. L. Lusk. Parallelizing the closure computation in automated deduction. In *10th Int. Conf. on Automated Deduction*, pages 28–39, Berlin, Heidelberg, 1990. Springer.

ACE: And/Or-parallel Copying-based Execution of Logic Programs

Gopal Gupta[1]
Dept. of Computer Science, U. of Bristol
Bristol BS8 1TR, U.K.
gupta@compsci.bristol.ac.uk

M. Hermenegildo[2]
Facultad de Informática, U. Madrid (UPM)
28660-Boadilla del Monte, Madrid - Spain
herme@fi.upm.es *or* herme@cs.utexas.edu

Abstract

The stack copying approach, as exemplified by the MUSE system, has been shown to be a quite successful alternative for representing multiple environments during or-parallel execution of logic programs. In this paper we present a novel execution model for parallel implementation of logic programs which is capable of exploiting both independent and-parallelism and or-parallelism in an efficient way and which combines the stack copying approach in the implementation of or-parallelism with proven techniques in the implementation of independent and-parallelism, such as those used in &-Prolog. The and parallelism is expressed via &-Prolog's conditional graph expressions. We show how all solutions to non-deterministic and-parallel goals are found without repetitions. This is done through recomputation as in Prolog (and &-Prolog), i.e., solutions of and-parallel goals are not *shared*. We also propose a scheme for the efficient management of the address space in a way that is compatible with the apparently incompatible requirements of both and- and or-parallelism. The resulting system retains the advantages of both purely or-parallel systems as well as purely and-parallel systems.

Keywords: And/Or-parallelism, Prolog, Stack copying, Conditional Graph Expressions.

1 Introduction

Recently, stack copying has been demonstrated to be a very successful alternative for representing multiple environments in or-parallel execution of logic programs, as exemplified by the MUSE system [2, 1]. In this approach, stack frames are explicitly copied from the stack of one processor to that of another whenever the latter processor needs to share a branch of the or-parallel tree of the former processor. By having an identical logical address space and allocating the stack of each processor in identical locations of this address space, the copying of stack frames can be reduced to copying large contiguous blocks of memory from address space of one processor to

---

[1]This author supported by UK SERC grant GR/F 27420.

[2]This author supported in part by ESPRIT projects "PEPMA"and "PRINCE" and CICYT project 361.208.

that of the other—an operation which most current architectures perform quite efficiently. The chief advantage of the stack copying approach is that program execution in a single processor is exactly the same as in a sequential system. Therefore, it is relatively easy to engineer such a parallel system from an existing sequential system; as is the case, for example, with MUSE which has been built using the sequential SICStus Prolog System.

The arguments that can be made for the stack copying approach regarding ease of implementation can also be made for an independent and-parallel system which *recomputes* non-deterministic and-parallel goals, as has been exemplified by the &-Prolog system [8] whose implementation is also based on the Sequential SICStus Prolog system.

In this paper we show how independent and-parallelism can be added to an or-parallel system which uses the stack copying approach. The resulting and-or parallel system is in the same category as PEPSys [12], ROPM [10] and the AO-WAM System [7]. However, our system is arguably better than the above systems in many respects, the chief ones being ease of implementation, sequential efficiency, and better support for the full Prolog language, in particular being able to incorporate side-effects in a more elegant way [6].

Returning to the issue of recomputation, recall that in the presence of both and- and or-parallelism, it is possible to *share solutions* as argued for example in [7]. That is, given two non-deterministic and-parallel goals a(X), b(Y), then rather than computing b in its entirety for every solution found for a, it would be much better if we computed all solutions for a and b and then combined these solutions through a join. Though this may apply to pure logic programs, it does not apply very well to logic programs which contain side-effects and extra logical features (as is the case with Prolog programs). For example, consider the case where, within b, the value of a variable is read from the standard input and then some action taken which depends on the value read. The solutions for b may be different for every invocation of b (where each invocation corresponds to a different solution of a). Hence solution sharing would yield wrong result in such a case. The simple solution of sequentializing such and-parallel computations results in loss of too much and-parallelism, because if a(X), b(Y) falls in the scope of some other goal which is being executed in and-parallel then that goal has to be sequentialized too, and we have to carry on this sequentialisation process right up to the top level query. If, however, the goals are recomputed then this sequentialisation can be avoided, and parallelism exploited even in the presence of cuts and side-effects. Hence, there is a strong argument for recomputing non-deterministic and-parallel goals, especially, if they are not pure, and even more so if we want to support Prolog as the user language.

In fact, for the above mentioned case of using Prolog as the source language, recent simulations of and-or parallelism [11] show that typical Prolog programs perform very little recomputation, thus providing further evidence that the amount of computation saved by a system which avoids recomputation may be quite small in practice. Presumably this behaviour is due to the fact that Prolog programmers, aware of the selection and computation rules of Prolog, order literals in ways which result in efficient search which minimizes the recomputation of goals. Notice that the use of full or partial recomputation can never produce any slowdown with respect to Prolog since Prolog uses full recomputation.

Having pointed out the advantages of stack copying or-parallel systems such as MUSE and independent and-parallel systems with recomputation such as &-Prolog our aim is then to develop an and-or parallel system which is a combination of the MUSE and &-Prolog systems and which is thus efficient and reasonably easy to implement.

The rest of the paper proceeds as follows: section 2 presents the issues involved in the combination of or- and and-parallelism using a stack copying model and the solutions proposed in our model. Section 3 then illustrates this through an example. Sections 4 and 5 deal with the important issues of address space management and work scheduling. Section 6 presents our conclusions.

Like in &-Prolog, we assume that programs are annotated with conditional graph expressions (basic CGEs[3] and combinations of the "&" operator and special builtins for performing run-time checks with standard Prolog constructs) before execution commences. The &-Prolog parallelization tools will be used to automatically generate such annotations from standard Prolog code. Alternatively, annotated programs can be given by the user.

2 The Stack Copying Approach to And-Or Parallelism

In our approach, the multiple environments that are needed to implement or-parallelism are supported through explicit copying, as in MUSE. To briefly summarize the MUSE approach, whenever a processor P1 wants to share work with another processor P2 it selects an untried alternative from one of the choice points in P2's stack. It then copies the entire stack of P2, backtracks up to that choice point to undo all the conditional bindings made below that choice point, and then continues with the execution of the untried alternative. In this approach, provided there is a mechanism for copying stacks, the only cells that need to be shared during execution are those corresponding to the choice points. Execution is otherwise completely independent (modulo side-effect synchronization) in each branch and identical to sequential execution.

If we consider the presence of and parallelism in addition to or-parallelism, then, depending on the actual types of parallelism appearing in the program and the nesting relation between them, a number of relevant cases can be distinguished. The simplest two cases are of course those where the execution is purely or-parallel or purely and-parallel. Trivially, in these situations standard MUSE and &-Prolog execution respectively applies, modulo the memory management issues, which will be dealt with in section 4.

Of the cases when both and- and or-parallelism are present in the execution, the simpler one represents executions where and-parallelism appears "under" or-parallelism (i.e. within or-parallel branches) but not conversely. In this case, and again modulo memory management issues, execution can still continue as &-Prolog (or in any other local way[4]). The only or-

---

[3]Although in &-Prolog more complex execution graphs can be built than those possible with CGEs, those graphs can be handled in a similar way to that given in the description that follows, which will thus for simplicity and without loss of generality be limited to CGEs.

[4]One can also conceive implementing Andorra-I [3] using stack copying in a simple way: since in Andorra-I and-parallel goals are always deterministic the combined parallelism is never "or-under-and" and therefore only the simpler case applies.

parallel branches which can be picked up appear then above any and-parallel node in the tree. The process of picking up such branches would be identical to that described above for MUSE.

In the presence of or-parallelism under and-parallelism the situation becomes slightly more complicated. Of course, exploitation of or-parallelism under and-parallelism can simply be disallowed in the system and the choice points created inside the and-parallel goals dealt with through backtracking in the usual way. However, simulation results [11] suggest that a significant amount of or-parallelism might be lost in that case, so we do support or-parallelism under and-parallelism in our model. In that case, an important issue is carefully deciding which portions of the stacks to copy. Our guiding principle will be to copy all branches that would be copied in an equivalent MUSE execution. And, as far as and-parallel execution is concerned we want to be as close to &-Prolog as possible, implementing the PWAM "point backtracking" strategy [9] used in &-Prolog. As we will see, this strategy results in copying the parts that &-Prolog reuses during backtracking and recomputing those that &-Prolog (and also Muse and Prolog) recompute.

Consider the case when a processor selects an untried alternative from a choice point created during execution of a goal g_j in the body of a goal which occurs after a CGE $(true => g_1 \& \ldots \& g_n), \ldots, g_j$. This is the case where there has been and-parallelism above the the selected alternative, but all the forks are finished. Then not only will it have to copy all the stack segments in the branch from the root to the CGE, but also also the portions of stacks corresponding to all the forks inside the CGE and those of the goals between the end of the CGE and g_j. All these segments have in principle to be copied because the untried alternative may have access to variables in all of them and modify such variables.

Also, a processor may select an untried alternative from a choice point created during execution of a goal g_i inside a CGE (see example above). Then it will have to copy all the stack segments in the branch from the root to the CGE, and it will also have to copy the stack segments corresponding to the goals $g_1 \ldots g_{i-1}$ (i.e. goals to the left). The stack segments up to the CGE need to be copied because each different alternative within g_i might produce a different binding for a variable, X, defined in an ancestor goal of the CGE. The stack segments corresponding to goals g_1 through g_{i-1} have to be copied because the different alternatives for the goals following the CGE might bind a variable defined in one of the goals $g_1 \ldots g_{i-1}$ differently.

3   An Example

We now illustrate by means of an example how or-parallelism can be exploited in non deterministic and-parallel goals through stack copying. Consider first the tree, shown in Figure 1.(i), that is generated as a result of executing a query a which during its execution calls a clause containing a CGE (true => b(X) & c(Y)). For the purpose of illustration we assume that there is an unbounded number of processors, P1 ... Pn. In Figure 1.(i) processor P1 has started execution of goal a, left an an untried alternative ("embryonic branch") a2, and then entered the CGE. In this case and-parallel execution can remain identical to that of &-Prolog, where a processor P2 can simply pick up the execution of goal c. At the same time, processor P3 can pick up the

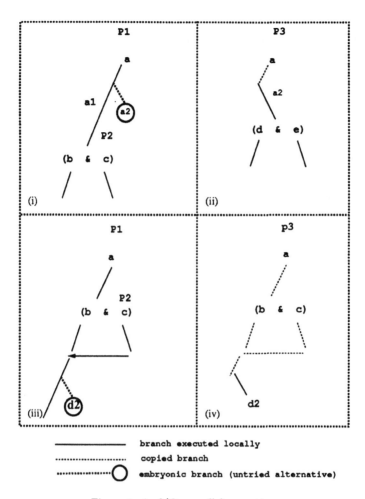

Figure 1: And/Or parallel execution

a2 branch left behind by P1. In order to do this P3 will copy the portion of the tree from the root to the embryonic node. Since there is no and-parallel work in this portion copying is as in MUSE. Execution then continues with the untried alternative (Figure 1.(ii)).

A different case is depicted in figure 1.(iii) processors P1 and P2 have finished execution of the CGE (leaving no alternatives behind) and then processor P1 has taken the continuation d and left an untried alternative d2. This alternative can be picked up by another processor (P3 in this case). In order to do this P3 has to copy the portion of the tree from the root to the CGE, the portions inside the CGE, and the portion of the continuation up to the embryonic node. Execution can continue then with the d2 alternative.

We now tackle the general case. Consider the tree, shown in Figure 2, that is generated as a result of executing a query q containing a CGE (true => a(X) & b(Y)). We have only shown the path from root of the tree to the CGE, there may be other or-parallel branches along this

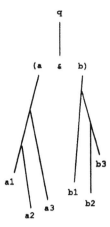

Figure 2: Execution tree with alternatives inside the CGE

path but we have omitted them for sake of simplicity since those nodes would corresponding to the cases presented before.

Execution begins with processor P1 executing the top level query q. When it encounters the CGE, it picks the subgoal a for execution, leaving b for some other processor. Let's assume that Processor P2 picks up goal b for execution (Figure 3.(i)). As execution continues P1 finds solution a1 for a, generating 2 choice points along the way. Likewise, P2 finds solution b1 for b.

Since we also allow for full or-parallelism within and-parallel goals, a processor can steal the untried alternative in the choice point created during execution of a by P1. Let us assume that processor P3 steals this alternative, and sets itself up for executing it. To do so it copies the stack of processor P1 up to the choice point (the copied part of the stack is shown by the dotted line; see index at the bottom of Figure 1), simulates failure to remove conditional bindings made below the choice point, and restarts the goals to its right (i.e. the goal b). Processor P4 picks up the restarted goal b and finds a solution b1 for it. In the meantime, P3 finds the solution a2 for a (see Figure 3.(ii)). Note that before P3 can commence with the execution of the untried alternative and P4 can execute the restarted goal b, they have to make sure that any conditional bindings made by P2 while executing b have also been removed. This is done by P3 (or P4) getting a copy of the trail stack of P2 and resetting all the variables that appear in it.

Like processor P3, processor P5 steals the untried alternative from the second choice point for a, copies the stack from P1 and restarts b, which is picked up by processor P6. As in MUSE, the actual choice point frame is shared to prevent the untried alternative in the second choice point from being executed twice (once through P1 and once through P3). Eventually, P5 finds the solution a3 for a and P6 finds the solution b1 for b.

Note that now 3 copies of b are being executed, one for each solution of a. The process of finding the solution b1 for b leaves a choice point behind. The untried alternative in this choice point can be picked up for execution by another processor. This is indeed what is done by processors P7, P8 and P9 for each copy of b that is executing. These processors copy the stack

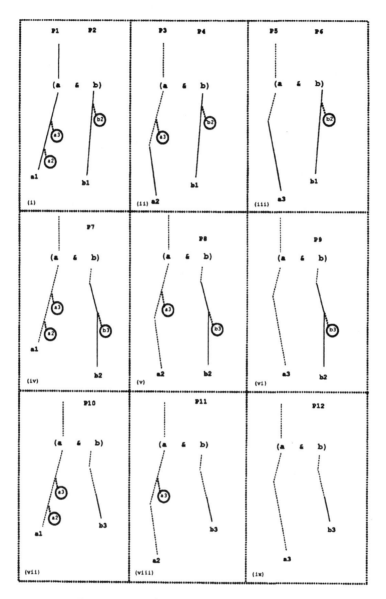

Figure 3: And/Or parallel execution (Cntd.)

of P2, P4 and P6, respectively, up to the choice point. The stack segments corresponding to goal a are also copied (Figures 3.(iv), 3.(v), 3.(vi)) from processors P1, P3 and P5, respectively. The processors P7, P8 and P9 then proceed to find the solution b2 for b.

Execution of the alternative corresponding to the solution b2 in the three copies of b produces another choice-point. The untried alternatives from these choice points are picked up by processors P10, P11 and P12, respectively. P10, P11, and P12 copy the stack segments for b up to the stolen choice point, as well as the stack segments corresponding to the solution for a, from P7, P8 and P9, respectively (Figures 3.(vii), 3.(viii), 3.(ix)). Note that if there were no processors available to steal the alternative (corresponding to solution b3) from b then this solution would have been found by processors P7, P8 and P9 (in the respective copies of b that they are executing) through backtracking as in &-Prolog. The same would apply if no processors were available to steal the alternative from b corresponding to solution b2.

In the above example, all other operations that are performed during and-parallel execution remain the same as in &-Prolog. Thus, execution of the continuation of CGE can begin only after at least one solution has been found for all goals in the CGE. Also, backtracking in CGE takes place just as in &-Prolog, i.e. goals to the right should be completely explored before a processor can backtrack inside a goal to the left. This leads to some constraints on scheduling processors and work, which might be considered a disadvantage compared to schemes such those as described in [7] which share environments rather than copy them, but the big advantage is that such a system has arguably lower sequential overhead, is easier to implement, and can be easily built out of existing systems. From the above example it may appear that intelligent backtracking is absent in our and-or parallel model. This is because if b were to completely fail, then this failure would take place in each of the three copies of b. We can incorporate intelligent backtracking by stipulating that an untried alternative can be stolen from a choice point, which falls in the scope of a CGE, only after at least one solution has been found for each goal in that CGE. Thus alternatives a2 and a3 in subtree of goal a, and b2 and b3 in subtree of goal b, would be allowed to be picked up by other processors only after P1 and P2 succeed in finding at least one solution for a and b respectively.

4 Managing the Address Space

One of the main features of the MUSE System, which greatly facilitates stack copying is that each processor has an identical logical memory address space. This enables one processor to copy the stack of another without relocating any pointers. In the presence of and-parallelism this may be hard to ensure. This is because each goal in a CGE may be executed in and-parallel by a different processor. Thus, as far as and-parallel execution is concerned all the participating processors should share a common address space. However, for or-parallel execution each processor should have an identical but independent logical address space so that stack segments can be copied without any pointer relocation. Thus, the requirements for or- and and-parallelism seem to be antithetical to each other. However, the problem can be simply resolved by dividing all the available processors into *teams*. All processors in a team share the same logical address space. If there are n processors in the team the address space is divided up into m memory segments ($m \geq n$). The memory segments are numbered from 1 to m. Each processor allocates its heap, local stacks, trail etc. in one of the segments. (This also implies that the maximum no. of processors that a team can have is m.) Each team has its own independent logical address space, identical to the address space of all other teams. Each team also has identical number of segments. And-parallel work can only be shared between processors of the same team. Or-

154

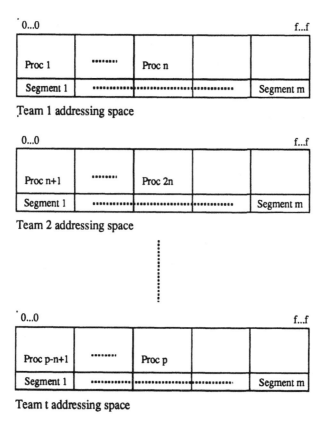

Figure 4: Address Space Management

parallel work can only be shared between teams. Processors are allowed to switch teams so long as there is a memory segment available for them to allocate their stacks in the address space of that team.

Consider the scenario where a choice point, which is not in the scope of any CGE, is picked by a team Tq from the execution tree of another team Tp. Let x be the memory segment number in which this choice point lies. The root of the Prolog execution tree must also lie in memory segment x since the stacks of a processor cannot extend into another memory segment in the address space. Tq will copy the stack from the xth memory segment of Tp into its own xth memory segment. Since the logical address space of each team is identical and is divided into identical segments, no pointer relocation would be needed. Failure is then simulated and the execution of the untried alternative of the stolen choice point begun. In fact, the copying of stacks can be done incrementally as in MUSE [2] (other optimizations in MUSE to save copying should apply equally well to our model).

Now consider the more interesting scenario where a choice point, which lies within the scope of a CGE, is picked up by a processor in a team Tq from another team Tp. Let this CGE be $(true \Rightarrow g_1 \& \ldots \& g_n)$ and let g_i be the goal in the CGE whose sub-tree contains the stolen choice point. Tq needs to copy the stack segments corresponding to the computation from the root up to the CGE and the stack segments corresponding to the goals g_1 through g_i. Let us assume these stack segments lie in memory segments of team Tp and are numbered $x_1, \ldots, x_k$. They will be copied into the memory segments numbered $x_1, \ldots, x_k$ of team Tq. Again, this copying can be incremental. Failure would then be simulated on g_i. We also need to remove the conditional bindings made during the execution of the goal $g_{i+1} \ldots g_n$ by team Tp. Let $x_{k+1} \ldots x_l$ be the memory segments where $g_{i+1} \ldots g_n$ are executing in team Tp. We copy the trail stacks of these segments and reinitialize (i.e. mark unbound) all variables that appear in them. The copied trail stacks can then be discarded. Once removal of conditional bindings is done the execution of the untried alternative of the stolen choice point is begun. The execution of the goals $g_{i+1} \ldots g_n$ is restarted and these can be executed by other processors which are members of the team. Note that the copied stack segments occupy the same memory segments as the original stack segments. The restarted goals can however be executed in any of the memory segments. Note that since the team Tq may have more than one processor, it is possible to (incrementally) copy the stack segments corresponding to g_1 through g_i in parallel.

Returning back to the earlier example (fig. 3), for execution to proceed as shown there, each pair of processors P1 and P2, P3 and P4, and P5 and P6 would have to be in the same team. Each of processors P7 through P12 will also have to be in a different team of its own. Assuming that P1 starts the execution of query q in memory segment numbered 1, and P2 starts the execution of b in memory segment numbered 2 (in the address space of the team to which P1 and P2 belong), then P3 and P5 would be forced to copy the stack segment corresponding to a in memory segment number 1 of their respective address space. P4 and P6 are, however, free to execute b in any memory segment (which will be a segment other than memory segment 1, because there is one processor to a memory segment and vice versa). Suppose P4 has its stacks located in segment 4 and P6 in memory segment 3, respectively, of its address space; therefore, they will execute b in memory segments number 4 and 3 respectively. When P7, P8 and P9 steal the alternative corresponding to solution b2 then each of them will copy stack segments corresponding to a in memory segment 1 of their respective address spaces, and the stack segment corresponding to b in memory segments 2, 4 and 3 of their respective address spaces. The same holds for processors P10, P11 and P12 when they steal the alternative corresponding to b3.

One might think that a potential problem during stack copying might be that, for example, when P7 wants to copy stack segments of a in memory segment 1 of its address space, then it may find that memory segment 1 is already being used by some other processor in its team to allocate its stack. This is not possible due to the following reason: Given that the process of picking a choice point, in the stack-copying approach, involves first obtaining the same computation state as the processor (or team, in our case) from which the or-parallel work is being stolen, there is never going to be the problem of finding a specific memory segment (which is needed for copying) being occupied, since in the worst case we can assume that all memory segments of the stealing team are empty.

Note that our model is a direct combination of the MUSE system and the &-Prolog system. Within each team, the computation is exactly as in &-Prolog. Among the teams the computation is exactly like MUSE. Thus, it is easy to see that in the presence of only and-parallelism our system would be as efficient as &-Prolog, while in the presence of only or-parallelism it will be as efficient as the MUSE system. Also notice that the amount of stack copying that will be done, in the presence of both and- and or- parallelism, would be identical to that done in the MUSE system provided, of course, that the scheduling strategy is the same. However, the set up time for executing the untried alternative choice points that falls within the scope of a CGE is arguably more than in MUSE, because of the need to copy more than one stack when a choice point from a CGE is stolen, but we hope that the difference would not be very significant.

It is also possible to implement our system on a hybrid multiprocessor—i.e. multiple shared-memory systems connected by a message passing network or a broadcast network. In this hybrid multiprocessor system each shared-memory multiprocessor constitutes a team with its own memory address space, and the various teams are connected by a message-passing or a broadcast network. And-parallelism is exploited within the shared-memory system while or-parallelism is exploited over the distributed network of these shared memory systems. This sort of approach can also be taken for implementing an and-or parallel system on NUMA (Non Uniform Memory Access) Machines such as the BBN Butterfly.

5 Scheduling

And-parallel work is shared within a team, thus a processor can steal and-parallel work only from members of its own team. Or-parallel work is shared at the level of teams, thus only an idle team can steal an untried alternative from a choice point. An idle processor first looks for and-parallel work in its own team. If no and-parallel work is found, it can decide to migrate to another team where there is work, provided it is not the last remaining processor in that team, and there is a free memory segment in the memory space of the team it joins. If no such team exists it can start a new team of its own, perhaps with idle processors of other teams, provided there is a free address space available for the new team. The new team can now steal or-parallel work from other teams.

Note that the need to schedule work arises at two independent levels: (i)and-parallel work at the level of processors within a team and, (ii) or-parallel work at the level of teams. This suggests that separate schedulers can be used for managing the and-parallel and or-parallel work respectively. Thus, and-parallel work can be managed exactly as in &-prolog: idle processor pick untried goals from *goal-stacks* of other processors; and, or-parallel work can be managed exactly as in Muse: idle teams request work from other teams. Schedulers developed for &-Prolog and for Muse can be used for this purpose. However, one has to be careful in balancing the number of teams and the number of processors in each team, to fully exploit all the and- and or-parallelism available in a given Prolog program. We plan to use some of the 'flexible scheduling' techniques that have been developed for the Andorra-I system [4] for this purpose.

6 Conclusions

In this paper, we presented a scheme capable of exploiting both independent and-parallelism and or-parallelism in an efficient way and which extends &-Prolog with or-parallelism by using the stack copying approach of MUSE. In order to find all solutions to a conjunction of non-deterministic and-parallel goals in our approach some goals are explicitly recomputed as in Prolog and unlike in other and-or parallel systems. This allows our scheme to incorporate side-effects and to support Prolog as the user language more easily. In addition the resulting system has a good potential for low sequential overhead, can be easily implemented by extending existing systems, and retains the advantages of both purely or-parallel systems as well as purely and-parallel systems.

7 Acknowledgements

The research presented in this paper has benefited from discussions with Kish Shen, Vitor Santos-Costa, Khayri Ali, Roland Carlsson, and David H.D. Warren, all of whom we would like to thank. Thanks also to Inês Dutra for her comments on a draft of this paper.

References

[1] K.A.M. Ali. Or-parallel Execution of Prolog on the BC-Machine. In *Fifth International Conference and Symposium on Logic Programming*, pages 253–268, MIT Press, 1988.

[2] K.A.M. Ali and R. Karlsson. The muse or-parallel prolog model and its performance. In *1990 North American Conference on Logic Programming*, MIT Press, October 1990.

[3] V. Santos Costa, D.H.D. Warren, and R. Yang. Andorra-I: A Parallel Prolog System that Transparently Exploits both And- and Or-parallelism. In *Proceedings of the 3rd. ACM SIGPLAN Symposium on Principles and Practice of Parallel Programming*, ACM, April 1990.

[4] Inês Dutra. A Flexible Scheduler for the Andorra-I System. In *ICLP'91 Pre-Conference Workshop on Parallel Execution of Logic Programs*, Computer Science Department, University of Bristol, June 1991.

[5] G. Gupta. Paged Binding Array: Environment Representation for And-Or Parallel Prolog. 1991. Submitted to FGCS'92.

[6] G. Gupta and V. Santos Costa. Cut and Side-Effects in And-Or Parallel Prolog. 1991. Submitted to FGCS'92.

[7] G. Gupta and B. Jayaraman. Compiled And-Or Parallelism on Shared Memory Multiprocessors. In *1989 North American Conference on Logic Programming*, pages 332–349, MIT Press, October 1989.

[8] M. Hermenegildo and K. Greene. &-Prolog and its Performance: Exploiting Independent And-Parallelism. In *1990 International Conference on Logic Programming*, pages 253–268, MIT Press, June 1990.

[9] M. V. Hermenegildo. *An Abstract Machine Based Execution Model for Computer Architecture Design and Efficient Implementation of Logic Programs in Parallel.* PhD thesis, Dept. of Electrical and Computer Engineering (Dept. of Computer Science TR-86-20), University of Texas at Austin, Austin, Texas 78712, August 1986.

[10] B. Ramkumar and L. V. Kale. Compiled Execution of the Reduce-OR Process Model on Multiprocessors. In *1989 North American Conference on Logic Programming*, pages 313–331, MIT Press, October 1989.

[11] K. Shen and M. Hermenegildo. *A Simulation Study of Or- and Independent And-parallelism.* Technical Report FIM-60.1/AI/90, Facultad de Informatica, U. P. Madrid, 28660 Boadilla del Monte, Madrid, Spain, October 1990.

[12] H. Westphal and P. Robert. The PEPSys Model: Combining Backtracking, AND- and OR- Parallelism. In *International Symposium on Logic Programming*, pages 436–448, San Francisco, IEEE Computer Society, August 1987.

Blackboard Communication in Prolog

Koenraad O.M. De Bosschere*

Electronics Laboratory
State University of Ghent, Belgium
kdb@lem.rug.ac.be

Abstract

This paper describes a formal model for parallel programming languages, based on macroscopical coarse grained parallelism and shared blackboard communication. Examples of such languages are Multi-Prolog [3, 4], and Shared Prolog [1]. Both languages support a blackboard which acts as a common communication medium between processes. The blackboard communication is explicit, by means of dedicated communication primitives. The parallelism exploited is not based on the properties of the logic (and-, or-parallelism), but on the visible parallelism in the application. A program consists of a number of communicating sequential (Prolog) processes [2].

1 Introduction

A formal model is created in two steps. In a first step, the semantics of Horn Clause logic is generalized to the semantics of *Communicating Horn Clause logic*, i.e., Horn clauses extended with two communication primitives, one to send information to and one to receive information from a blackboard.

The declarative semantics is a generalization of the model-theoretic semantics of Horn clauses. An associated operational semantics is defined and proved to be sound and complete. This shows that the theory of Communicating Horn Clauses, although it is not side-effect free (blackboard communication is clearly a side-effect), is not in conflict with the logic programming paradigm.

In a second step, a number of Communicating Horn Clause processes are put around the *blackboard* and can start cooperating to solve a goal. In this model, we look at processes as sets of traces, because the complete blackboard input/output behavior of a process can be described by means of the set of traces it can generate. A trace now becomes a blackboard transforming function.

Declaratively, a goal is true iff a trace t_1 associated with the goal, and a trace t_2 generated by the other processes, can be combined in such a way that one of the resulting traces can be executed successfully on the current blackboard. This is an example of a *may-semantics* [6]. This means that there must be 'a way to do it', but not every way must be successful, although it might.

---

*Research Assistant with the Belgian National Fund for Scientific Research.

An operational semantics that covers the declarative semantics is also defined. However, at this point, due to the may-semantics, two selection functions must be introduced: one to decide the order in which processes are going to communicate (process selection function to solve the inter-process non-determinism), and one to decide which process trace is going to be used next (trace selection function to solve the intra-process non-determinism).

2 Related work

This work is related to both Distributed Logic [9] and Linda [5]. At first sight, it seems to be a weakened version of Distributed Logic. However, a closer look reveals quite the contrary. In Distributed Logic, the creation and termination of processes have a *logical* meaning. The concurrent execution of a conjunction of two goals is true iff both goals can be proved true. In contrast, the creation and termination of processes in communicating Horn Clauses do *not* have a logical meaning. They are extra-logical.

Moreover, the communication is open, rather than channel-based. That means that a message is broadcast to the blackboard, where precisely one process can pick it up and produce an answer. Messages may even stay there for a while before they are picked up. So, the communication in Communicating Horn Clauses is asynchronous, in contrast to Distributed Logic where it is synchronous.

The resemblance with Linda is, to say the least, quite strong. The blackboard is an implementation of Linda's tuple space. The communicated ground terms correspond to Linda's tuples. The use of terms is appropriate for a logic programming language, because terms are a natural way to represent information, and unification is a built-in mechanism to do the pattern matching on the tuples.

Communicating Horn Clauses could also be seen as a model for the language Shared Prolog [1]. An application in this language also consists of a number of sequential processes (called 'theories') which cooperate to execute a task by means of activation patterns. However, the communication in Shared Prolog is more structured (preactivation and postactivation parts). Our model makes fewer assumptions on the program structure, and is therefore more general.

3 Syntax and Informal Semantics

The syntax of Communicating Horn Clause logic is very similar to the syntax of traditional Horn Clause logic. The alphabet consists of connectives, punctuation symbols, functors, predicate symbols, variables, and communication modes.

So as to express parallelism and communication, the language must have at least two additional operators: one to create processes, and one to communicate between processes. At this point, we consider the creation of processes as a side effect without a direct logical meaning; for the time being, it is considered extra-logical. We introduce two communication primitives: one to send information to the the shared blackboard, and one to receive information from it.

The introduction of communication operators introduces sequentiality in the underlying logic model. That is, the truth value of a predicate is not necessarily a timeless function. It may depend on the current state of the blackboard, which might have been affected by earlier communication operations.

The dependence on a blackboard state implies that the declarative and refutation semantics of Communicating Horn Clauses must anew be proved equivalent [7].

There are two communication modes: ! to write to, and ? to read from the blackboard. Communication (blackboard) goals are built from the communication modes and terms. The expressions !john and ?mary are examples of communication goals. The goal !john will write the term john to the blackboard, while ?mary will search for a term mary in the blackboard, and remove it as soon as such a term is found. Operationally, the requesting process will block until an answer is produced. A communication goal will generate communication events, or simply *events*.

At this point, it is necessary to introduce some notation and auxiliary concepts.

Definition 3.1 A *formula* is an atom, a blackboard goal, or a conjunction of formulas.

Definition 3.2 A *blackboard communication goal* is of the form $?\tau_1$, or $!\tau_2$, where τ_1 and τ_2 are ground terms.

At run time, the $!\tau$ goal can only put ground terms onto the blackboard. This is a consequence of the fact that processes of Communicating Horn Clauses are considered as independent agents. The communication of non-ground terms would be in conflict with this principle because a non-ground term actually creates a direct connection between two processes. Hence, streams as they exist in other parallel logic programming languages do not exist in Multi-Prolog.

Definition 3.3 The *basic clauses* of Communicating Horn Clauses are:

$$f \leftarrow$$
$$f \leftarrow g_1 \; , \; g_2$$
$$f \leftarrow e$$

where e is a blackboard communication goal ($!\tau$ or $?\tau$), f an atom, g_1 and g_2 are formulas.

To ease our task in proving theorems, we use the following lemma.

Lemma 3.4 (structural induction) *Every set of clauses can be rewritten to a form using only basic clauses while preserving unsatisfiability.*

4 Traces generated by a Horn Clause process

The semantics of Horn Clause logic only depends on the set of clauses, not on the selection rule used during resolution. However, the introduction of communication events in Horn Clause logic creates the notion of time, which affects the semantics. In our model, time is formalized by means of a *trace of communication events*. Since a trace is an ordered collection, it imposes an ordering on the clauses generating it, and also on the selection function used to implement resolution. The selection function we shall assume in the sequel is left to right. The most important consequence of this restriction is that Communicating Horn Clause logic is semantically not equivalent with traditional Horn clause logic. It resembles more the semantics of Prolog.

Although the loss of commutativity, which is one of its consequences, may seem a severe restriction, this is not the case. It only shows that the model is more closely related to Prolog, which evaluates left to right, and in which the conjunction does not commute either. Our model can be used to study the behavior of Prolog more carefully than is possible with Horn Clause logic.

The external behavior of a set of Communicating Horn Clauses can be characterized by the set of traces it can generate. For example, the trace of a process that first writes the term a onto the blackboard, and afterwards reads b from the blackboard is <!a,?b>. This trace completely describes the external behavior of the process. We shall now formalize this notion.

Definition 4.1 The set of *communication events* H_E on a set H_U is given by $H_E = \{!,?\} \times H_U$

Definition 4.2 A *trace* t is a finite sequence of communication events. The set of all traces $(H_E)^*$ is denoted by H_T [2, 10].

For example, for the Herbrand universe $H_U = \{a,b,c\}$, the set of Herbrand events H_E is given by $\{!a,?a,!b,?b,!c,?c\}$. An example of a trace on H_E is given by <!a,?b,!b>. The order of events in a trace is significant, and must not be changed.

In the sections that follow, we study the behavior of one single sequential communicating process. Such a process interacts with a trace by means of its communication goals. We first discuss the modified concepts of interpretation and model. Afterwards we discuss the formal semantics.

5 Interpretations and Models for Communicating Horn Clauses

In traditional Horn Clause logic, an interpretation for a set of clauses can be described as a subset of the Herbrand base containing the ground atoms that are taken to be true [8]. Unfortunately, in Communicating Horn Clauses, such a subset of the Herbrand base is no longer sufficient to make a communication goal true. The truth value of a goal depends on the state of the blackboard, that is, the cumulative effect of all previous communication operations. Therefore, an interpretation must also depend on that blackboard. We shall use traces for this purpose. Atoms are now considered true in the presence of some trace, and false in the presence of others. A Herbrand interpretation I is therefore a subset of $H_T \times H_B$.

A Herbrand interpretation I can be structured *atom-wise*. For every element a of I, let I[a] be the set of traces that make a true, i.e., $I[a] = \{t \in H_T: (t,a) \in I\}$.

Definition 5.1 Let a be a ground atom, and let t a trace. Then, the expression $t \models_I a$ means that, under the interpretation I and in the presence of trace t, the formula a is true, i.e., $(t,a) \in I$.

In the sequel we shall always use the notation $t \models_I f$ because of its convenience. The set-interpretation will only be used in proofs.

Notice that, to make a true, the trace t must be completely consumed. If the atom a is true by using a strict prefix of t, $t \models_I a$ is not true. The expression $<> \models_I a$ means that the truth of the atom a only depends on the program, not on the trace. It is trivially the case that $\diamond \models_I \text{true}$.

It is useful to extend the definition of $\models$ to non-atomic expressions in the following way:

1. by $(t \models_I g, h)$ we mean $(t_1 \models_I g \wedge t_2 \models_I h \wedge t = t_1 + t_2)$, for g and h ground formulas;

2. by $(t \models_I a \leftarrow f)$ we mean $(t \models_I f) \rightarrow (t \models_I a)$, for a and f ground formulas;

3. by $(t \models_I \leftarrow f)$ we mean $\neg (t \models_I f)$, for f a ground formula;

4. by $(t \models_I e)$ with e a ground communication event, we mean that t unifies with $\langle e \rangle$.

In case the formulas are not ground, the above expressions must hold for all ground instances of the formulas.

So far, we have only considered isolated traces. However, a process is modeled by a *set* of traces. This set of traces describes all possible blackboard communication operations a process can ever perform. It is useful to extend the definition of $\models$ to a set of traces T: $(T \models_I f)$ iff $\exists t \in T: (t \models_I f)$.

Let us now turn to the concept of a *model* of a set of clauses S. We say that an interpretation I is a model iff every clause of S is **true** under I. To make clear distinction between a classical model (subset of the Herbrand base), and our model, based on traces and the Herbrand base, we shall call our model a *generalized model*.

6 Declarative Semantics

The *declarative semantics* of a set of clauses S is the least generalized Herbrand model of S.

In this section, we use a fixpoint argument to characterize the least general model of a set of clauses S. As stated above, an interpretation for a set of clauses S is a subset of $H_T \times H_B$. Let $\mathcal{I}$ be the set of all interpretations for S. With S we associate an operator $\mathcal{S}: \mathcal{I} \mapsto \mathcal{I}$ (the least consequences operator). Given an interpretation I, the set $\mathcal{S}(I)$ is constructed as follows:

1. let $a \leftarrow$ be a ground instance of a fact $a' \leftarrow$ of S. Then, it follows that $(\langle \rangle, a) \in \mathcal{S}(I)$;

2. let $a \leftarrow g_1, g_2$ be a ground instance of a clause $a' \leftarrow g_1', g_2'$ of S. If $t_1 \models_I g_1$ and $t_2 \models_I g_2$, then $(t_1 + t_2, a) \in \mathcal{S}(I)$;

3. if $t \models_I e$ (that is, $t = \langle e \rangle$), and S contains a clause $a' \leftarrow e'$ of which $a \leftarrow e$ is a ground instance, then $(t, a) \in \mathcal{S}(I)$.

The above conditions imply that $I \subseteq \mathcal{S}(I)$; obviously, $\mathcal{S}(I)$ is also an interpretation. More importantly, the construction of $\mathcal{S}(I)$ suggests a way to construct a generalized model for S, as indicated by the following theorem.

Theorem 6.1 *An interpretation I is a generalized model for a set of clauses S iff I is a fixpoint of $\mathcal{S}$.*

Example 6.2 The program S

```
p(a)←
q←p(X),!X
r←?X, X=a
X=X←
```

is rewritten as a set of basic clauses S'

```
p(a)←
q←p(X), x'(X)
r←x"(X), X=a
X=X←
x'(Y)←!Y
x"(Z)←?Z
```

We choose the empty set $\emptyset$ as initial interpretation.

$$I_0 = \emptyset$$
$$I_1 = \{(<>,p(a)), (<!a>,x'(a)), (<?a>,x"(a)), (<>,a=a)\}$$
$$I_2 = \{(<>,p(a)), (<!a>,x'(a)), (<?a>,x"(a)), (<>,a=a),$$
$$(<!a>,q), (<?a>,r)\}$$
$$I_3 = I_2 = M$$
$$\ldots$$

The restriction to the Herbrand base of the initial set of clauses gives

$$M = \{(<>,p(a)), (<!a>,q), (<?a>,r), (<>,a=a)\}$$

7 Refutation Semantics

The refutation semantics is a formal model for the operation of a derivation procedure. The set $S \cup \{←f\}$ is unsatisfiable iff $←f$ is false in all generalized models of S, and therefore in the minimal generalized model. The fact that $←f$ is false in the minimal generalized model of S is equivalent to the fact that there is at least one instance $←f_0$ of $←f$ which is false in the minimal generalized model of S. That means that there is at least one f_0 which derives true for the set S. The derivation procedure is purely syntactical.

We start with a formalization of the derivation procedure, which is modeled as a rewriting system. Let S be a set of basic clauses and b be an atom. The rewriting rules for the basic clauses listed below must be understood as follows: assume that the atom b is unified with the head of the clause f, using the unifier θ. Then, the atom b is replaced by the right hand side of the clause (or simply omitted), and the substitution θ is applied to the remaining formula. For the blackboard goals, an event will be consumed as well. In summary, we have:

clause	rewriting rule
$f←$	$b,g:<>,\theta \rightarrow_s g\theta$
$f←g_1,g_2$	$b,g:<>,\theta \rightarrow_s (g_1,g_2,g)\theta$
$f←e'$	$b,g:<e>,\theta \rightarrow_s g\theta$

For the clause $f \leftarrow e'$, the substitution θ consists of two parts: θ_1, resulting from the unification of b with f, and θ_2, resulting from the unification of e' with e. A goal consisting of one atom b can be rewritten by replacing the goal by b,true.

Definition 7.1 We say that in the set of clauses S, g derives h directly with trace t and substitution θ, denoted as, $g:t,\theta \rightarrow_s h$, if, by using the trace t, the substitution θ, and one of the rewriting rules mentioned above, g can be rewritten into the formula h.

Definition 7.2 We say that, in a set of clauses S, the formula g *derives* h with trace t and substitution θ, $g:t,\theta \Rightarrow_s h$, if there exists a finite sequence of *direct derivations*

$$g=g_0:t_1,\theta_1 \rightarrow_s g_1:t_2,\theta_2 \rightarrow_s \ldots \rightarrow_s g_{n-1}:t_n,\theta_n \rightarrow_s g_n = h$$

such that $t = t_1 + \ldots + t_n$ and $\theta = \theta_1 \ldots \theta_n$. If g is equal to true, the derivation is said to be successful. The rule that a number of direct derivations can be combined into one derivation is known as the *transitivity rule*. The concept of direct derivation allows us to give a precise definition of refutation semantics of a formula f.

Definition 7.3 The *refutation semantics* of a set of clauses S is the set of all ground pairs (t,a) of traces and atoms for which there exists a successful derivation $a:t,\{\} \Rightarrow_s \text{true}$.

Example 7.4 For the program consisting of the basic clauses S' of example 7.2 it is straightforward to produce a successful derivation for q

$$q = q,\text{true}:<>,\{\} \quad \rightarrow_{s'} \quad p(X),x'(X),\text{true}:<>,\{X/a\}$$
$$\rightarrow_{s'} \quad (x'(X),\text{true})\{X/a\} = x'(a),\text{true}:<!a>,\{Y/a\}$$
$$\rightarrow_{s'} \quad \text{true}$$

or, as one derivation $q:<!a>,\{X/a,Y/a\} \Rightarrow_{s'} \text{true}$. Since q is a ground atom, the derivation can be rewritten as $q:<!a>,\{\} \Rightarrow_{s'} \text{true}$.

Similar derivations can be produced for the other atoms of the Herbrand base.

$$r:<?a>,\{\} \Rightarrow_{s'} \text{true}$$
$$a=a:<>,\{\} \Rightarrow_{s'} \text{true}$$
$$p(a):<>\{\} \Rightarrow_{s'} \text{true}$$

The refutation semantics is given by $\{(<>,p(a)), (<!a>,q), (<?a>,r), (<>,a=a)\}$.

8 Soundness and Completeness

To prove that the declarative semantics and the refutation semantics are equivalent, we must show that the refutation semantics is *sound* and *complete*. The soundness property means that *no wrong* results are derived by the refutation algorithm, while the completeness property indicates that *all* solutions are generated. The proofs are not given here.

Theorem 8.1 (Soundness) *If* $f:t,\theta \Rightarrow_s \text{true}$ *for a set of clauses S, then* $S \cup \{\leftarrow f\}$ *is unsatisfiable, i.e.,* $t \models_M f_0$ *for at least one ground instance* f_0 *of f.*

Theorem 8.2 (Completeness) *If* $S \cup \{\leftarrow f\}$ *is unsatisfiable, and if* $t \models_M f_0$, *for some trace t, and some instance* f_0 *of f, then* $f:t,\theta \Rightarrow_s \text{true}$, *where θ is a substitution such that* f_0 *is an instance of* $f\theta$.

9 Communicating Horn Clauses connected to a Blackboard

Now, we change our point of view. We no longer consider the 'internal' semantics of a process, and turn our attention to the 'external' semantics, i.e., the input/output behavior of a process. This behavior is described by a set of traces. It describes the 'reaction' of a process on an input from the blackboard. The set $\{<?a,!c>,<?b,!c>\}$ tells us that the event !c will be generated after the event ?a or the event ?b has occurred. In practice, a number of processes will execute simultaneously. We shall describe the behavior of a number of concurrently running processes in the same way as one single process, i.e., by means of a set of traces.

Example 9.1 Consider the program

$p_1 \leftarrow ?a,!b$
$p_2 \leftarrow ?b,!c.$

We create two processes by spawning p_1 and p_2. The set of traces from p_1 and p_2 is given by $\{<?a,!b>\}$ and $\{<?b,!c>\}$, respectively. As both processes are running independently, their events may occur in any order, as long as the event order per process remains the same. The set of traces generated by the concurrent operation of p_1 and p_2 is given by the *interleaving* $\oplus$ of the traces for p_1 and p_2 :

$$\{<?a,!b>\}\oplus\{<?b,!c>\} =$$
$$\{<?a,!b,?b,!c>,$$
$$<?a,?b,!b,!c>,$$
$$<?a,?b,!c,!b>,$$
$$<?b,?a,!b,!c>,$$
$$<?b,?a,!c,!b>,$$
$$<?b,!c,?a,!b>\}$$

It should be clear that the resulting set of traces effectively contains all allowable orderings of the individual communication events. Hence, the newly generated set of traces describes the combined behavior. That means that the concurrent operation of two processes can be treated as one single (virtual) process. This statement has an important consequence. Instead of studying the interaction of one process with a set of processes, we can restrict ourselves to the communication between *two* processes: the process at hand and the 'virtual process' constituted by all the other processes in the system (these processes constitute the environment).

Definition 9.2 Let $P_1,\ldots,P_n$ be n processes running in parallel. The *environment* E created by the joint operation of these processes is given by the interleaving of their sets of traces, $E = P_1\oplus\ldots\oplus P_n$, augmented with all the prefixes of these traces.

The reason why the prefix closure is taken is related to the fact that traces, generated by the environment do not have to be consumed entirely.

Example 9.3 The environment E of the sample program

$p_1 \leftarrow ?a,!b$
$p_2 \leftarrow ?b,!c$

with two processes p_1 and p_2 is given by

```
{<<?a,!b,?b,!c>,<?a,!b,?b>,<?a,!b>,<?a>,<>,
 <?a,?b,!b,!c>,<?a,?b,!b>,<?a,?b>,
 <?a,?b,!c,!b>,<?a,?b,!c>,
 <?b,?a,!b,!c>,<?b,?a,!b>,<?b,?a>,<?b>,
 <?b,?a,!c,!b>,<?b,?a,!c>,
 <?b,!c,?a,!b>,<?b,!c,?a>,<?b,!c>}
```

It contains all traces or prefixes of traces which could ever be generated by the processes when running independently. The set E is called the *prefix closure* of {<?a,!b>} $\oplus$ {<?b,!c>}.

Definition 9.4 A *Herbrand blackboard* is a bag of terms of the Herbrand universe.

Examples of Herbrand blackboards for $H_U = \{a,b,c\}$ are: [a,b,a,a], [a,a], [], etc. The blackboard is a model for the common 'communication space' of all processes. We denote the set of all Herbrand blackboards as H_{BB}.

The execution of events by a process will give rise to changes in the blackboard. The event !a will put the term a onto the blackboard, while ?a will get a from the blackboard, as soon as it is available. The blackboard will only contain the net effect of both operations. We say that the blackboard is modified by the *execution of a process trace*, and that a trace is a blackboard-transforming function. Therefore, we give a more useful definition of a trace

Definition 9.5 A *trace* $t: H_{BB} \mapsto H_{BB}$ is a blackboard-transforming function. For s a Herbrand blackboard, and τ a ground term, the function is defined as a set of rewriting rules:

```
<>s ~ s
(<!τ>+t)s ~ t(s∪{τ})
(<?τ>+t)(s∪{τ}) ~ ts
```

Example 9.6 The application of the trace <?a,!b,!c,?c> on the blackboard [b,a] can thus be rewritten as

```
<?a,!b,!c,?c>[b,a] ~ <!b,!c,?c>[b] ~
       <!c,?c>[b,b] ~ <?c>[b,b,c] ~ <>[b,b] ~ [b,b]
```

When the rewriting rules are used left to right, the length of the trace is always decreasing. Eventually it will be the empty trace, which can be omitted, resulting in a Herbrand blackboard. However, some trace applications cannot be rewritten as a Herbrand blackboard, such as, <!a,?b,!c>[] ~ <?b,!c>[a]. The expression <?b,!c>[a] cannot be simplified further.

The rewriting equations describe an equivalence relation between trace applications on a Herbrand blackboard. This equivalence relation introduces a partition on the set of trace applications on Herbrand blackboards.

Definition 9.7 A trace t is *fully executable* on a blackboard s if the trace application t s is equivalent to a Herbrand blackboard (the element of the partition to which t s belongs, contains also *one* Herbrand blackboard).

We call H_T the set of fully executable Herbrand traces on the empty blackboard. The property of full executability is thus equivalent to set membership of the set H_T.

Example 9.8 The set of fully executable traces H_T over the alphabet $\{!a,?a\}$ is given by $\{<>,<!a>,<!a,?a>,<!a,!a>,<!a,!a,!a>,<!a,!a,?a>,<!a,?a,!a>,\ldots\}$.

10 Declarative Semantics: Formalization

Definition 10.1 The *declarative semantics* of a number of processes connected to a blackboard is given by the subset of the Herbrand base that is true.

Let $P_1,\ldots,P_n$ be n processes connected to the blackboard, let E be the environment created by these processes, and let M' be the (global) generalized model of the program. The declarative semantics is then given by

$$\{a\in H_B : \exists t\in M'[a] \ \wedge \ \exists t'\in E \ (t\oplus t')\cap H_T\neq\emptyset\},$$

where $M'[a]$ denotes the set of traces that can make a true: $M'[a] = \{t\in H_B : (t,a)\in M'\}$. The declarative semantics equals the subset of the Herbrand base of which the elements are **true** by using a trace generated by the environment. In other words, there must be at least one trace, needed to make a **true**, and one trace, generated by the processes in the system, which give rise to at least one fully executable interleaving.

Example 10.2 Consider the program

```
t(a)←
t(b)←
p₁←?x,t(x),!c
p₂←?c,!d
main←!a,?x,x=d.
```

The Herbrand universe H_U is given by $\{a,b,c,d\}$. The program contains two processes p_1 and p_2 with the sets of traces $\{<?a,!c>,<?b,!c>\}$ and $\{<?c,!d>\}$. The generalized model M' is given by

$$\{(<>,t(a)),(<>,t(b)),(<?a,!c>,p_1),(<?b,!c>,p_1),$$
$$(<?c,!d>,p_2),(<!a,?d>,main),(<>,a=a),(<>,b=b),$$
$$(<>,c=c),(<>,d=d)\}.$$

All atoms which need the empty trace to be **true** are automatically part of the semantics of the program ($<>\oplus<>\cap H_T\neq\emptyset$ because $<>\in H_T$) The atoms p_1 and p_2 cannot be proved because there is no trace from the environment which can make the traces for p_1 and p_2 fully executable.

The interleaving of the trace $<!a,?d>$ (cfr. main) and the trace $<?a,!c,?c,!d>$ from the environment $\{<?a,!c>,<?b,!c>\}\oplus\{<?c,!d>\}$ contains precisely one fully executable trace $<!a,?a,!c,?c,!d,?d>$. This means that main belongs to the declarative semantics. which is given by $\{t(a),t(b),main,a=a,b=b,c=c,d=d\}$.

It is remarkable that the semantics of a program, consisting of a number of concurrently operating processes can be expressed in the same way as the semantics for a sequential program. This shows that a set of cooperating logic programs is a valid way to introduce parallelism in logic programming, and that the use of a blackboard for communication is not in conflict with the logic programming paradigm. The semantics of both a sequential and a parallel program can be expressed by the same means.

Here also it becomes clear why we need a prefix closure for the environment E. Consider the process p←!a,?b and the goal ←?a. After spawning the process p, the goal ←?a can be solved, although the process p will suspend on the event ?b. According to the definition, the set <!a,?b>⊕<?a> does not have a fully executable trace, but the set <!a>⊕<?a> has. Actually, as soon as our goal can be made true, we do not bother about the other processes any longer. Their state has become unimportant, so they may get blocked.

11   Operational Semantics: Formalization

Definition 11.1 The *operational semantics* of a program consisting of a number of processes, connected to a blackboard is given by the set of atoms which can be proved **true** by executing a finite sequence of events.

In the previous section, a blackboard was considered as a bag of terms from the Herbrand universe. The application of a trace to a blackboard yieds a blackboard if the trace is fully executable. Hence, the application of a fully executable trace on a blackboard is also a representation of a blackboard. Moreover, every Herbrand blackboard can be rewritten as a trace application on the empty Herbrand blackboard.

$$[\tau_1,\ldots,\tau_n] \text{ is equivalent to } <!\tau_1,\ldots,!\tau_n>[]$$
$$t([\tau_1,\ldots,\tau_n]) \text{ is equivalent to } (<!\tau_1,\ldots,!\tau_n>+t)[]$$

This representation can be further generalized to non-fully executable traces. By doing so we can specify more general blackboards than we could up to now. We therefore give a definition of a generalized blackboard.

Definition 11.2 A *generalized blackboard* is defined as a trace application on a Herbrand blackboard or on a generalized blackboard. It belongs to the set $(H_T)^+ \times H_{BB}$.

Examples of generalized blackboards are: <><><><>[], <!a,!b,!c>[], <>[a,b,c], <?a>[a], <?b>[a], <!a><!b>[], and so on.

The operational semantics of generalized blackboards is slightly different from the semantics of Herbrand blackboards. With $t \in H_T$, $s \in H_{BB}$, $s' \in H_{BB}$, the derivation rule for a generalized blackboard is as follows,

$$t_1 \ldots t_{j-1} t_j t_{j+1} \ldots t_n \ s \ \longrightarrow \ t_1 \ldots t_{j-1} t_j' t_{j+1} \ldots t_n \ s' \text{ where}$$
$$t_j \text{ is the selected trace } \wedge \ t_j = <e>+t_j' \ \wedge \ <e>s \sim <>s'$$

Due to the fact that more than one trace t_j may be ready to be executed, we introduce a selection function S_p. It is a formalization of the *interprocess non-determinism*. At any moment in the derivation process, it returns the process (or trace) that will generate the next event on the blackboard. It is a function $(H_T)^+ \times H_{BB} \mapsto H_T \cup \{\textbf{success}, \textbf{deadlock}\}$. The function returns **success** if the trace in front of the generalized blackboard is equal to <>, and returns **deadlock** if there is no event which can be executed on the blackboard.

Example 11.3 An example may clarify the semantics of a general blackboard (the selected trace is underlined).

$$\begin{aligned}
&\underline{<!a,?b>}<?a,!b><?a,!c>[\,]\twoheadrightarrow\\
&<?b>\underline{<?a,!b>}<?a,!c>[a]\twoheadrightarrow\\
&<?b>\underline{<!b>}<?a,!c>[\,]\twoheadrightarrow\\
&\underline{<?b>}<>\!<?a,!c>[b]\twoheadrightarrow\\
&<><>\!<?a,!c>[\,]
\end{aligned}$$

Of course, the selection function could have been different, as is shown in the next example.

$$\begin{aligned}
&\underline{<!a,?b>}<?a,!b><?a,!c>[\,]\twoheadrightarrow\\
&<?b><?a,!b><?a,!c>[a]\twoheadrightarrow\\
&<?b><?a,!b>\underline{<!c>}[\,]\twoheadrightarrow\\
&<?b><?a,!b><>[c]
\end{aligned}$$

In this case, the computation ends with a **deadlock**. One process is waiting for b, the other for a. Neither of them will ever be generated on the blackboard.

A generalized blackboard is a formalization of the interaction of primitive processes (i.e., single trace processes) on a blackboard. However, it is not yet a formalization of real processes. In order to create a full description of such a system, we need to introduce one more generalization, which is another source of non-determinism. Indeed, the description of a general process is not a single trace, but a set of traces. Not every trace will give rise to a successful computation. The choice of a particular trace out of this set of traces, is done by the trace selection function S_T.

Definition 11.4 A general blackboard is *successfully executable* if there exists a selection function S_p such that $t_1 \ldots t_n[\,]$ can be rewritten as $<>t_2' \ldots t_n'b$.

Definition 11.5 A *goal expression* is a set-based general blackboard, i.e., it belongs to the set $((H_T)^+)^+ \times H_B$.

Example 11.6 Examples of goal expressions are:

$$\{<>\}[\,]$$
$$\{<!a>,<!b>\}[\,]$$
$$\{<!a>,<!b>\}\{<?a>,<?b>\}[c]$$

Goal expressions can be rewritten as a set of generalized blackboards; e.g., the goal expression

$$\{<!a,?d>\}\{<?a,!c>,<?b,!c>\}\{<?c,!d>\}[\,]$$

is equivalent to the set of generalized blackboards (i.e., single-trace processes)

$$\{<!a,?d><?a,!c><?c,!d>[\,] \,,\quad <!a,?d><?b,!c><?c,!d>[\,]\}\,.$$

Hence, the transition from an program with primitive single-trace processes to an program with multi-trace processes is just a matter of creating a set of single-trace processes *and* selecting one single-trace process. This way of treating the *intra-process non-determinism* is allowed because a process will generate *at most* one trace.

Definition 11.7 A goal expression is *successfully executable* if it contains a generalized blackboard that is successfully executable.

In order to check whether a goal expression is successfully executable, we need two selection functions. One to select a generalized blackboard from the set of generalized blackboards (the trace selection function S_T), and one to select the order in which processes will generate the communication events (process selection function S_P).

Definition 11.8 The operational semantics of a program with generalized model M', and consisting of n processes $P_1, \ldots, P_n$ is given by

$$\{a \in H_B : \quad M'[a] P_1 \ldots P_n[] \text{ is successfully executable}\}$$

The operational semantics is sound, i.e., if an atom a belongs to the operational semantics, then it also belongs to the denotational semantics.

The operational semantics is non-deterministically complete. This means that an atom that belongs to the denotational semantics, can be proved operationally, iff the proper trace selection function and process selection function is available.

12 Conclusion

The main contribution of this work is that the semantics of a set of cooperating processes connected to a blackboard can be described in precisely the same way as for a sequential program, i.e., as a subset of the Herbrand base. This means that, given a subset of a Herbrand base, one could choose either a sequential, or a parallel implementation of that semantics. It shows that the concepts of macroscopical parallelism and blackboard communication are not in conflict with the logic programming paradigm.

13 Future Work

We are now implementing Multi-Prolog, a programming language based on the model described. It would be interesting to investigate whether it is possible to automatically detect the application parallelism by inspecting the relations between procedures. It is probably possible to give the application programmer a hint how to create processes. This task is not trivial because the decomposition is not based on the syntax of the program, but on the semantics. It is related to the modularity of knowledge and locality in the program.

14 Aknowledgement

The author would like to express his gratitude towards Prof. J. Van Campenhout for the valuable discussions on this topic. He also wants to thank L. Wulteputte for the prototype implementation of this language.

References

[1] Brogi, A., and Ciancarini, P., "The Concurrent Language Shared Prolog", *ACM Transactions on Languages and Sytems*, 13(1), 1991.

[2] Brookes, S.D., Hoare, C.A.R., Roscoe, A.W., "A Theory of Communicating Sequential Processes", in *Journal of the ACM*, Vol. 31, no. 3, July 1984, pp. 560–599.

[3] De Bosschere, K., "Multi-Prolog, Another Approach for Parallelizing Prolog", in *Proceedings of Parallel Computing 89*, Leiden, NL, august 1989.

[4] De Bosschere, K., "Multi-Prolog, a Process-oriented Prolog", in *Proceedings of Software Engineering for Real-Time Systems*, Cirencester, UK, september 1989.

[5] Gelernter, D., "Generative Communication in Linda" in *ACM Transactions on Programming Languages and Systems*, 7(1), p. 80–112, jan 1985.

[6] Hennessy, M., *Algebraic Theory of Processes*, in MIT Press Series The Foundations of Computing, Cambridge, Massachusetts, 1988.

[7] Lloyd, J.W., *Foundations of Logic Programming*, Springer Verlag, Berlin, 1984.

[8] Manna, Z., *Mathematical Theory of Computation*, McGraw Hill, New York, 1974.

[9] Monteiro, L., *Distributed Logic, A theory of distributed programming in logic*, Report Computer Science Dept., University of Lisbon, Portugal, 1986.

[10] Van de Snepscheut, J.L.A., *Trace Theory and VLSI Design*, Lecture Notes in Computer Science, no. 200, Springer-Verlag, Berlin, 1985.

Data Parallelism in Logic Programming

Giancarlo Succi & Giuseppe Marino

DIST - Università di Genova
via Opera Pia 11a
I-16145 Genova
ITALIA

Abstract

Many researchers have been trying to use the implicit parallelism of logic languages parallelizing the execution of independent clauses. However this approach has the disadvantage of requiring a heavy overhead for processes scheduling and synchronizing, for data migration and for collecting the results. In this paper it is proposed a different approach, the *data parallel* one. The focus is on large collections of data and the core idea is to parallelize the execution of element-wise operations. The target language is SEL, a Subset Equational Language. An abstract machine for it, the SAM (Subset Abstract Machine), is outlined, which, under certain points of views, belongs to the WAM family. The data parallel structure of the SAM is here explained and some examples of how it works are given. Eventually it is explained the role of abstract analyzers in this framework and it is presented the plan for the future research.

1 Parallel Implementations of Logic Languages

One of the biggest appeals of logic programming languages is what is commonly referred to as "Implicit Parallelism"; i.e. the parallelism a compiler can automatically, and easily, identify and exploit, since no explicit constraint on the execution order is posed in the abstract logic evaluation scheme. Several attempts have been made for using this property in order to design and implement a language which can fully exploit the (parallel) architecture of its target machine, possibly without resorting to ad-hoc constructs and/or annotations.

Various forms of parallelism has been evidenced, such as *and-*, *or-* and *stream-* parallelism (and, of course, their combination), but nevertheless the results that have been achieved are not as expected. Probably the initial goals were set too high, but anyway we claim that too much attention has been devoted to the most "expensive" form of parallelism, expensive in terms of time and space overhead required for communications, synchronizations and processes management.

On the other side, very little attention has been given other simple forms of intrinsic parallelism, which could have clearer and simpler definitions, and that can due to more straightforward implementations.

This paper analyzes the *data parallel* approach for this problem. Section 2 introduces the concept of *data parallelism*, section 3 gives a general overview of the language used in this approach, section 4 describes the SAM, the abstract machine under development, aimed to exploit the data parallelism, section 5 presents the data parallel instructions, in section 6 some sample compilations for the SAM are presented, section 7 is devoted to some comments on abstract analysis for the SAM and section 8 draws the conclusions together with some plans for future research.

2 Data Parallel Declarative Programming

We can divide the intrinsic parallelism of logic programs in two classes:

- *process parallelism,*
- *data parallelism.*

Process parallelism is the form of parallelism which parallelizes the execution of independent parts of a program, usually with the following approach:

1. identify closures which can be executed independently,

2. decide whether to execute them or not,

3. schedule the ones we have decide to execute on the processors,

4. collect the results.

Using this classification, *and-*, *or-* and *stream-* parallelism fall in this class, despite at a first sight they seem to act quite differently one from another.

It is evident that this approach have some intrinsic limitations since it requires quite a lot of communications between processes for exchanging data and synchronizing, a lot of time for forking and joining processes and a lot of bookkeeping to have a consistent execution. Furthermore there is the undecidable problem of how to choose what processes should run on what processors.

A different design can be devised and a good candidate for it seems *data parallelism*, which is almost unexplored within the field of logic programming. It can be described by the following approach:

1. identify the collections of objects globally handled by our program,

2. decide how to spawn them onto the available processors,

3. manipulate them applying, as much in parallel as possible:

- "element-wise" operators,
- filters,
- "folding" operators;

in order to obtain either new collections or just scalar elements.

This approach seems quite appropriate for an implementation on both MIMD parallel architectures and the SIMD ones, like the Connection Machine and it overcomes most of the limitations of process parallelism.

This design requires a language suitable for the representation of collections of objects and an effort of programmers to adapt their mind to this new paradigm. The question is then which kinds of languages and of collections we should use and how we should spawn the collections onto the available processors.

3 SEL and Sets

The target language for our *data parallel* approach is SEL, the Subset Equational Language developed by Jayaraman et al. [JN88] at UNC/Chapel Hill and at SUNY/Buffalo. This language handles sets in a clean, neat and simple way. Choosing sets as the core collection has also the advantage that lots of people have experience from many different fields in representing problems as relations between sets.

A SEL program is a sequence of two kind of assertions:

equational assertions of the kind $f(terms) = expression$.

subset assertions of the kind $f(terms) \supseteq expression$.

The meaning of this assertions is:

equational assertion : the function f applied to the ground instances of *terms* is equal to the corresponding ground instances of *expression*;

subset assertion : the function f applied to the ground instances of *terms* contains the corresponding ground instances of *expression*,

The language incorporates the *collect-all assumption* for subset assertions, which states that the result of a function application to ground terms is the union of all the subsets obtained by all the subset assertions matching the ground terms with all the possible matching. We do not go into details here, and for a complete description of the language [Suc91] can be consulted.

Some examples of SEL programs can help understanding our approach. The first program we examine is aimed to compute the sets of the squares of a given set.

```
squareSet({x|_}) contains {x*x}.
```

Here it is present a remarkable feature of SEL, i.e., the *multiple matching:* since no order is imposed over the elements of a set, a matching of the kind $\{x|\_\}$ produces the matching of x with all the elements of the argument set; therefore, by the *collect all* assumption, the result is the set containing the squares of all the elements.

A data parallel implementation on a SIMD architecture, for instance, can perform this operation in just one shot: if the argument set is already distributed among the processors what it is needed is just to ask each processor to square the element stored on it (and this can be done in parallel) plus some extra (constant time) bookkeeping.

In the same way it behaves the cartesian product of two sets:

```
cartProd({x|_},{y|_}) contains {[x,y]}.
```

Here we have two nested set mappings, but the general philosophy is the same, and so can be the implementation.

Also more complicate patterns can be handled in this way, like:

```
perms({}) = {[]}.
perms({x|t}) contains distr(x,perms(t)).

distr(x,{t|_}) contains {[x|t]}.
```

which determines all the possible permutations of the elements of a set. In this case the computation proceeds first generating all the sets matching the pattern in linear time (assuming to have enough available processors, otherwise we need some sort of virtualization) and then applying to all the sets `distr`.

Filters can be implemented with this approach too:

```
filter({x|_}) contains if p(x) then {x} else {}.
```

The function `filter` selects the elements of its argument set that satisfy the predicate p; again we can have a data parallel implementation in just one shot, provided that we have enough processors.

4   The SAM

We take the quite usual approach of dividing the implementation in two phases [Jay91]:

- the development of a compiler for the language targeted to an *abstract* machine,

- the implementation of the *abstract* machine to our *real* architecture.

The abstract machine we are developing is called **SAM**, Subset Abstract Machine. Its general philosophy comes from the WAM [AK90] and it is quite closely related to the SEL-WAM[Nai88]. We do not give a detailed description of the SAM here, our emphasis is on its data parallel structure; for a complete survey see [SM91b].

Like the SEL-WAM, the SAM treats an n arguments assertion like a *(n+1)* arguments clause whose first n are input arguments and the *(n+1)-th* is the output. Like the SEL-WAM, also, there is no need of unification capabilities, which has the consequences that:

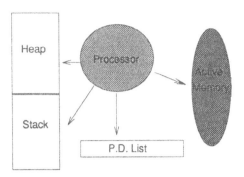

Figure 1: General Structure of the SAM

- there is no need of "trail",

- faster **store** and **match** instructions replace the **unify** ones, since in the SEL framework it is decidable at compile time where we need to match and where to store.

Differently from the SEL-WAM, the SAM has the capability of handling functors, it uses a table of constants and it performs the environment trimming optimization. The usage of functors does not require any big complication neither in the original language -despite not being implemented, they were always present its formal description- nor in the compilation or in the execution. However, to simplify the compilation, we decided to require the user to write annotations of the kind:

> **functor f,g,h.**

specifying that **f, g** and **h** are functors and not function, therefore they must not be reduced. The table of constants and environment trimming are aimed mostly to space optimization, nevertheless they allow also some time saving.

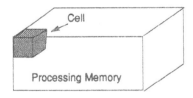

Figure 2: The Processing Memory

Quite new is the compilation of assertions: equational assertions are speeded up by means of an enhanced clause indexing strategy and the management of sets is entirely revised. The SAM includes a *processing memory*, that is a memory whose cells both store results and perform computations. Sets are stored here instead of on the heap and some "set-oriented" operations are executed virtually in parallel on it.

Dealing with sets, it is sometimes convenient to use *basing* techniques. When there are some sets differing one-another only for few elements, it may be useful to store in

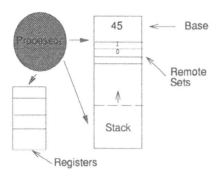

Figure 3: Structure of a Cell

the processing memory a superset of all of them, the *base*, and to represent each of the original sets (called *remote sets*) with a bitvector -a 1 in its i-th position means that the i-th element of the base belongs to the remote set, and a 0 that it doesn't.

Figure 2 describes the processing memory: it can be viewed as an array of cells. The cells are outlined in figure 3. Each one contains a processor, a memory and some registers. The local memory is divided in three parts: the first for storing the base element (in the example the number 45); the second for the bits of the remote sets (here the first remote set contains the number 45 while the second doesn't). The last portion is devoted to a stack for local computations.

For this reason the adj-like instructions are replaced by map instructions, which generate a new set in terms of another one, and there are folding instructions -for computing element oriented set properties- and filtering instructions aimed to the definition of subsets of a given set.

We try to minimize the usage of the processing memory has to be parsimonious, since it is a scarcer resource than "standard" memories. Moreover, architectural constraints may impose to allocate the processing memory cells at loading time. Hence abstract analyzers play a relevant role in the design of the SAM.

We can devise various implementations of the processing memory: presently it just coincides with the standard one; a single processor approach using hashing tables has been described in [Suc91] and an implementation on the Connection Machine is under development.

5   Data Parallel Instructions

As it is said before, ad hoc instructions have been designed to properly handle sets. They can be divided in three groups:

- *mapping* instructions,

- *filtering* instructions,

- *folding* instructions.

5.1 Mapping Instructions

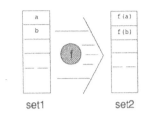

Figure 4: **set2** is obtained mapping **set2** through **f**

A clause of the kind:

```
squareSet({x|_}) contains {sqr(x)}.
```

is quite common in SEL: it computes a new set as a mapping of an already existent set through a mapping function (here **square**). This situation is suited for a data parallel approach since all the mappings can be executed in (data) parallel over the elements of the set distributed on the active memory. The class of the **map** instructions is used here, which determine a new set in terms of an already existing one and a mapping function. The SAM code for this situation is:

```
squareSet/2:
        ..   ..   ..
        map_over <argument_set> <resulting_set>
        <compute square of the element>
        end_map_over <storing the result>
        ..   ..   ..
```

Figure 4 represents this situation: **set2** is obtained mapping **set1** through **f**. Note that if a potentially unlimited number of processors is available, this operation can be performed in constant time.

5.2 Filtering Instructions

As it was previously mentioned, certain classes of subset assertions can be defined as filters, e.g., they selects which elements of a given sets belong to another one. Their general form is:

```
filter({x|_}) contains if p(x) then {x} else {}.
```

Here the resulting set contains those elements of the argument set satisfying the predicate p. The assertion **selectEven**:

```
selectEven({x|_}) contains if even(x) then {x} else {}.
```

is an operation of this kind. For this purpose the SAM uses the instructions of the class
`filter`. They have the format:

```
selectEven/2:
    ..   ..   ..
    filter_over <argument_set> <resulting_set>
    <compute even on the element>
    end_filter_over <storing the result if true>
    ..   ..   ..
```

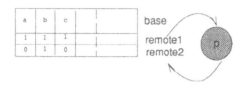

Figure 5: `remote2` is computed filtering `remote1` with p

Figure 5 evidences how this approach can be performed taking a data parallel approach.
The predicate is computed over the elements of `remote1`; for those satisfying it (only b)
a 1 is stored in `result2` while for those not satisfying it (a and c) a 0 is stored.

5.3   Folding Instructions

The last group of operations targeted by this approach are those of the kind:

```
f({}) = k.
f({x|t}) = z(x,f(t)).
```

Here there is the chance of performing a tree-like computation on a parallel architecture which could be performed in logarithmic time. Figure 6 describes how this can be
exploited. The argument set contains the letters between a and m and the function z is
applied to couples of them and of partial results in a binary tree fashion until a single
element i obtained.

The SAM uses the `fold` class of instructions for taking advantage of the potential
paralelism of this situation. They have the form:

```
fold <argument set> <result> <zero> <folding function>
```

where `<result>` is the result of the computation (`res` in figure 6), `<zero>` is the value for
the empty set (`k` in the example) and `<folding function>` is the function to be applied
in parallel (here `z/3`).

Note that this class of operations is not deterministic, since no order is imposed on
the sets, e.g., the (pseudo) function `nonDet`:

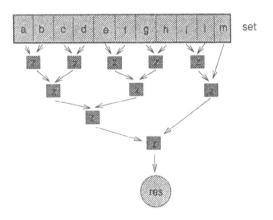

Figure 6: The result is determined folding set with z

```
nonDet({}) = 0.
nonDet({x|t}) = minus(x,nonDet(t)).
```

applied to the set $\{1,2,3\}$ can give 0, 2 or 4 as result, depending on which matching we choose. However [MS89] demonstrated that if the folding function is commutative and associative the result is the same no matter of the matching; so since plus is both associative and commutative, the result of applying det:

```
det({}) = 0.
det({x|t}) = plus(x,det(t)).
```

to $\{1,2,3\}$ is always 6.

6   Compilation Examples

Sample compilations can help understanding the design of the SAM; we present the SAM code for the squareSet program we explained in the previous section.

```
squareSet/2:
            allocate
            get_set A1 Y1
            get_variable A2 Y2
            map_over Y1 Y3 Y4 end
    begin:
            put_value Y4 A1
            put_value Y4 A2
            put_variable Y5 A3
            call mult/3
            end_map_over Y2 Y3 Y4 A3 begin
```

```
end:
        deallocate
```

Here we perform a mapping of the original set -pointed by Y1- on the new one -pointed by Y2. The instructions between map_over and end_map_over determine the operations that have to be done on all the elements of the set, which are pointed by Y3, and therefore these instructions can be executed in parallel on all processors of a parallel architecture.

A little bit more involved is the case for the clause intersect:

$$intersect(\{x|\_\},\{x|\_\})\ contains\ \{x\}.$$

which can be handled like filters, since the second matching poses a logic (and implicit) constraint on the fact that the element of the first set belongs to the result; the compilation of this assertion is therefore:

```
intersect/3:
        get_set A1 X3
        get_set A2 X4
        get_variable A3 X5
        filter_over X3 X6 X7 end
begin:
        match_set_element X7 X4 X8
        end_filter_over X4 X6 X7 X7 X8 begin
end:
        proceed
```

7 Abstract Analysis

Abstract analyzers play an important role in the process of building an efficient implementation of a logic language: their aim is to infer important properties of programs analyzing them without executing. Then ad hoc compilers can take advantage of these informations to produce a faster code. There is already a wide usage of abstract analyzers for computing the "mode" of a variable, for determining whether the same object can be shared or need to be copied, and so on. All these techniques can be extended to this framework. However there are more reasons for partial eveluators here.

It has already noted that the usage of the processing memory has to be minimized, since its availability is much lower than that of "standard" memories and that architectural constraints may impose to allocate the processing memory cells needed at loading time. Hence it is strictly necessary to design abstract analyzers to determine at compile time good approximations of the objects involved in the executions and of their sizes. In this design they are divided in two classes:

- *object size analyzers*, aimed to determine the sizes of the objects,

- *persistency analyzers*, targeted to compute the lifetime of objects.

A full description of them can be found in [SM91a].

8 Conclusions and Further Research

In this paper it is presented a new model for exploiting the intrinsic parallelism of logic programming, the data parallel one. A suitable language is overviewed and a suitable abstract machine is described quite in detail. Examples are given on how the data parallelism works on this machine and on its pseudo assembler.

At the present time we have almost completed an implementation of the SAM on a RISC Sun4 and we have started its Connection Machine porting which should be ready by October.

Obviously there are still lots of open questions about this project. It would be interesting to see how much we could integrate this two forms of parallelism: we could allow some very limited and conservative forms of process parallelism coupled with data parallelism which should be able to exploit a high degree of parallelism. The point is then what kind of architecture we should use for this approach.

9 Acknowledgments

The first author thanks prof. Jayaraman for being introduced by him to this field and for his precious comments.

References

[AK90]   H. Aït-Kaci. *The WAM: A (Real) Tutorial.* Digital - Paris Research Laboratory, January 1990.

[Jay91] B. Jayaraman. Implementation of Subset-Equational Programs. *The Journal Of Logic Programming*, 1991.

[JN88]   B. Jayaraman and A. Nair. Subset-Logic Programming: Application and Implementation. In *5th International Logic Programming Conference*, Seattle, August 1988.

[MS89]   J. Marino and G. Succi. Data Structure for the Parallel Execution of Functional Languages. In G. Gries and J. Hartmanis, editors, *PARLE '89*, pages 346–356. Springer-Verlag, June 1989.

[Nai88] A. Nair. Compilation of Subset-Logic Programs, December 1988. University of North Carolina at Chapel Hill – Master Thesis.

[SM91a] G. Succi and J. Marino. Abstract Analyzers for Data Parallel Declarative Languages. Technical report, DIST - Università di Genova, 1991.

[SM91b] G. Succi and J. Marino. A New Abstract Machine for Subset Equational Languages. Technical report, DIST - Università di Genova, 1991.

[Suc91] G. Succi. Set Representations in a Subset-Equational Language, February 1991. State University of New York at Buffalo – Master Thesis.

AN EFFICIENT BINDING MANAGEMENT IN OR-PARALLEL MODEL

H. BOURZOUFI, G. GONCALVES, P. LECOUFFE, B. TOURSEL

Université de LILLE1
Laboratoire L.I.F.L. (UA 369 CNRS)
59655 Villeneuve d'Ascq Cedex
FRANCE
e-mail : bourzouf@lifl.lifl.fr
or goncal@lifl.lifl.fr
fax : (33) 20 43 65 66

Abstract

A new binding scheme is presented which allows a depth first scheduling strategy in order to manage efficiently side effect predicates. The dereferencing mechanism is based on a set of N key registers associated to each processor. Each key register K_i selects conditional bindings made by processor P_i and which are valid for a given processor P_k .

1. Introduction

Over last years, much research activity has been focused on finding efficient ways of exploiting parallel execution mechanisms within Prolog programs. Broadly speaking, two forms of parallelism have been intensively studied :

- AND parallelism exploited in deterministic problems
- OR parallelism introduced in non-deterministic problems.

Both of these approaches have been widely implemented ([LUS88], [BAR88], [LIN88]) on shared-memory multiprocessors (Sequent, Encore machines) as an extension of the WAM sequential implementation. The rest of this paper focuses on the second form of parallelism (i.e. OR-parallelism) based on shared-memory multiprocessors.

One of the challenges in OR-parallelism is to manage side effect predicates in such a way that parallel execution of a Prolog program produces the same set of results while keeping the same order as a sequential execution. Because side effect predicates like I/O predicates, database predicates and CUT are strongly dependent on the depth first execution strategy of Prolog, an usual way to handle side effect predicates in OR-parallel system is either to suspend their execution until the corresponding branch is the leftmost active one of the search tree [HAU88] or to activate OR-parallelism in a depth first manner [BOU90] [DEL91].

Depending on the scheduling strategy, the processor is free or not to look for another task before resuming the older one. In this case a great deal of attention must be provided to preserve data (i.e. stacks) of suspended tasks. Moreover, as the number of suspended tasks grows, memory management becomes increasingly complex due to both the crumbling of a single physical stack into several logical stacks and the increasing cost of task switching.

One way to overcome this problem is firstly to suspend temporarily the processor executing a side effect predicate until its branch becomes the leftmost of the search tree and secondly to provide a scheduling strategy which minimize the elapsed time of a suspended processor.

In order to do this, a depth first scheduling strategy is chosen in which an idle processor attempts to grab deeper work from the processor the branch of which is the leftmost.

This scheduling strategy has two secondary side effects :

- The first one is concerned with the granularity of tasks. As deeper task is chosen as smaller the granularity may be. So task switching may occur more frequently and the number of shared variable installation/deinstallation should be higher than in a topmost scheduling strategy. One needs a binding scheme which allows fast task switching.

- The second one is the scheduling strategy ability to give preference to non speculative work over speculative one (i.e. branch which can be cut away). In [HAU90] it was shown that the lowest speculative tasks reside usually in the leftmost branch and speculativeness of the tasks decreases with the depth of the tree.

Ours aim is to provide a binding scheme well suited for a depth first scheduling strategy (i.e. task switchings are fast and free of the current position of the processor in the search tree) while keeping access to variable bindings within bounds.

In the following sections we propose a new multiple binding mechanism which seems a good compromise between the cost of creating and accessing variable bindings and the cost of creating multiple tasks.

2. Basic binding mechanisms

Another challenge in OR-parallelism is to do the management of multiple bindings in such a way that both cost of variable binding and cost task switching are minimized. Because several processors can explore distinct branches of a program search tree emanating from a common ancestor node, one must provide a mechanism to manage the binding of a single ancestor Prolog variable to multiple alternative bindings.

Many approaches have been proposed over the five last years but all have one of these two particularities [WAR87a] :

- When the dereferencing mechanism does not suffer a real overhead, the cost of parallel task installation decreases the system performance (see SRI model [WAR87b])

- When the parallel task installation does not penalize the system performance, this one is decreased by the overhead introduced by the dereferencing mechanism used (see Argonne [BUT86] and PEPSys models [BAR88]).

In the SRI model, accesses to conditional bindings are constant time operations because one private binding array is provided to each processor and makes direct accesses to them possible. However it imposes an overhead on task switching proportional to the number of bindings to be installed or deinstalled in the binding array. So several scheduling strategies have been studied (in the Gigalips project) [CAL89] [BUT88] to keep the non-constant time for task creation relatively small. The basic idea are the following ones :

- firstly to maximize the granularity of tasks (i.e. minimizing the occurrence of task switching) by providing the topmost available task

- secondly to minimize the number of required binding installation/deinstallation by getting new task closer to the old one.

In the Argonne/PEPSys model, shallow binding is used as far as possible (i.e. favoured binding) otherwise deep binding is performed in a private hash-window (i.e. non-favoured binding). Because this mechanism allows the sharing of non-favoured bindings through a chain of hash-windows, task switchings are rapidly done but non-favoured accesses are rather slow operations. However in the optimized Pepsys model, the dereferenced values of non-favoured OR shared variables are cached in the local hash-window, so further accesses will be reduced. The advantage of this model is that it put less restriction onto a scheduling strategy because the inherited OR shared bindings are only copied as needed.

In the scope of a depth first scheduling strategy, none of the above binding models seems to be quite suitable because of the following reasons:

- The SRI binding model has a prohibitive task switching when a high number of binding installation/deinstallation occurs (i.e. proportional to the depth of the choice point from which the new alternative is chosen) .

- The PEPSys binding model may produce arbitrary long chains of hash windows which are also proportional to the depth of choice points.

In the next part, we propose a new mechanism to handle multiple bindings while keeping good characteristics of the above models and in which the side effect predicates can be done in a straightforward way (i.e. with a depth first scheduling strategy).

3. A key-based binding sharing model

As discussed before, a depth first scheduling strategy has shown two drastic constraints that should be taken into account in an efficient implementation.:

- To allow fast task switchings
- To get constant dereferencing operations

However the binding scheme presented in the following is strongly dependent on the depth first execution scheduling strategy we used. This scheduling strategy will be described in more details in a forthcoming paper. In short, three points characterize this strategy :

- when a processor becomes idle, it looks for the deeper leftmost available work. As soon as a processor takes an alternative from a non local choice point, a new task is started until the corresponding subtree is totally explored.

- when a processor backtracks to a local node (i.e. a choicepoint it has created before) in which available alternatives exist, it takes the next ones (otherwise see next point) .

- when there are no alternatives left, but some child processors are still working below this node, the processor try to help the leftmost child where some available work exists, otherwise the bactracking process of the processor is suspended until all of its children processor have terminated their corresponding tasks.

As the most obvious way to get fast task switching is the binding sharing, our model is based on a similar technique in which all conditional bindings are tagged with a CPN (Choice Point Number) . This CPN is related to the total number of "active" choice points (i.e processors are working below this choice point) created by that processor and it plays the same role as OBL in the PEPSys implementation which validates the scope of an OR shared variable binding.

A key-based binding validity check

The problem now is how a processor can determine conditional bindings made by other ancestor processors and which are valid for itself.

In this way, the processor use a set of key registers which will define its scope over binding made by the others.

Every time an OR node is created by a processor, the current CPN value is memorized in the OR node data structure before incrementing, so when an idle processor takes an available alternative from that node it inherits the CPN value of its father processor.

To validate a conditional binding, the processor uses a set K of key registers [K1,K2,....,KN] where N is the number of processors. Each register Ki contains the CPN corresponding to the last ancestor node (i.e. choice point) created by the processor P_i. When a processor starts a new branch at a given choice point, it inherits its key registers from the state of the processor task creating the choice point. In fact it firstly makes a copy of the current key register values of its father processor, then it updates the father key register value relative to its father processor with the inherited value of the OR node and finally it increments its CPN value (see figure 1 showing an OR search tree example with three processors).

On the example, circles with number represent choice points with their corresponding CPN values and Ki are sets of key registers. It should be noted that CPN value of a processor P_i is always the same than the corresponding key register Ki value.

The snapshot shows processor P_0 is going to help its children by taking an available alternative from processor P_2, other children choice points were completed. Processor P_0 makes a copy of the key registers K=[2, 1, 1], replaces the K2 value 1 by the CPN choice point value 0 and increments its CPN (i.e. key register K0) by one.

So the cost to pay for installing a new parallel task is just the overhead due to copying the key registers of father node from which the alternative is taken.

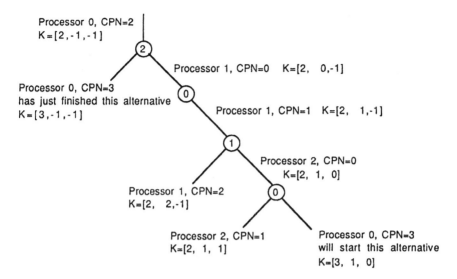

Processor 0, CPN=2
K=[2,-1,-1]

Processor 1, CPN=0   K=[2, 0,-1]

Processor 0, CPN=3
has just finished this alternative
K=[3,-1,-1]

Processor 1, CPN=1   K=[2, 1,-1]

Processor 2, CPN=0
K=[2, 1, 0]

Processor 1, CPN=2
K=[2, 2,-1]

Processor 2, CPN=1
K=[2, 1, 1]

Processor 0, CPN=3
will start this alternative
K=[3, 1, 0]

figure 1 : a snapshot showing Processor 0 which has terminated its alternative
and starts a new one.

Storage implementations

Three possible storage implementations of the above key based binding model have been considered and are briefly described in the following. These implementations are now under integration in a simulator.

The first one is a straightforward implementation based on sharing through hash-windows as in the Argonne/PEPSys. The difference with the PEPSys implementation is the limited number of hash-windows in a dereferencing chain. At any time, we only have one hash-window per processor (instead of one hash-window per task) because of the depth first scheduling strategy we used. So the length of dereferencing chain cannot be greater than the number of processor in the system and leads to bounded costs in dereferencing operations. The drawback of this implementation may be the hashing operation cost for addressing a memory location in a hash-window.

In the second implementation, when a first binding to conditional variable is detected, a N components vector is dynamically allocated for it as in Version Vector model [HAU87] (N is equal to the number of processors). The value cell of this variable is then set to the address of the new vector. In fact, when a processor Pi tries to bind a conditional variable, it stores the binding value in the component i of the corresponding variable vector. The major drawback of this method is the needed synchronization during the variable vector creation.

191

Finally the third implementation uses local binding array to store conditional bindings :

- All conditional bindings are deep ones and every time a variable is created, its value is assigned with an index to the PBA (Processor Binding Array) as in SRI model
- All conditional bindings are tagged with a CPN (Choice Point Number) as in PEPSys model thus it allows both shared-bindings and fast task switchings.

By this way, we can achieve bounded access time operation on OR shared variable while keeping fast task switching. In the next section, we describe in more details the last implementation.

4. A key-based binding sharing model - Processor binding array Version

Every time a variable is created , its value cell is assigned with an index that identifies a location in its associated PBA (Processor Binding Array). The difference with the SRI model is that there is only one binding array per processor instead of one binding array per task because the scheduling strategy makes it possible.

To bind a variable, if the binding is unconditional the value cell is just over-written with the new value as in the classic WAM stack model. Otherwise, if the binding is conditional, the binding value is stored in the corresponding PBA location and only the variable address is trailed.

In order to allow the sharing of conditional bindings among possible children processors, binding values are tagged with the current value of the father processor's CPN (Choice Point Number) . The CPN plays the same role as OBL in the PEPSys implementation which validates the scope of an OR shared variable binding.

The difference with the PEPSys approach is that on the one hand the CPN of an idle processor is initialized to "-1" and it is incremented by one each time the processor starts processing a new task anywhere in the OR search tree. It is also incremented every time an OR node is created by the processor. On the other hand the CPN is decremented when either the backtracking process of a choice point ends or the current task is over. Moreover, only one CPN per processor is needed because of the scheduling strategy instead of one OBL per task as in PEPSys model.

Dereferencing mechanism

Assume that [K1,K2,....,KN] are the key registers of a processor P_j dereferencing a variable. In practice a Kh key register value "-1" means that the corresponding processor P_h is not in the scope the current processor P_j (i.e. not an ancestor processor) , so no conditional bindings made by processor P_h are valid for P_j.

To dereference a non local variable several accesses are generally needed. A first access is made to value cell of the processor P_k stack creating this variable in order to check if the binding is unconditional or not. If it is the dereferencing is over, otherwise one keeps the index i of the corresponding PBA location. Then a second access to the PBA_j location i is necessary to check if the variable has been already bound by processor P_j. Failing that, a search operation for a valid binding is performed in the other PBA_k location i for each k ≠ j and Kk ≠ -1. A deep binding of a PBA_k is valid if it is tagged by a number lower or equal to Kk value.

In the example of figure 2, the processor P_0 has created an environment in which variable X has been unconditionally bound to empty list [] (i.e. flag u is set) and variable Y was still unbound at the next choice point creation (i.e. flag c is set).

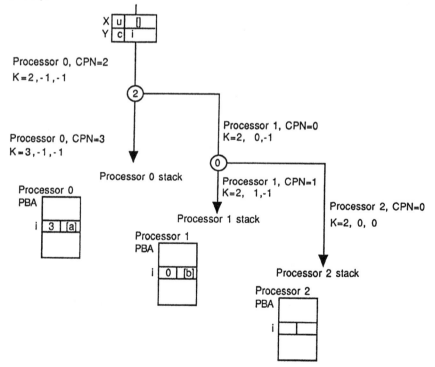

figure 2 : an example showing different conditional bindings of variable Y

After this point, the variable Y has been conditionally bound by both processor P_0 and processor P_1. The first component of a conditional binding is the tag value and the second component is the binding value.

When the processor P_2 wants to dereference the variable Y, a search operation for a valid binding selects only the binding made by processor P_1 which is in the scope of processor P_2 (i.e. K1 is lower or equal to the i location tag of processor P_1).

Thus deep binding dereferencing requires a maximum of N+1 memory accesses.

5. Simulation and data structures

The binding mechanism described above, has been just developed and integrated in a OR-parallel simulator of Prolog programs extending a Prolog sequential interpreter. The program has been written in Le_Lisp programming language and it runs on SUN workstation.

In this section we describe the data structures we added to the classical WAM approach in order to implement the above key based binding mechanism.

In particularly WAM choicepoints are expanded to include extra-fields needed for the parallel execution of OR-nodes. The most important field which have been added in the node structure is the CPN field. This field contains the CPN current value of the processor at the node creation time.

The value of key registers for the current active task of a processor are memorized in the N words starting at the basis of the local environment stack. In order to access the key register values, one special stack base register SS points to the basis of the current active processor task. When a processor suspends its current task for helping its children processor, it starts a new local environment task at the top of the previous one, and then a new set of key registers is calculated and pushed.

Finally, an additional stack called "job stack" have been added to the other classic WAM stacks to distribute work among processors. Each time a new OR-node is created by a processor, a pointer to its node structure inside the environment stack and the value of SS register are pushed together in the corresponding job stack. During the execution of a program, all the processor job stacks could be read by any processor. The basis of these stacks are known by all processors and they contain a pointer to their top of stack. By this way, both the key registers and the CPN values of a father node can be inherited by a child processor.

A structure of stack has been chosen because it provides a natural way to implement a depth first scheduling strategy (i.e. the deeper task is always located at the top of job stack). The remaining problem of how to determine the leftmost processor P_i is resolved by a token which value indicates the P_i number and will be presented in a forthcoming paper.

The figure 3 shows stacks of processor P_0 and P_2 at the moment when processor P_0 starts a new alternative created by processor P_2 (see figure 1).

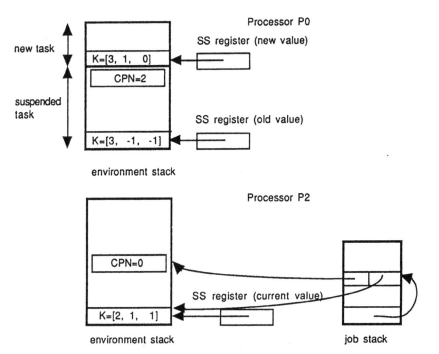

figure 3 : Processor P_0 has started a new task from job stack of Processor P_2

Today, we are currently investigating the evaluation of our approach with regard to other existing models (i.e. SRI, Argonne model) through a set of significant benchmarks.

6 Conclusion

We have proposed a new alternative to handle multiple binding environments minimizing overhead of both binding accesses and task switchings which often occur in a depth first scheduling strategy. Furthermore conditional binding a:~esses are bounded-time operations (i.e. searching operation over a fixed number of PBA processor).

References

[BAR88] U. BARON, J. CHASSIN DE KERGOMMEAUX, M. HAILPERIN, M. RATCLIFFE, P. POBERT : "The Parallel ECRC Prolog System PEPSys : an overview and evaluation results". FGCS'88, Nov-Dec 88, pp 841-850

[BOU90] H. BOURZOUFI, G. GONCALVES, I. HANNEQUIN, P. LECOUFFE, B. TOURSEL : "Depth First Or Parallelism in the LOG-ARCH Project". Parallel and Distributed Computing, and Systems, October 1990, pp42-45

[BUT86] R. BUTLER, E. L. LUSK, R. OLSON, R.A OVERBEEK : "ANLWAM, a parallel implementation of the Warren Abstract Machine", international report, Argonne National Laboratory, 1986

[BUT88] R. BUTLER, T. DISK, E. L. LUSK, R. OLSON, R. OVERBEEK and R. STEVENS : "Scheduling OR parallelism: an Argonne Perspective", Fifth International Logic Programming Conference and Fifth Symposium on Logic Programming 1988

[CAL89] A. CALDERWOOD and P. SZEREDI : "Scheduling OR Parallelism in Aurora - The Manchester Scheduler" 6th International Conference on Logic Programming, Portugal, pp 419-435, June 1989

[DEL91] I. DELIGNIERES-HANNEQUIN : "Proposition d'un Modèle d'Evaluation Parallèle de Prolog". Thèse de Doctorat, Fevrier 1991, LIFL, Université de Lille1

[HAU87] B. HAUSMAN, A. CIEPIELEWSKI, S. HARIDI : "OR-Parallel Prolog made efficient on shared memory multiprocessor ". 4th symp on Logic Programming, San Francisco, Sept 87, pp 69-79

[HAU88] B. HAUSMAN, A. CIEPIELEWSKI, A CALDERWOOD : "Cut and Side effects in OR-Parallel Prolog", FGCS'88, Nov-Dec 88, pp 831-840

[HAU90] B. HAUSMAN : "Handling of speculative work in OR-Parallel PROLOG : Evaluation Results" in Proceeding of NACLP 1990, pp 721-736

[LIN88] Y. J. LIN, V. KUMAR : "Performance of AND-Parallel execution of Logic programs on a shared-memory multiprocessor", FGCS'88, Nov-Dec 88, pp 851-860

[LUS88] E. LUSK, R. BUTLER, T. DISZ, R. OLSON, R. OVERBEEK, R STEVENS, D. H. D. WARREN, A. CALDERWOODD, P. SZERIDI, S. HARIDI, P. BRAND, M. CARLSON, A. CIEPIELEWSKI, B. HAUSMAN : "The Aurora OR-Parallel Prolog System".FGCS'88, Nov-Dec 88, pp 819-830

[WAR87a] D. H. D. WARREN : "OR-Parallel Execution Models of Prolog". TAPSOFT 87, Pisa, March 87, pp 243-255

[WAR87b] D. H. D. WARREN : "The SRI model for OR_Parallel execution of Prolog-Abstract design and implementation issues", 4th symp on Logic Programming, San Francisco, Sept 87, pp 92-102

Lecture Notes in Computer Science

For information about Vols. 1–481
please contact your bookseller or Springer-Verlag

1991.

Vol. 524: G. Rozenberg (Ed.), Advances in Petri Nets 1991. VIII, 572 pages. 1991.

Vol. 525: O. Günther, H.-J. Schek (Eds.), Advances in Spatial Databases. Proceedings, 1991. XI, 471 pages. 1991.

Vol. 526: T. Ito, A. R. Meyer (Eds.), Theoretical Aspects of Computer Software. Proceedings, 1991. X, 772 pages. 1991.

Vol. 527: J.C.M. Baeten, J. F. Groote (Eds.), CONCUR '91. Proceedings, 1991. VIII, 541 pages. 1991.

Vol. 528: J. Maluszynski, M. Wirsing (Eds.), Programming Language Implementation and Logic Programming. Proceedings, 1991. XI, 433 pages. 1991.

Vol. 529: L. Budach (Ed.), Fundamentals of Computation Theory. Proceedings, 1991. XII, 426 pages. 1991.

Vol. 530: D. H. Pitt, P.-L. Curien, S. Abramsky, A. M. Pitts, A. Poigné, D. E. Rydeheard (Eds.), Category Theory and Computer Science. Proceedings, 1991. VII, 301 pages. 1991.

Vol. 531: E. M. Clarke, R. P. Kurshan (Eds.), Computer-Aided Verification. Proceedings, 1990. XIII, 372 pages. 1991.

Vol. 532: H. Ehrig, H.-J. Kreowski, G. Rozenberg (Eds.), Graph Grammars and Their Application to Computer Science. Proceedings, 1990. X, 703 pages. 1991.

Vol. 533: E. Börger, H. Kleine Büning, M. M. Richter, W. Schönfeld (Eds.), Computer Science Logic. Proceedings, 1990. VIII, 399 pages. 1991.

Vol. 534: H. Ehrig, K. P. Jantke, F. Orejas, H. Reichel (Eds.), Recent Trends in Data Type Specification. Proceedings, 1990. VIII, 379 pages. 1991.

Vol. 535: P. Jorrand, J. Kelemen (Eds.), Fundamentals of Artificial Intelligence Research. Proceedings, 1991. VIII, 255 pages. 1991. (Subseries LNAI).

Vol. 536: J. E. Tomayko, Software Engineering Education. Proceedings, 1991. VIII, 296 pages. 1991.

Vol. 537: A. J. Menezes, S. A. Vanstone (Eds.), Advances in Cryptology – CRYPTO '90. Proceedings. XIII, 644 pages. 1991.

Vol. 538: M. Kojima, N. Megiddo, T. Noma, A. Yoshise, A Unified Approach to Interior Point Algorithms for Linear Complementarity Problems. VIII, 108 pages. 1991.

Vol. 539: H. F. Mattson, T. Mora, T. R. N. Rao (Eds.), Applied Algebra, Algebraic Algorithms and Error-Correcting Codes. Proceedings, 1991. XI, 489 pages. 1991.

Vol. 540: A. Prieto (Ed.), Artificial Neural Networks. Proceedings, 1991. XIII, 476 pages. 1991.

Vol. 541: P. Barahona, L. Moniz Pereira, A. Porto (Eds.), EPIA '91. Proceedings, 1991. VIII, 292 pages. 1991. (Subseries LNAI).

Vol. 543: J. Dix, K. P. Jantke, P. H. Schmitt (Eds.), Nonmonotonic and Inductive Logic. Proceedings, 1990. X, 243 pages. 1991. (Subseries LNAI).

Vol. 544: M. Broy, M. Wirsing (Eds.), Methods of Programming. XII, 268 pages. 1991.

Vol. 545: H. Alblas, B. Melichar (Eds.), Attribute Grammars, Applications and Systems. Proceedings, 1991. IX, 513 pages. 1991.

Vol. 547: D. W. Davies (Ed.), Advances in Cryptology – EUROCRYPT '91. Proceedings, 1991. XII, 556 pages. 1991.

Vol. 548: R. Kruse, P. Siegel (Eds.), Symbolic and Quantitative Approaches to Uncertainty. Proceedings, 1991. XI, 362 pages. 1991.

Vol. 550: A. van Lamsweerde, A. Fugetta (Eds.), ESEC '91. Proceedings, 1991. XII, 515 pages. 1991.

Vol. 551:S. Prehn, W. J. Toetenel (Eds.), VDM '91. Formal Software Development Methods. Volume 1. Proceedings, 1991. XIII, 699 pages. 1991.

Vol. 552: S. Prehn, W. J. Toetenel (Eds.), VDM '91. Formal Software Development Methods. Volume 2. Proceedings, 1991. XIV, 430 pages. 1991.

Vol. 553: H. Bieri, H. Noltemeier (Eds.), Computational Geometry - Methods, Algorithms and Applications '91. Proceedings, 1991. VIII, 320 pages. 1991.

Vol. 554: G. Grahne, The Problem of Incomplete Information in Relational Databases. VIII, 156 pages. 1991.

Vol. 555: H. Maurer (Ed.), New Results and New Trends in Computer Science. Proceedings, 1991. VIII, 403 pages. 1991.

Vol. 556: J.-M. Jacquet, Conclog: A Methodological Approach to Concurrent Logic Programming. XII, 781 pages. 1991.

Vol. 557: W. L. Hsu, R. C. T. Lee (Eds.), ISA '91 Algorithms. Proceedings, 1991. X, 396 pages. 1991.

Vol. 558: J. Hooman, Specification and Compositional Verification of Real-Time Systems. VIII, 235 pages. 1991.

Vol. 559: G. Butler, Fundamental Algorithms for Permutation Groups. XII, 238 pages. 1991.

Vol. 560: S. Biswas, K. V. Nori (Eds.), Foundations of Software Technology and Theoretical Computer Science. Proceedings, 1991. X, 420 pages. 1991.

Vol. 561: C. Ding, G. Xiao, W. Shan, The Stability Theory of Stream Ciphers. IX, 187 pages. 1991.

Vol. 562: R. Breu, Algebraic Specification Techniques in Object Oriented Programming Environments. XI, 228 pages. 1991.

Vol. 563: A. Karshmer, J. Nehmer (Eds.), Operating Systems of the 90s and Beyond. Proceedings, 1991. X, 285 pages. 1991.

Vol. 564: I. Herman, The Use of Projective Geometry in Computer Graphics. VIII, 146 pages. 1991.

Vol. 565: J. D. Becker, I. Eisele, F. W. Mündemann (Eds.), Parallelism, Learning, Evolution. Proceedings, 1989. VIII, 525 pages. 1991. (Subseries LNAI).

Vol. 566: C. Delobel, M. Kifer, Y. Masunaga (Eds.), Deductive and Object-Oriented Databases. Proceedings, 1991. XV, 581 pages. 1991.

Vol. 567: H. Boley, M. M. Richter (Eds.), Processing Declarative Kowledge. Proceedings, 1991. XII, 427 pages. 1991. (Subseries LNAI).

Vol. 568: H.-J. Bürckert, A Resolution Principle for a Logic with Restricted Quantifiers. X, 116 pages. 1991. (Subseries LNAI).

Vol. 569: A. Beaumont, G. Gupta (Eds.), Parallel Execution of Logic Programs. Proceedings, 1991. VII, 195 pages. 1991.